I WILL BE CALLED
JOHN

Lawrence Elliott was born in Brooklyn, New York,
in 1924 and was educated there and at City College
of New York. After service in World War II and a
tour as a writing editor on *Coronet* magazine, he
began working for *Reader's Digest*, first as a roving
editor covering Alaska and Western Canada, then
as European correspondent, based in Paris. He and
his wife, Gisèle, now live in Columbia County, New
York. *I Will Be Called John* is Elliott's sixth book.

I WILL BE CALLED
JOHN

A Biography of
Pope John XXIII

LAWRENCE ELLIOTT

FONTANA/COLLINS

First published in the United States of America 1973
by Reader's Digest Press, New York, and simultaneously
in Canada by Clarke, Irwin & Company Limited, Toronto
and Vancouver

First published in Great Britain 1974
by William Collins Sons & Co Ltd London

First issued in Fontana 1976

Copyright © 1973 by Lawrence Elliott

Made and printed in Great Britain by
William Collins Sons & Co Ltd Glasgow

CONTENTS

For Gisèle, with love

Grateful acknowledgment is made for permission to quote from *Journal of a Soul* by Pope John XXIII, copyright 1965, Geoffrey Chapman Ltd; and from *Letters to His Family* by Pope John XXIII, copyright 1969, Geoffrey Chapman Ltd.

FOREWORD

In the spring of 1967, Maurice Ragsdale, the book editor of *Reader's Digest*, asked me if I would be interested in writing something about Pope John, a little memoir, perhaps, that might convey John's warmth and his enormous attraction to people of all faiths. Although I was at work on another project, I said yes at once, for the idea greatly appealed to me. We discussed it a bit more and then—I had already gotten up to go—Ragsdale said, "By the way, are you Catholic?"

"No," I replied, and wondered if I had just lost the assignment.

"Good!" he said emphatically. "I think what we're after here is the story of a man. He happened to become pope, but people didn't love him because he was high and mighty but, just the opposite, because he was so human. And the human side of it— the whole business of his terrific appeal to non-Catholics—is probably easier told from the outside looking in."

So I begin my acknowledgments for aid and encouragement in the writing of this book with thanks to Maurice Ragsdale. The "little memoir" grew to a proportion unimagined on that spring day more than five years ago, and has taken far longer to write than the six or eight months I'd originally allotted to it. But I hope the reader still finds in these pages the essence of Ragsdale's idea: the story of a man who won the world's heart.

As always, I am grateful to the other editors of *Reader's Digest* who believed in this work over the long slow years during which it took shape; and to the *Digest*'s European editorial office in Paris, and to researchers in Milan, Rome, Stuttgart—indeed, all over Europe—who kept digging up the raw material of history for me and faithfully responding to my queries. If, in spite of their efforts, there are errors in this work, they are my own.

Sincere special thanks to Susan Vadnay, one of the most astute members of the Rome press corps, who took time from her own work to serve a long hitch as my interpreter, guide, and adviser; whose persistence opened Vatican doors that would otherwise have been closed to me; and whose wide friendships resulted in key interviews with church personages who almost never see writers.

I am, in fact, grateful to all the members of the Italian press corps who so generously offered leads and expertise in a field to which I came as a novice. In particular I want to note the names of Luigi Bortolozzi (Borlui), Vittorio Carrara, Alice Leone-Moats, Alfred McElwain, Barrett McGurn, Sandro Meccoli, James O'Neill, Corrado Pallenberg, Curtis Bill Pepper, Prince Guglielmo Rospigliosi, Alexandra Wasiqullah, George and Charlotte Weller; and to thank them all.

My debt to the many who contributed directly to this biography by sharing with me their personal recollections of Pope John is obvious, and in most instances their names and relationships to His Holiness are evident in the context of the book itself. I am deeply appreciative of the time they gave me, and of the patience and thoughtfulness with which they answered what must have seemed like an endless string of questions. Yet there remain some without whose particular help this work simply would not have been possible, and I must offer my thanks to them individually.

No one, now or in the future, who attempts any serious evaluation of the life and influence of John XXIII can hope for any measure of real success unless he begins with the source material made available by Msgr. Loris Capovilla, the late pontiff's secretary and loyal aide. If the biographer has the personal assistance of Monsignor Capovilla, he is doubly blessed. My gratitude to him is beyond measure. It was the time we spent together in Chieti that convinced me I had to expand my projected work on Pope John to its full biographical dimensions, and the concrete help and guidance he gave me that encouraged me to begin. In addition, the extensive and ongoing labors of Monsignor Capovilla in the editing of Pope John's journals and letters have opened a treasure trove of the most pertinent material, and permission to quote from it is gratefully acknowledged.

Among the many members of Pope John's family who granted me interviews, I am especially indebted to his nephew, Msgr. Battista Roncalli of Bergamo, and his niece, Enrica Roncalli of Sotto il Monte. Their contributions are readily evident in this book, and the intimate memories they shared with me have helped to shape it.

I thank all the church dignitaries who responded to my requests for information and made time to see me in the midst of often pressing duties. I am particularly appreciative of the openness with which Pope John's former friends and aides spoke of him. In that regard I want to mention and thank His Eminence Cardinal Egidio Vagnozzi; Msgrs. Andrea Spada and Thomas Ryan; and Archbishop William Carew, who provided me with a wealth of data about Vatican geography and Pope John's years in the apostolic palace. Finally, I want to record a special debt to His Eminence, the late Cardinal Angelo Dell'Acqua, who was one of Pope John's closest collaborators.

At this point it might be well to say that no one who contributed memories or material for this book has any responsibility for the use I have made of it. The interpretations and viewpoints, as well as such mistakes as may have crept in, are entirely my own. I am human enough to hope that those who helped me will think well of what I have written, but I am bound to add that if they do not the fault is probably mine.

Lawrence Elliott

New York City

I

SEDE VACANTE

It began on a day when the summer had slipped almost imperceptibly into golden autumn. It began in the olive hills southeast of Rome, in Castel Gandolfo, where for three centuries and more the popes had gone in summer to escape the heat of the city. There, Pius XII died, worn out by his years, exhausted by the burdens of holy office in a world of skepticism and rage. And so it began, as the record of man's painful progress often does, with an ending.

The bells of the village church tolled. A Jesuit father of the Vatican Radio, face shadowed by the long vigil, read the final bulletin: "The supreme pontiff is dead. Pope Pius XII, the most esteemed and venerated man in the world, one of the greatest pontiffs of the century, with sanctity passed away at 3:52 today, October 9, 1958."

The stately, dispassionate machinery of the Vatican started to turn. The immemorial rituals attendant on *sede vacante* (a break in the papal rule) were set inexorably moving. The cardinals of the church, posted in twenty-one different countries on the five

1

continents, having been forewarned that the pope's illness was terminal, now made last preparations for the journey to the holy city, there to bury the pope, and there to choose his successor. Those resident in Rome met in "preparatory congregation" on the very day of Pius's death, as bidden by clerical law. There was much to do. The princes of the church are its governors during an interregnum, administrators of all its widespread religious and temporal offices. Together, they constitute the sacred college of cardinals, and when from fifteen to eighteen days had passed, time enough for the farthermost among them to reach Rome, they would shut themselves up in secret conclave, not to reappear in the sight of men until two-thirds plus one of their number agreed on which one of them would be the new pope.

Cardinal Benedetto Aloisi Masella, a particular force in the *Curia Romana*, was elected *camerlengo* (cardinal chamberlain) or chief among equals, but, of course, without papal power. He immediately took charge of the properties of the Holy See, decreed that the Fisherman's ring, symbol of the pope's rule, be brought to the cardinals and destroyed in their presence. The papal apartment was sealed. Preparations were made for the *novendialia* (nine funeral masses for the dead pope), and for receiving the diplomatic delegations which would soon be calling to offer condolences. A date, October 25, was chosen for the opening of the conclave.

On Friday, October 10, the mortal remains of Eugenio Pacelli were returned to the Vatican. By the time the procession reached Rome, it was two miles long, with thousands of high ecclesiastics marching solemnly behind, and hundreds of thousands of mourners standing in the streets in the dazzling bright sun. It moved slowly past the Colosseum where, in another age, Christians were martyred, past the house on the Via degli Orsini where the pontiff had been born nearly eighty-three years before, and so to the Basilica of Saint Peter where drums rolled and a contingent of the Swiss Guard led the way to a bier at the papal altar. The funeral chant rose to the soaring dome. It echoed distantly, hauntingly, against the silent stone.

For nine days the Holy City was draped in black, and the cardinals put aside their scarlet cassocks for the purple of mourning. On the third day, the body of Pius was laid to rest in the Sacred Grotto beneath the basilica, close to the tomb of Saint Peter. On the ninth day, the solemn requiem mass, attended by representatives of fifty-three governments, ended the *novendialia*. By now, arrangements were nearly completed for convocation of the conclave.

All but a few of the cardinals had arrived. Over the years, death had cut their full rank from seventy to fifty-five, and their age and frailty were sadly emphasized when two of their number proved too ill to attend the conclave, and two others died just as it was about to begin. The rest remained secluded in the monasteries and ecclesiastical colleges where they had been quartered in Rome. They left only for Vatican ceremonies and scrupulously avoided contact with the troops of reporters who poured into the city. Even when they received members of the Vatican diplomatic corps, they did so in a mass audience, and it was understood that this was their way of shielding themselves from any hint of outside influence.

Meanwhile, theory, conjecture, and wild guesses ran rampant in the secular world surrounding the Holy City during these critical days. There were those who held that the church's need was for a pastoral pope, one who would shore up its inner structure. Pius had come to the throne of Saint Peter only months before the outbreak of World War II and his pontificate had been preoccupied with nations in turmoil and a world in flames. Now, according to one thesis, it was time to turn inward, to modernize the ancient machinery of the church and adapt its venerable traditions to the convulsive social changes wrought in the twentieth century.

But no, said others, the greater dangers were still from without, from powers mighty enough to destroy the world if they unleashed their full force against each other, from hostile ideologies that denied Catholics their God and the ministrations of their priests. Look, they said, hammering the argument home, of the three cardinals from Communist Europe, only one, Cardinal Wyszinski of Poland, had been allowed to travel to Rome for the conclave, and China's exiled Cardinal Tien, who had come to vote for the new pope, was unable to return to his homeland. No, they insisted, the times were dark and the church still needed a diplomatic pope, another Pius.

In the final hours before the sacred college locked itself away from the world, all the wide-ranging speculation was reduced to a single question: Who would it be? But just as no dominant point of view had emerged, neither had a commanding candidate. There was no answer.

On Saturday, October 25, Msgr. Antonio Bacci, Secretary of Papal Briefs to Princes, implored the cardinals to give the church a worthy successor to Peter, vicar of Christ. "We need a pontiff who knows how to tell the truth even to those unwilling to hear it, who can resist the enemies of God and of the church with unconquerable courage, who can defend the rights of Christians and human civilization, but at the same time open the arms of pardon to all, even to those who make bloody the heart of our common father."

At 3:30 P.M., the cardinals, wearing their scarlet robes once more, walked in solemn single file through the frescoed halls of the Vatican Palace and into the Sistine Chapel. A choir sang the ancient invocation, "Come, Holy Spirit." Cardinal Eugène Tisserant, the French prelate and scholar who was dean of the sacred college, assumed the responsibility of presiding. His proud eyes glowed above a russet beard as he instructed all but the cardinals to leave the chapel. Then he read the Apostolic Constitution which would govern their task.

Before the first conclave, which had elected Gregory X in 1271, the college of cardinals was often at the mercy of imperious, conniving sovereigns, or of a riotous populace. Since then, the papal electors have closeted themselves away to make their decision, subject only to church law and the dictate of God. On this day, the opening of the seventy-eighth conclave in the history of the Catholic church, the cardinals stepped forward one by one, each to swear that he would faithfully observe the Apostolic Constitution, that if chosen pope he would strenuously defend all the rights of the church, that he would keep the secrets of the conclave, and that he would neither receive nor convey the veto of a civil power. Of the fifty-one, only sixteen had been cardinals when Pius XII was made pope in 1939; thus, only these men had ever participated in a papal election.

At 5:30 P.M. the great bell in the courtyard of Saint Damasus rang out, warning all unauthorized persons to leave the conclave enclosure. The prefect of ceremonies marched along crying, "*Extra Omnes!*" ("everyone outside"), and the meticulous work of sealing off walls and passages began. The windows had been whitewashed and revolving sections had been installed in the doors, through which food would be passed in to the conclavists. Now all telephones were disconnected and radios removed.

Journalists who had been shown through the two hundred-room enclosure remarked on its makeshift accommodations. It was in an imposing and celebrated part of the Vatican, centering on the Courtyards of Parrots and Saint Damasus, but it was sadly short of sleeping and bathing facilities. Most of the cardinals were assigned narrow cots in provisional bedrooms. The newsmen jauntily added that as the cooking for Their Eminences would be done in improvised kitchens by the Sisters of Santa Marta, an order not noted for its culinary excellence, the conclave was apt to be a short one.

A ceremonial search party now held its lanterns in the dark corners of the enclosed area and reported that none but the cardinals and their authorized attendants remained inside. At 6:08 P.M., the last entryway, a set of double doors leading to the courtyard of Saint Damasus, was locked from the outside. The cardinals were alone with their awesome task. They would not come out until one of them was elected pope.

The immense piazza in front of Saint Peter's was never empty. Day and night, priests came to pray, nuns to sing hymns, and the people of Rome to gossip and exchange rumors, and all of them to wait. Four times each day, twice in the morning and twice each afternoon, there was a heart-stopping moment during which they all fell absolutely still, every eye fixed on the slender stovepipe on the roof of the Sistine Chapel and the wisp of slate-colored smoke winding up out of it. Tradition has it that the cardinals burn each of their ballots, adding damp straw to the unavailing ones to produce black smoke, a signal to the waiting world that they have not yet reached agreement.

In fact, the result was sometimes confusing. On Sunday, the smoke seemed white enough and the Vatican Radio and at least one news agency flashed word that a pope had been chosen. But as the minutes passed without light or any sign of activity in the Hall of Benedictions on the second floor of Saint Peter's, and the facade of white-curtained windows remained dark and mute, the people in the piazza and the millions around the world who also waited realized that the watch still went on.

Sunday passed, and Monday, and the guessing game of *papabili* (possible popes) intensified and seemed finally to infect everyone. *L'Osservatore Romano*, the Vatican newspaper, deplored the speculation but could not stop it. Within the arms of the regal Bernini colonnade, the people milled around the great piazza, watching the smoke and the silent windows, and kept nagging the journalists and television crews, "Well, is there anything?"

But there was nothing, only new rumors. Some said that the early favorites—Agagianian, Siri, Lercaro, Ottaviani—had lost their chances. This one was too young, they said, and that one too conservative, and the other one was Armenian and the time not yet come for a non-Italian pope. New names were entered into the lists of *papabili*, new theories. Now it was said that the cardinals were seeking an interim pope, a pope of transition, and one heard that the likely candidate was Masella, or Mimmi, or the fat one from Venice, Roncalli. But the truth, as deep-down everyone knew, is that no one knew. Alone in the chapel dominated by Michelangelo's powerful and portentous fresco, The Last Judgment, the fifty-one princes of the church would perform the supreme act of their ministry without external pressure and in absolute secrecy.

On Tuesday, October 28, at a few minutes past 5:00 P.M., white smoke puffed up from the chimney on the Sistine Chapel. It turned into a thread and was soon lost in the dusk, and no one was certain whether it was the long-awaited signal or another false alarm. Then a light appeared, and others. There was a flurry of movement behind the windows in the Hall of Benedictions, and when a floodlight picked the central balcony of the basilica out of the darkening stone and held it in whitest light, there was no longer any doubt: The conclave was broken; a pope had been elected.

"*Viva il Papa!*" some people cried out, and it was taken up and rolled, a joyous, roaring wave, up to the lighted windows. A group of nuns close to the graceful obelisk in the center of the piazza began to sing, "*Christus vincet, Christus regnat*" ("Christ triumphs, Christ reigns").

The news spread. From the farthest corners of the city, the crowds started moving toward Saint Peter's. A strike of Rome's streetcar and bus operators did not stop them, nor did the monumental traffic jam they themselves created. They abandoned their autos and continued on foot, streams of people filling the streets and converging into a vast torrent of humanity bound for the Vatican, every one of them with the same question: "Who is he? *Chi?*"

It may have been the greatest crowd ever assembled in one place. The journalists guessed that three hundred thousand people were there but no one really knew the actual number. All that was known was what could be seen, that the piazza of Saint Peter's was black with people, and that still more came moving in, slowly, relentlessly, across the broad reach of the Via della Conciliazione, all of them standing in the fine evening rain and waiting to hear the name of the new pope.

Everywhere in the world people waited, the faithful and the strays, the humble and heads of state, for the spiritual leader of 500 million Catholics, whether he wills it or not, is a force in the affairs of all men. But the moment belonged to the fervent throng in the great square of Saint Peter's. Here the historic drama would be played out, here the new page turned in a two thousand-year-old story. For this night, at least, the new pope was *their* pope. They would be first to see him as he came to stand on that brilliantly illumined balcony to bestow his blessing on Rome and all the world.

There were "Huzzas" for the band of a carabinieri honor guard crossing the piazza: Red plumes bobbed on their ceremonial tricorns and the brassily buoyant pontifical march rang out through the dusk, signifying an end to mourning and a new beginning. Then there were more lights, another stirring in the Hall of Benedictions, and the triple-barred golden papal cross was carried out to the balcony, now filling with monsignors who were careful to leave an open space in the center. Only fifty-five minutes after the first wisp of white smoke was seen, in an electric hush heightened by the hugely amplified whisperings of the microphones, eighty-four-year-old Cardinal Nicola Canali, senior cardinal deacon, suddenly appeared at the railing. He cleared his throat. Speaking in Latin, in a voice so charged with emotion that it broke in the midst of the historic pronouncement, he said, "*Nuncio vobis gaudium magnum. Habemus Papam!*" ("I announce to you a great joy. We have a pope!")

There were cheers, hand-clapping. But the response was automatic and the sounds tentative. The people waited for the rest, for the answer to the supreme question, "*Chi?*"

"He is my most eminent and reverend lord, Cardinal Angelo Giuseppe Roncalli."

There was a split second of astonishment. If Roncalli's name was on anybody's list of *papabili*, it was usually near the bottom, appended as a sort of afterthought. He was old, rarely seen in Rome and, though ten years patriarch of Venice, still thought of as a Vatican emissary, forever shuffling between distant capitals. So they were to have an interim pope, after all.

But no matter—"*Habemus Papam!*" A thundering roar broke loose from the crowd and swept off to the darkening sky. Cardinal Canali cleared his throat again. He was a small man, barely visible above the stone railing, but the crowd was his and fell instantly silent. Now he announced the name by which the new pope had chosen to be known, not in traditional Latin, but in cadences of rich, rolling Italian, "*Giovanni Ventitresimo*" ("John XXIII").

Another moment of surprise—no pope had been called John since the Middle Ages—and again the exuberant crowd boomed its approval. The faithful crossed themselves and there were shouts, "*Viva il Papa!*" Some tried to squirm closer to the balcony, while nearly a thousand journalists, reporting to perhaps two billion people, were making for special telephones and cable stations, or were broadcasting the momentous news from where they stood.

Mostly the crowd did not budge. The people had come here to see the new pope, to be blessed by him, and that transcendent moment was still to come. They watched as a huge tapestry was unfurled over the edge of the balcony. It was the coat of arms of Pius XII, a dove bearing an olive branch. They saw windows thrown open on either side of the balcony and groups of cardinals, having just come from the Sistine Chapel, standing and watching, too.

Now bugles of the carabinieri band cut through the murmuring night. The monsignors and canons on the balcony shuffled among themselves, then fell back. There were voices: "Is he coming? Do you see him yet?"

Almost unexpectedly he was there, a solid, thickset figure in white. Other popes had been borne to the balcony in portable thrones amid the full splendor of the Vatican court. John XXIII came alone and on foot, and he stood there so still and unassuming that seconds passed before most of those below were aware of what had happened. Then they raised a mighty cheer and waved their handkerchiefs, and the pope smiled with unmistakable pleasure as he raised both arms in greeting and benediction.

To those at the farther ends of the piazza, he seemed a tiny figure, glimpsed over a sea of heads and waving arms. But when someone whispered to him about some apparent procedural matter, the microphones caught a vigorous, resonant voice: "I know, I know," he said briskly, and began to intone the time-honored *Urbi et Orbi*, the apostolic blessing on the city and the world, while members of the papal court sang the responses. Thousands crossed themselves and dropped to their knees, and women held their babies aloft, as though to fully imbue them with the significance of the moment.

The pope asked for indulgence, absolution, and the remission of sins. His words were those used by his predecessors for centuries past, "May the blessing of Almighty God, the Father, the Son and the Holy Ghost descend upon you and remain with you always."

"Amen," sang the attending clerics.

For a long last moment the pope stood there, arms extended to the people of Rome as they clambered up from their knees. Then he turned and disappeared behind the curtains.

The crowd began to break up. The rain had stopped and there was a certain calm in the night that had hold of the people. They moved slowly toward the Via della Conciliazione, or slipped through the colonnade to the side streets that would lead them home. They spoke of this John XXIII, of the way he seemed to them as he stood there on the balcony, his peasant's face beaming. And there were questions: "Whoever thought they would pick *that* one? Where does he stand?"

And speculation: "He is so old—what, seventy-eight? Surely he has been chosen only to mark time for a younger, more vigorous pontiff."

And again and again: "Will he be good?"

II

SOTTO IL MONTE

In the yellow hills that rise from the Lombard plain in the north of Italy, on a long slope above the valley of the Po River, there is a cluster of stuccoed houses called Sotto il Monte. It means "under the mountain," and its people have tilled the same stony, stubborn soil for ten centuries, never expecting more in recompense than an evening meal of soup and polenta, an occasional glass of wine and the continued blessing of God. In summer, the vineyards and little plots of corn languish in the heat. In winter, a bitter wind sweeps down from the Alps, blowing snow or freezing rain across the hills, rattling windows, chilling bones.

On such a day long ago, on the morning of November 25, 1881, a child was born to Giovanni Battista Roncalli and his wife Marianna, a first son after three daughters. By midafternoon, although the wind still raged and cold rain fell steadily, the mother had risen from her bed and, with her husband, prepared to set out for the parish church. For devout parents in that remote place and uncertain time, it could not be otherwise. Would that the little mite to whom they had given life grow to robust manhood; but if it were to be otherwise, if the good Lord summoned him this very day, he would go to the heavenly father properly baptized. And so they marched out into the storm, Marianna carrying the blanket-swathed infant—men did not carry babies—with Giovanni walking ahead with his Uncle Zaverio, known as "Barba" for his fierce beard. He was head of the Roncalli household and was to stand as godfather.

They crossed the piazza to the spare little church of Santa Maria of Brusico, its stones smoothed by the years, shutters banging in the wind, to learn that the parish priest was in the neighboring village visiting the sick. "When would he return?" they asked.

The sexton shrugged: *"Chissà?"* ("Who knows?")

There was no question of returning home. While Marianna and the uncle waited, Giovanni dashed through the rain to the municipal registry to record the birth of his son, then rejoined them in the rectory, where they sat, stiff and silent on the single hard bench, in their dark, proudly aged church clothes.

The father was dark and wiry, with a great black mustache and the arched nose and prominent ears that, in manhood, would characterize the son. The mother, born Maria Anna Mazzola, was then twenty-seven years old and already ample in shape. She had the warm perceptive eyes, the open face that would be her son's. Both were of the peasantry, that well of humanity that the old world casually exploited for a millennium, on which it counted to grow its food and fill its armies and, of those who came seeking opportunities in the cities, to man its factory machines. All these things the peasants of Europe did, all the while infusing family and village and nation with their steady, leavening values in good times and bad, maintaining a stoic and unbreakable link between past and present.

It is said that the name Roncalli comes from the Italian word *ronchi*, a sort of terrace benched into the hillside for the planting of grapevines. The first Roncalli to settle in Sotto il Monte had come over the hills from the Imagna Valley in the Bergamo district around 1430. His name was Martino and he built himself a good sound house which still stands, although it passed from the family's hands centuries ago. Then the Roncallis owned nothing. They had only each other and an abiding faith in God, and like other families in the yellow hills, they clung to the soil with peasant tenacity, generation after generation. They were *mezzadros* (tenant farmers) on the land of Count Ottavio Morlani. They labored in the fields, children and sometimes women, as well as the men, from daybreak to dusk, with none but the simplest tools, and so earned food for the table and perhaps a few lire besides.

In 1881, the year this new baby was born, the Roncallis worked four hectares of land, about eight acres, and had four cows in the stall, of whose milk they were allowed to keep half. But a family was a family then, with grandparents and uncles and aunts and their children all living under the same roof, and each night there were twenty-eight mouths to feed. Forty years were still to pass before an unexpected profit in silkworms enabled Giovanni Battista to make a down payment on the four hectares of land called Colombera Farm and the house that stood on it. The infant now sleeping in his mother's arms would be called on to add his name to the list of family signatures so that, in 1921, the bank in Bergamo would advance the first installment on the agreed price of fifty-five thousand lire. Then twenty years more would go by before the debt to Count Morlani was paid, before, for the first time in five hundred years, the Roncallis were no longer tenant farmers. They owned their own land at last, and their home—and remained as poor as ever.

It was already late in the evening when the priest, Don Francesco Rebuzzini, returned. He was shivering wet and no doubt looking forward to taking his shoes off and sipping a cup of warm wine, quietly, before a fire. Instead, he was confronted by the new parents and the proud uncle, all standing now, Marianna thrusting the baby toward him.

"He came this morning," she said. "A boy."

"We came for the baptism," Giovanni said.

"If it is not too late," Uncle Zaverio added.

The priest sighed. No, it was not too late. He led them into the little chapel, cold and bare, candles flicking dark shadows at the walls. They stood before the marble font and Uncle Zaverio took his godson into his arms, the mother and father edging closer as Don Francesco began the service. Outside, the wind howled on and sometimes they heard a sheet of rain clatter against the shutters. So the child was received into the church. On the baptismal certificate, his name is recorded as Giuseppe Angelo Roncalli, but that may have been due to Don Francesco's weariness, for he was actually Angelo Giuseppe. Nor was there any sign, any spectral omen, that the day would come when he would accede to the throne of Saint Peter.

In the beginning, they lived in the three hundred-year-old farmhouse on the Via Brusico where he had been born. It is still there, though somewhat changed, a two-story, log-beamed structure with whitewashed walls and red brick floors. It had no running water, no fireplace, and in winter the animals were kept on the lower floor and grain stored in the courtyard. They lived with poverty, as did the other villagers, and all accepted it with cheer and peasant forbearance. Angelo—who, as a child, was called Angelino—was to say later, "We were very poor, but so was everyone so we didn't realize that we lacked anything." There were no surprises at supper. There was always polenta, a cornmeal dish of the Lombardy region, and at Christmas a little wine and homemade cake. And if a beggar came to the kitchen door at evening, he was seated at their table and shared the little they had.

Angelo remembered the fields, wet at planting time and dusty dry at harvest. Even when he was too young to work, he went with his mother, trotting along behind as she plodded up the long hill toward home at twilight. His father rode the donkey, for such was the custom of the country people. It would never have occurred to him to let Marianna ride.

Years later when he had become pope, he recalled his father

with a flash of that tender humor that linked him to all men and all faiths, "There are three ways of ruining oneself—women, gambling, and farming. My father chose the most boring."

The bell of the friars at Boccanello, a mile away, was their clock. It told them when to waken, when to pray, when to eat. When it rang the Angelus at five in the morning, the boy could hear his mother stirring in the next room, her voice calling, "Wake up, Giovanni! The angel of the Lord declared unto Mary. . . ." When it rang before noon, she stopped whatever she was doing and said, "Time to put the polenta on."

In October 1887, when Angelo was nearly six, he was enrolled in Sotto il Monte's only school, a one-room building with three benches, one for each grade, conducted by the parish priest, Don Francesco. He had a quick mind and a good memory and he liked learning new things. His younger brother, Zaverio, who began going to school with him the following year, said, "Imagine—he *wanted* to go to school! Me, I did not go to school for twenty years, just one, and then only when it was raining. If it was fair, I went to the fields. I suppose that's why he grew up to be the pope and I grew up illiterate."

Angelo's other classmates were not so impressed with his industry. One day a district inspector came to their school and asked them which weighed more, a quintal of iron or a quintal of straw. Everyone cried out eagerly: "Iron! The iron!" And as the last of their voices faded, Angelo stood and, perhaps a trifle smugly, said, "A quintal is a quintal. They weigh the same."

"The inspector praised him," one of his schoolmates was to remember, "but we beat him up." Battista Agazi is gone now, but his daughter, who still lives in the house across from Colombera Farm, recalls her father's rueful glee in retelling that story of his youth. "Yes, yes, it is true," he would say to everyone. "We waited for him on the street and we beat him up—just a little."

When Angelo had completed the three primary grades, Don Francesco, who seemed to sense that there dwelt in the boy some special destiny, sent him with his father to Carvico, a neighboring parish, where the priest, Don Pietro Bolis, was said to be an excellent teacher of Latin. "He is not stupid," said the father, "so if he falls behind, beat him." Don Bolis needed no encouragement: Boxed ears and rapped knuckles were the secret of his pedagogic success, and Angelo learned Caesar's *Commentaries on the Gallic Wars,* as he himself put it, "at the rate of one page per clout."

The pattern of his life at home was unchanging, the rhythms dependable, comfortable. On holy days, there was an invariable pilgrimage to one of the nearby shrines, his mother carrying bread and cheese for the midday meal. Every day began with mass and ended with a recitation of the rosary. In the evening, Angelo sat with the others at the long kitchen table and listened raptly as Uncle Zaverio read aloud from the Bible or the Catholic newspapers of Bergamo.

This uncommon man, almost entirely self-taught, took the boy in his charge and seemed to instill in him a Christian ethic that went beyond rite and piety, a concern and curiosity about the vast world that stretched away beyond the mountains. Angelo remembered the other elders of the household as "a bit surly but truly good and worthy folk." More than half a century later, he recalled them in a letter to his younger brother Giovanni: "Fortunately you brothers do not imitate our old people . . . who hardly ever spoke to each other except to grumble. . . . I remember that when I was a child I used to implore the Lord most fervently to make the old Roncallis talk to each other a little. And I used to wonder: how will they ever get to Heaven if the Lord says we must all love each other. . . ."

Around this time the family moved to Colombera Farm, a rambling three hundred-year-old house built around a courtyard. It had an imposing red tile roof and eighteen rooms, but marked only a modest change in the Roncalli fortunes. They were *mezzadros* still, and apart from the congestion of uncles, aunts, and cousins—there were now twenty children in the household, of whom Angelo was the oldest boy—a certain number of rooms had to be saved for the animals.

In October 1891, when not quite ten years old, Angelo entered a secondary school at Celana, on the far side of San Giovanni

Mountain. His father, doubtful at first that a boy who was going to be a farmer needed all that education, was persuaded by Don Francesco that times were changing. In the modern world in which they now lived, the priest said, it was not enough for a bright boy like Angelo to grow up, as they had, speaking only the provincial dialect of the Bergamo district. He must learn "the Italian of the books," Don Francesco said, and geography and arithmetic. Giovanni shrugged and marched his son over the mountain to the San Marino Valley, there to install him with some relatives who lived close to the Episcopal College at Celana.

But they did not go all the way together. "When my father accompanied me along the road toward the Faida woods," Angelo Roncalli wrote long afterward, "and left me there to go on by myself to Pontida where I had to stay with our uncle and aunt at Ca' de Rizzi in order to attend the Celana college as a day boy, as soon as I found myself in the cold and in the woods, all alone, I wept at the thought of the home I had left."

His estrangement did not last long, however. The relatives at Pontida fell into a tumultuous wrangle among themselves over an inheritance, and one night Marianna came and took her boy home. Now he had to walk the five miles over Monte San Giovanni to school each day, leaving Sotto il Monte at 6:00 A.M., his shoes most often slung over his shoulders to preserve them, and a slice of cold polenta wrapped in his pocket for lunch. By the time he returned home at night, tired and chilled, he hadn't the energy to do more than eat and fall into his bed. In the morning, stumbling in the cart tracks that led to Celana, he doggedly held a book open in front of his eyes, trying to grasp the day's lesson. But geography and arithmetic danced fuzzily in his head. "I was no hero at Celana," he said later, and his half-yearly grades, an average of five on a marking scale of ten, bore him out.

There were other unhappy complications. The episcopal college at Celana had been founded in the sixteenth century by Saint Charles Borromeo, a Bergamesque who became archbishop of Milan and would figure again in Angelo's life. But in 1891 it was a diocesan school and nearly all the students, besides being older than the dark, chunky boy from Sotto il Monte, were of a some-what more exalted social class. They made fun of his poor cloth-ing and rustic mountain dialect, and once he was almost expelled for a wrong that was really theirs. It was all a burdensome thing for a ten-year-old.

Once he said, "I do not remember a time when I did not want to be a priest." Religious faith had come to him as spontaneously as breathing. The church was vibrantly alive in his heart. Its saints were his heroes and the stories of its past stirred and uplifted him. God was real. Angelo felt His presence, not only when he prayed, but whenever he looked out across the hills or crumbled the winter earth in his fingers, knowing that in spring it would again yield up and nourish the tender shoots of corn.

To his small boy's way of thinking, there could be no nobler calling than to serve God as a parish priest. The priest was the father of the village, wise and kindly shepherd of souls. He taught the catechism, celebrated mass, heard confession. He knew every family, all its hopes and needs and secret fears. When he preached, he spoke with the voice of God, and nothing in the world seemed real or final, neither betrothal nor birth nor even death, until the priest stood up in the pulpit and announced it.

Angelo did not speak of his aspiration to the priesthood, feeling it to be presumptuous for a *mezzadro*'s son. But somehow Don Francesco knew. Catching the boy staring with awe at his cassock and stiffly starched clerical collar, he teased, "Don't you ever become a priest, Angelino. Look how we sweat in this clothing. And how the collar hurts!"

But he coached him in Latin and allowed him to make his first Communion when he was only eight, then chose him to inscribe the names of the other children in the Apostleship of Prayer. And in the autumn of 1892, despite Angelo's poor showing at Celana, it was Don Francesco who managed to have him accepted at the junior seminary in Bergamo.

Still, he was not committed to the priesthood. At that time, the seminaries offered the only opportunity for a Catholic boy to gain a higher education. He went to the seminary whether he wanted to become a doctor, lawyer, journalist, or priest. But by now Giovanni also knew what path his boy would take. He gave his assent reluctantly, for every father looked forward to the help of his first-born son in the fields, and he said, "He's the son of a poor farmer. He'll become an impoverished priest."

It had been arranged, also through the intercession of Don Francesco, that the tuition would be paid by the brother of the landowner, Count Morlani, who was prior of a religious order at Santa Maria Maggiore. But Marianna said that a boy far from home needed to have a few lire in his pocket. She and Giovanni had nothing. Their family had grown to twelve—eventually Angelo would have thirteen brothers and sisters, of whom three died in childhood—and whenever there was any money it went for shoes or a warm coat. Nevertheless, Marianna set out to petition each of the relatives for a little money with which to send the boy off. She was gone all morning and most of the afternoon. When she returned, her lips trembled and she sagged down at the long kitchen table, defeated. Then she wept bitterly. Angelo, who had never seen the strong, self-possessed woman break down before, never forgot that moment.

"What is it, Mama?" he pleaded. "What's the matter?"

Unable to speak, she shook open her worn purse for reply. Some small coins clattered down on the table. They added up to two lire, worth about forty cents.

And with that, and a heartful of youthful hope, Angelo Roncalli, almost eleven years old, set out to become a priest.

III

MOST CATHOLIC OF CITIES

Bergamo is only eight miles from Sotto il Monte but to Angelo Roncalli, who arrived there early in November 1892, it was another world. It shone with urbanity and pulsed with wit and life. Its shops were full of finery such as he hadn't even imagined, and peering into the cafés he saw coolly elegant men and women who bore no resemblance to anyone he had ever known. The seminary was in the Città Alta, the ancient city, whose walls go back to the time of the Etruscans, and whose domed medieval churches and Renaissance palaces sit high above the tumble of red roofs in the new town below. At night, the Città Alta was a dazzle of lights afloat on the darkness of the mountain.

And though it was a small city—no railway or great road ran through—it was rich in a tradition of music and drama and art. Here the pantomime and masked characters of the *commedia dell'arte* were conceived and flourished from the sixteenth century. Here had lived the great composer Donizetti and the Catholic writer Alessandro Manzoni, whose epic novel, *The Betrothed*, set in the Bergamo countryside, had enthralled three generations of

Italians and was to become a favorite of young Angelo Roncalli. He responded to the uniquely Bergamesque sense of life's spectacle. Its gently mocking humor would fuse well with his peasant nature.

It was also, in those turbulent last years before the century turned, the most important center of Catholicism in the land. *L'Osservatore Romano* called it "*Catholicissima Città*" ("most Catholic of cities"). It was the time of *risorgimento*, a surge of Italian nationalism that had beaten and battered away at the temporal sway of the church. In 1870, the last of the pope's once vast domains, Rome and the Papal States, had been annexed by King Victor Emmanuel, and the bitter response of Pius IX was to declare himself a prisoner in the Vatican and, by a decree of *non-expedit*, to forbid Catholics to vote or hold any national office. Twenty years would pass before Italian Catholicism began again to be integrated into the political life of the country. And that beginning was made in Bergamo.

For beneath its brilliant veneer, there smoldered in the city a poverty as stark and demeaning as any in Italy. Here, as elsewhere, the headlong sweep of the industrial revolution had overrun and enslaved thousands of guileless men and women. Lured to the factories, they worked brutally long hours for little pay. They endured the stress of dirty, clangorous workshops and went home to crowded hovels and lived without hope for themselves or for their children. When their health broke or they grew too old to work, they were cast out.

There were those, priests among them, who held that this was a proper concern of the church. They saw that the political unification of Italy would be meaningless without a social rebirth. Their leader was Camillo Guindani, bishop of Bergamo, and in 1891 their cause was immeasurably inspirited when Pius's successor, Pope Leo XIII, issued his epochal encyclical letter, *Rerum Novarum* (The Condition of Labor). It was a dramatic call for the righting of old wrongs, and new regard for those who toiled with their hands for a livelihood.

"Some remedy must be found, and quickly found," it began,

"for the misery and wretchedness which press so heavily at this moment on the huge majority of the very poor." And it went on, for the first time in memory, to assert the church's responsibility, not only for the religious lives of its people, but for their earthly welfare, as well. It was a clear call to conscience, and in Bergamo clergy and Catholic laymen responded by lining up on the side of working men and leading the quest for just and practical solutions to the curse of poverty. They fought for the rights of laborers and peasants to organize so they could help themselves. They established communal kitchens and insurance programs. By 1895 there were nearly a hundred Catholic unions, cooperatives, and credit associations with more than forty-two thousand members in the Bergamo district.

All these efforts, summed up in the term Catholic Action, predictably shocked certain segments of church and laity. Also predictably, they were derided by the anticlerical left. But someday it would be seen that Catholic Action was a reasonable path out of the political impasse between undue temporal interference by the church and rabid anticlericalism, and as the genesis of the Christian Democratic movement, it remains a vital force in Italian life to this day. And Angelo Roncalli, who was to spend eight of his most formative years in Bergamo, where the spirit of *Rerum Novarum* thrived, who grew to manhood there and returned again and again to its humanist and intellectual ferment—Angelo Roncalli would abide by Pope Leo's admonition that labor is nothing to be ashamed of, that we must respect in every man his dignity as a man.

The Roman Catholic church is not a democratic institution. It is based on the principle of authority and administered by a hierarchy that does not take kindly to dissent. But even a hundred years ago, when social classes in Europe were rigidly stratified, when a poor boy could look forward only to becoming a poor man, there was opportunity for the lowborn to move upward in the church ranks, even to reach the heights of power and influence as cardinal, member of the Roman Curia or diplomat of the Holy See. The fact is that young seminarians, regardless of their origins and from the very beginning of their studies, were carefully watched for signs of special promise, the selected few to be sent to Rome, wellspring of the church leadership, to complete their training.

From the record of his first years in Bergamo, no one would have predicted that Angelo Roncalli would be so honored. He himself lamented his inability to grasp the fundamentals of the exact sciences, particularly mathematics, and he had an unfortunate tendency to make little jokes in the classroom, which he invariably regretted since it did not fit his early concept of priestly piety, but could not resist. On the other hand, he had begun to read widely in history and theology, and while other boys were undone by the rigorous seminary routine, the long hours of study and devotions beginning at six every morning, young Roncalli's farmer's stamina saw him through without flinching. At the end of two years, his grades were satisfactory if unspectacular.

Sometime in the spring of 1895, the young Angelo acquired a notebook with a stiff black cover. It was probably no different from the one he used for schoolwork, sixty-four pages, square-ruled sheets, but it was to have particular significance. On the inside front cover he wrote a Latin motto which translates as "Faults which are trifles in the mouths of lay people are blasphemies in the mouths of priests." Then he copied out the "Rules of Life to Be Observed by Young Men Who Wish to Make Progress in the Life of Piety." They had been given him by his spiritual director and enumerated the long list of precepts he meant to follow every day and "at all times": "Devote at least a quarter of an hour to mental prayer before you get out of bed"; "Beware of praising yourself and of wishing to be esteemed more than, or even as much as, others."

These were the first entries in a spiritual diary that Angelo Roncalli would faithfully keep for the rest of his life. Wherever he went in the next half century and more, that diary went with him. He came to call it his journal, the journal of a soul, and it grew eventually to thirty-eight notebooks and folders. Msgr. Loris Capovilla, who became personal secretary to Pope John, calls it "an account begun by a fourteen-year-old seminarist . . . the faithful record of a most intimate and sincere communication between a Christian and his God." As boy, priest, bishop, and pope, Roncalli wrote in it by candlelight, oil lamp, and electric light. He set down his deepest thoughts and meditations. And the earliest pages had turned yellow and brittle when on July 9, 1961, Pope John XXIII made this entry: "A peaceful Sunday. Msgr. Loris showed me my old notebooks, which he has kept and is now carefully arranging. He would like to publish them; I feel a certain reluctance. They are a more intimate part of me than anything else I have written; my soul is in these pages."

Then, wrote Monsignor Capovilla, "He paused to read over again the pages of 1895–1899, and with his mild eyes suffused with tears he went on: 'I was a good boy, innocent, somewhat timid. I wanted to love God at all costs and my one idea was to become a priest. Meanwhile I had to fight an enemy within myself, self-love. I imposed severe sacrifices on myself. I took everything very seriously. . . .' "

In the end, he made some minimal corrections of fact and agreed to the publication of the notebooks. "They might do some good to souls who feel drawn to the priesthood," he said. And in 1964, a year after his death, *Journal of a Soul* was published and eventually translated into many languages.

It is not hard to see the stocky, solemn boy in those early entries, earnestly scolding himself and struggling against countless little misdemeanors:

"I will be less of a chatterbox during recreation and will not let myself become too merry."

"I must not doze during meditation, as I did this morning."

"There is another thing—I am really very greedy about fruit."

And again and again as he grew older, he cautioned himself about the temptations of the opposite sex: "Never converse familiarly or play or jest or in any other manner show too much confidence with women, whatever may be their state in life, their age or relationship." Later, he wrote, "As regards purity, it is true that, thanks to my Immaculate Lady, I do not have any strong temptation contrary to this virtue—yet I must confess that I have two eyes in my head which want to look at more than they should."

But the truth is that all these fidgetings of conscience were more an echo of seminary discipline in the 1890s than an actual picture of Angelo Roncalli as a teen-ager. He *was* a good boy. And occasionally the essential gladness inside him broke through the solemnity and we catch a glimpse of his true self. Bewailing his "excessive mirth," he cannot help adding, "But after all, it is always better to be merry than to be melancholy. And remember: 'Rejoice in the Lord.'"

If he had any genuine concerns in those years, they were over a nagging sense of estrangement from his family. Sotto il Monte was close enough that he was often home, but from the first it was not the same. He sat again at the long kitchen table, but now his cousins addressed him by the formal *voi* (you) instead of the old familiar *tu* (thou). And the seminarian's cassock and round hat which seemed so natural in Bergamo immediately set him apart in Sotto il Monte. Some elders now deferred to him, which he found embarrassing, and others, "even those who have taken an interest in me, now look at me askance." Once it was reported to the seminary directors that he put on airs and expected preferential treatment at home. He was duly rebuked and accepted it in silence.

There was in all this, of course, envy of an equal suddenly set apart, the one boy in all the village who had been chosen for the seminary. But there was also the inevitable turmoil in Angelo's own heart between the essential boy he was and the seminarian with the mark of his calling already on him. And he knew it. He saw how easily he fell into the little conceit of declaiming on problems far beyond his wisdom to solve, of taking sides in the endless petty feuds that beset every family. Then he would be contrite: "This is a natural failing with me, wanting to be a Solomon, to sit in judgment, to lay down the law left and right. What presumption, what pride!"

The periods at home grew more trying for him. "Those cursed holidays. . . . I have had three days of my vacation and already I am tired of it. At the sight of so much privation, in the midst of such suspicions, oppressed by so many anxieties, I often sigh and am sometimes driven to tears."

The poverty of his family wore heavily on him, and as his studies took him further and further from their circumscribed world of hard work and simple piety, there seemed less and less to talk about. For their part, the parents felt the rift with at least as much poignancy: here was the son in whom they had such pride, in whom they'd vested such hope, growing away from them. And it must have been hard for them to see how it was his education, the dawning of perceptions they couldn't share, that was responsible, and not Angelo himself, whose love for his mother and father never faltered. Nor could it have been easy for them, in the face of life's day-to-day trials, to sit and listen to the half-formed judgments of their sixteen-year-old seminarian.

Sometimes simmering resentments erupted. In September 1898, his little brother Giovanni fell seriously ill and it seemed to Angelo that his parents were accepting the danger passively. He spoke sharply to them. They replied in kind. Later, oppressed with guilt, he wrote in his journal, "This morning everything was a bit disordered; afterwards, I was ill-mannered with those present when we were talking about the best way to cure my beloved brother. Now I see that if at all times I keep silent, even for the best of reasons, I must suffer for it, and I have to bottle everything up and feel stifled, but I will offer up all this to Jesus and Mary for the greater good of my soul and that of my little Giovanni."

In the evening, his brother seemed better and Angelo walked up the street to see Don Francesco Rebuzzini, his patron and pastor. He was to remember their talk with poignancy—how much better Don Francesco's encouragement made him feel, and the cheerful "*Arrivederci!*" when they parted For when he returned to the church early next morning, Sunday, September 25, to assist with the mass, he found his devoted friend dead at the foot of the altar, mouth open and red with blood. These are the words with which he tells his feelings:

> My good Father, who did so much for me, who set me on the road to the priesthood, has died. I had no tears. I did not weep—but inside I turned to stone. To see him there on the ground with his eyes closed, I thought he looked to me—oh, I shall always remember that sight—like a statue of the dead Jesus, taken down from the Cross. And he spoke no more, looked at me no more. Where is my Father now? He is there, close to the heart of Jesus. May the prayers which he said for me and the prayers I now say for him make me truly like him. That will make sense of last night's "*Arrivederci*" and mean that we shall embrace again in paradise.

He was given Don Francesco's copy of *Imitation of Christ* as a keepsake, and in the hope that he, too, would be called to spend his life as a simple country priest, carried it close for a long time.

There was to be more sorrow in his young life, more family hurts. But he was moving toward an understanding of himself, and of his parents. On a summer evening in 1900, after another unhappy episode at home, he wrote:

> This evening there was an incident which made a profound and painful impression on me. My mother was rather hurt by something I said (which, I confess, might have been put more gently). She said things to me which I had never expected to hear from my mother. . . . This was too much for the heart of a son. This gave me the most bitter sorrow. How could I help giving way to tears? O mother, if only you knew how much I love you, and how I long to see you happy, you would not be able to contain your joy!
>
> Will you, my Jesus, accept this sacrifice which I place in your heart, offering it to you that you may grant me more

meekness and gentleness, and grant my poor, kind mother
greater fortitude.

He was happy in Bergamo. His mind was stirred, his spirit uplifted, and he moved purposefully through the milestones that
mark the life of a seminarian. At fourteen, he had been received
into the sacred tonsure, a ceremonial shaving of the head symbolizing Christ's crown of thorns and marking his admission to
the ecclesiastical state. Three years later, he took the minor
orders.

His horizons were broadening. His vision and philosophy of
life deepened into an attitude of humanism, a conviction that the
priesthood was a service of love. Often, as he sat in the great
cathedral with his fellow students and listened to the brave and
forward-looking sermons of Bishop Guindani, he was fired with
the missionary sense of his calling. He became more absorbed in
his studies—liturgy, world literature, history and the Latin of
Cicero, Virgil, and Ovid. His once-indifferent scholastic record,
though short of brilliant, now put him near the top of his class. In
1896, he was made prefect of his dormitory. A certain special
destiny was becoming clearer.

As it happened, the diocese of Bergamo had for two and a half
centuries maintained a small college in Rome. It had been established in 1640 by the will of a simple priest, Canon Flaminio
Cerasola, and provided scholarships for the most promising students of the diocesan seminary. Over the years, the little school
was absorbed into the Pontifical Roman Seminary, usually called
the Apollinare, among whose graduates were some of the
church's most distinguished ecclesiastics. For a time, following the
bitterness of 1870 when the king's troops marched into Rome, the
Cerasolian scholarship program was dropped. But in 1900, after
tedious negotiations, it was reinstated and three Bergamo seminarians were sent on to the Apollinare to continue their studies.
Among them, Angelo Roncalli was first to be chosen.

IV

THOU ART A PRIEST
FOREVER

In the year before he came to Rome, young Angelo Roncalli, the seminarian from Sotto il Monte, was still grappling with conscience, still doggedly insistent on his own insignificance. In February, during a retreat, he wrote in the journal, "Who am I? Where do I come from? Where am I going? I am nothing. Everything I possess, my being, life understanding, will and memory—all were given me by God. Twenty short years ago all that I see around me was already here; the same sun, moon and stars, the same mountains, seas, deserts, beasts, plants and men; everything was proceeding in its appointed way. And I? I was not here. Everything was being done without me, nobody could imagine me, even in dreams, because I did not exist."

Now it was January 3 in the second year of the new century and Angelo had more immediate cause to feel his obscurity. He was on a train hurtling south through the winter night, across the sleeping Lombard plain and over the high spine of the Apennines of Tuscany, dozing a little, then jolting awake by the sudden thunder of the rails in the mountain tunnels. With his two classmates, Achille Ballini and Guglielmo Carozzi, he was bound for the city of Rome and his new life at the Pontifical Roman Seminary. Once before, as a tourist, he had visited the scurrying, storied city, on a pilgrimage with other Bergamo students. Now he was to live there, to study in one of the great seminaries of the world.

They arrived at 6:30 on the morning of January 4, in the dark of a winter dawn. The Apollinare, when he first saw it, looked dark and forbidding, too. It sat in a maze of little twisting streets, the gloomy stone seminary between the Piazza Sant' Agostino and Via della Scrofa linked by enclosed bridge to the Church of Sant' Apollinare, and both chilled gray by the centuries. His room had a single barred window high in the wall, a hard bed, table, bookshelf, and running water. The ancient stone floor never seemed quite dry. Yet in his first letter home he wrote:

I could never have imagined I would be so fortunate! The food here is different from what we have in Sotto il Monte or what I had in Bergamo: we live like lords! In fact, they tell me that I grow fatter every day. The welcome I received and the affection shown me by my reverend superiors are truly beyond all praise. I have found excellent companions so that I now feel quite at home in the seminary. The lectures and homework are no trouble to me at all; in fact I enjoy them. Every day I go out for a walk and so far I have been able to visit many holy places and pray there for myself and for you. I have already been twice to Saint Peter's and today I have been to the tomb of Saint Philip Neri. The other evening I was present at a congress held in the College of *Propaganda Fide* during which forty seminarians who had come here to study in order to return as missionaries to their own lands recited their own compositions in forty different languages. If only you could have seen them! They were all colors, white, yellow, red—and some with faces and hands as black as charcoal.

I was able to see the pope on Sunday evening in Saint Peter's, in the midst of great splendor. I got quite near to him so that I could see him plainly and receive his blessing.

In that solemn and moving moment I thought of you all, and of all my other relatives, benefactors and friends, and he, that good old man, blessed you all.

But now I want to have news of you. Good-bye. God bless you.

This is my address: To the Reverend Seminarian Angelo Roncalli. Seminario Pontifico S. Apollinare. Piazza S. Apollinare. Rome.

It was Rome that captivated him first, as it must anyone with feeling for the past. Just beyond the walls of the seminary, beneath the very ground on which the city was built, lay the record of western civilization from its beginnings in a pagan village on the Capitoline Hill. And the ruins and restorations of the pagan village, and of the Roman Republic and the empire, the remains of primitive churches and Christian hiding places, the splendors of the Renaissance—all this was now his, and he could not get enough of it.

More than forty years later, he wrote of this time, "Oh, those churches and altars, and the ceremonies, and the examples of the martyrs and confessors! One feels one cannot grow old in Rome, or perhaps growing old there is always lit by the fervor of youth."

It was a holy year. Pilgrims from all over Europe, even from America, come for the apostolic blessing of ninety-year-old Pope Leo XIII, filled the streets. Along with awed seminarians from other lands, with whom he now shared a spiritual Roman citizenship, Angelo roamed the historic city at every opportunity. It came alive in his heart. In the silent stone, he read the stories of emperors and popes who rebuilt the past and added their own monuments to the future: the great Roman Forum, the Colosseum, the Arch of Constantine. Below the pavement, in dank catacombs that seemed still to echo a two thousand-year-old tragedy, Angelo Roncalli felt the chill terror that engulfed Christ's first followers, and caught the flame of courage that had seen them through their martyrdom.

He worked hard at the Apollinare. He was keenly aware that his presence there was a particular honor—and that it imposed on him particular obligations—and his journal for this period is peppered with cautions and reminders. A photograph, taken in January 1901, shows him in cassock and vestment, hair carefully brushed to the side, eyes gazing levelly back at the camera, and on his face an expression of such innocence and calm as to refute the turmoil of unworthiness in his notes. Underneath he wrote, "First portrait of the cleric Angelo Roncalli, at twenty years."

Although he had already completed a year's study of theology at Bergamo, he was now obliged to start the course from the beginning because of his youth. The teachers at the Apollinare were among the best in the secular clergy and Angelo would have reason to remember them well. There was an assistant lecturer in canon law, a thin, ascetic-looking young man with steel-rimmed glasses and a gentle, abstracted manner whose understated brilliance marked him, even then, even in the unripened judgment of a young seminarian, for a larger future. He was Don Eugenio Pacelli, to be known one day, and ever after, as Pope Pius XII.

Angelo's spiritual director from 1902 until after his ordination was Don Francesco Pitocchi, a Redemptorist father, who suffered an illness that made it impossible for him to lift his head from his chest. But his spirit soared. He listened more than he spoke—"he read our eyes; he read our hearts"—and listened with constant kindness. His spiritual teaching was summed up in the words, "Always obey, with simplicity and good nature, and leave everything else to the Lord." Later, as pope, John would say, "Ah, Padre Francesco! If finally we managed to make something of our lives we must say it came from him."

His professor of church history, Msgr. Umberto Benigni, was to make a mark of another sort. He was a flurried, intense man who spoke with a slight stutter and published a church paper, *Voce della Verità*, in the seminary basement. Correcting proofs in class, he would often convey the news of the day to the students in little asides; they themselves were forbidden to read newspapers, even the Vatican's own *L'Osservatore Romano*, but in light of Msgr. Benigni's later activities, one must question the even-handedness of his pronouncements. After World War I, the discovery of a secret cache of papers in Belgium revealed him to be ringleader of a virulent anti-Modernist cabal.

The bursar was a harried little man named Garroni to whom Angelo frequently had to turn for the loan of small sums. This exasperated him and may have colored his judgment of the harried bursar, whom he describes as scuttling between the refectory tables during the midday meal and cautioning the students against eating too much. "One would have thought the responsibility for provisioning all Rome weighed on his shoulders."

Three weeks after Easter in that first year, he made his first retreat since coming to Rome. "How am I?" he wrote in the journal. "Certainly I cannot complain about the graces Jesus has sent me. As for myself, however, I must confess that I have not changed at all from what I was before. . . . I must never think of my studies during religious duties. I will make my visit to the Blessed Sacrament with special fervor and modesty. Most of all, a careful watch over my eyes during our walks, especially in certain districts."

In June, he was awarded the baccalaureate in theology and won a prize for studies in the Hebrew language. It was an early indication of what was to be his lifelong devotion to the Scriptures. He had a Mediterranean sense of tradition, a reverence for the early church fathers and saints, for Dante and Cicero, whose works he learned intimately and quoted at length. His Latin was excellent—the old pedant of Carvico, Don Pietro Bolis, had done his work well—and he could easily lose himself reading medieval history.

Only a few days after arriving at the Apollinare, he had written home, "And you, my beloved Mother, do you remember that last morning, when neither of us had the heart to say a word to the other? Here in Rome I forget nothing." Now, the school year over, he told her joyously, "Next week I shall leave Rome for home. Please make my usual little room ready for me because I am coming home to study hard, not to amuse myself. I am just the same as before so I don't want you to go to any special trouble.

Just imagine I am coming home from the seminary in Bergamo. My respectful greetings to the reverend parish priest and curate, and tell them I am very glad to be coming home to bother them again."

The Italian government remained antagonistic to the church. Among the other small irritations it imposed was a military conscription edict that took no notice of canon law forbidding priests to bear arms and made no provision for excepting seminarians from service. So it was that on November 30, 1901, a few days past his twentieth birthday, Angelo Roncalli had no choice but to present himself for duty in Bergamo, at the garrison of the Seventy-third Infantry Regiment of the Lombardy Brigade. Its motto was "*Accerrimus Hostibus*" ("Irresistible to the Enemy").

At the beginning it must have seemed to him like stepping into a cold bath. The abrupt transition from the devout and monastic shelter of the seminary to the rough world of the barracks, a world in which obscenity and blasphemy were part of ordinary discourse and where carnal hungers were cheerfully discussed and avidly pursued, was a psychological jolt to young Roncalli, one he would not soon forget. Yet he could not help liking his new comrades. That was his nature. His innate decency and warmth seemed to call forth the best in them, and some became his longtime friends.

One of the first letters, to Father Pitocchi and the rector at the Apollinare, reflected his confused feelings: "Mine is a life of the greatest sacrifice, a true purgatory." He found the requirements of military discipline "very wearing, principally in the beginning. Suffice it to say that this miserable letter of mine was begun perhaps a week ago without my ever being able to finish it." Then he conceded certain solaces, "I have excellent officers who make it clear that they like me very much; they show me great respect and make certain that I have the utmost freedom to fulfill my religious obligations. Among my comrades in the ranks, most of whom are from Bergamo and Brescia, I have observed thus far only marks of reverence and affection."

The fact that he could visit Sotto il Monte and his old teachers at the Bergamo seminary buoyed him, too. And the discipline, though of a different sort, was in fact not so confining as that with which he had already lived nearly ten years. The drills and long mountain marches toughened him and were no more arduous than the time when he had to walk over Monte San Giovanni every day to get to school. Soon he was taking it all in stride. He was promoted to corporal and just before his discharge in November 1902, to sergeant, and returning home to visit his family, cut a rather elegant figure in black uniform with silver piping and a fine military mustache.

But his initiation into the ingrained immorality of the world left a mark. Back in Rome, during a long and soothing retreat at the end of the year, he filled his journal with reflections and resolve:

O my good Lord, shall I too be sent to hell? I know what life in a barracks is like—I shudder at the very thought of it. What blasphemies there were in that place, and what filth! And would hell be any better? If I were to end up there, while my fellow soldiers, the poor wretches, who grew up surrounded by evil, were sent to paradise—no wonder I tremble at the thought! I must pity all sinners and never cease to thank my God for the kindness he has shown to me. . . .

Even if I were to be pope, even if my name were to be invoked and revered by all and inscribed on marble monuments, I should still have to stand before the divine judge, and what would I be worth then?

Meanwhile, what matters is that I should never be ashamed of my poverty, indeed I should be proud of it. I am of the same family as Christ—and what more can I want? I am not at all what I believe myself to be or what my pride wishes me to be taken for. My father is a peasant who spends his days hoeing and digging, and I, far from being better than my father, am worth much less, for my father is simple and good, while in me there is nothing but malice . . . self-love.

I shall always remember 1902: the year of my military service, the year of conflicts. I might, like so many other poor wretches, have lost my vocation—and I did not lose it. I might have lost holy purity and the grace of God, but God did not allow me to do this. I passed through the mire and by his grace I was kept unpolluted. I am still alive, healthy, robust as before, better than before. Jesus, I thank you, I love you.

It was only later, in the perspective of the years, that Angelo Roncalli understood how his months in the army had widened his experience, how they had deepened his compassion and helped him better understand the frailties of men. As pope, with his judgments tempered by time, he made some notes for an autobiography and, writing in the third person, said this about being a soldier, "He will always cherish the most precious memory of these twelve months, as an experience of strict discipline, a means of getting to know the youthful spirit of Italy's sons, and of finding out the best practical ways of drawing them to all that is good."

Some sixty years after his military service, Pope John recognized the chaplain-general of the Italian army at an audience in the Vatican. The chaplain knelt to kiss the papal ring and the pope helped him to his feet. "We were a sergeant once," he said wistfully.

Returned to the sanctuary of the Apollinare, Angelo lost himself in study and prayer. In later years, because he took such pleasure in recalling his peasant beginnings, most people never suspected the high level of his intellectual achievement, the high value he placed on learning, the effort he put into gaining it, and the special satisfaction it gave him. Around this time, he was much in the thrall of Saint Philip Neri, the sixteenth-century Florentine who exalted and reformed the religious life of Rome when it was at low ebb, and of Philip's disciple, Cardinal Cesare Baronius. To the broad spectrum of Romans who came to the cell-like room known as the Oratory, Philip offered instruction, inspiration, and the grace of God. To the young Baronius, he was a source of constant encouragement in an epic undertaking, *Annales Ecclesiastici*, a history of the early church unrivaled in scholarship until the advent of modern research.

Could it be, Roncalli sometimes wondered, that his priestly destiny might take him in a similar direction, that instead of becoming a pastor of souls in some little village, he would add to the written record of the church? As it happened, he would indeed compile several works of historic value, first among them a life of Cesare Baronius. He would tell how the good cardinal made a pilgrimage every day to the unfinished Basilica of Saint Peter's, stopping to give a penny to the beggars and, once inside, kneeling to kiss the bronze foot of the Apostle, to whom he vowed *"obedientia et pax"* ("obedience and peace"). Angelo was to take these words for his own motto, but, though he would have been content as a church historian, a larger task awaited him.

Meanwhile he worked on, learning and maturing. Soon after the new year, he recorded a fresh insight in the journal:

> The concept of holiness which I had applied to myself was mistaken. In every one of my actions, I used to call to mind the image of some saint whom I had set myself to imitate down to the smallest particular. I used to say to myself: in this case Saint Aloysius would have done so and so, or: he would not do this or that. However, it turned out that I was never able to achieve what I thought I could do, and this worried me. The method was wrong. From the saints I must take the substance, not the accidents, of their virtues. I am not Saint Aloysius, nor must I seek holiness in his particular way, but according to the requirements of my own nature. I must not be the dry, bloodless reproduction of a model, however perfect.

Similarly, he listened to a gathering storm of controversy over "Modernism"—a characterization that lumped together every new idea for dealing with the needs and problems of the church—and he applied to it a cool intelligence and the earthy, inborn realism to which millions would later respond. To avoid the extremes, to recognize that in the arguments of both sides passion often spoke more loudly than perception, this was the course he chose. He had come of age in the stir and excitement of Bergamo's zeal for social innovation and was inevitably receptive to new ideas. The time would come when the rabid defense of Orthodoxy concerned him more than the danger of Modernism. But he remained scrupulous in his faithfulness to the Catholic canon and dogma. He refused to read pamphlets and papers surreptitiously circulated. And when he had been twenty years a priest he could still caution, "The spirit of modernity, liberty and criticism is like good wine—bad for weak heads."

It was one of the small miracles of the Italian seminary system at the turn of the century that young men who had donned the cassock at age twelve and been shut away from the doings of the world for the next decade could still most often emerge as warm and sensitive pastors. In all those growing-up years, in the critical time of transition from boy to man, they were severely supervised, admonished to shun women, forbidden to read a newspaper, discuss politics, or hear a deviating point of view. They had only their love of God and fellow men to fall back on.

In the summer of 1903, Pope Leo lay dying, the end of his long reign at hand. Only a few months before, on February 20, Angelo had written, "A great day today. Our Holy Father has completed the twenty-fifth year of his pontificate. The Catholic world has been at his feet to present him with its congratulations and homage on this happy occasion, which has occurred only twice in nineteen centuries."

· It was not the Catholic world alone which paid homage to Leo in the spring of that anniversary year. Triumphantly the seminarian records the arrival in the Vatican of England's Edward VII:

Rome is officially celebrating . . . flags, festoons, decorations in the streets. He is king of one of the greatest nations, and so he deserves to be honored and respected. But a gorgeous livery, a waving plume are enough to excite men and throw them into ecstasy, and meanwhile no one has a thought to spare for God. . . . Yet this man, a Protestant, did one really good thing while he was in Rome: Showing himself superior to certain tendentious currents of anticlericalism; a highly significant event this, a heretical king of Protestant England, which has persecuted the Catholic church for more than three centuries, going in person to pay his respects to the poor old pope, held like a prisoner in his own house.

And a few weeks later, this ebullient note about the visit of Emperor William II of Germany: "It is truly an act of Divine Providence, a real triumph for the papacy. A Protestant emperor, after centuries of hostility, ascends the Vatican stairs and humbles himself before the greatness of the papal throne!"

Like most of the faithful of Rome, Roncalli's appraisal of these events reflected more his devout personal wish, that the apostates would return to the fold, than the fact, which was simply a matter of the respect due and paid to a great and long-lived spiritual leader. How little he yet understood the rest of the Christian world, how much his views would broaden before the time of his own ecumenical papacy, is seen in this journal entry of a year later: "Our excellent father director has begged me to take as my companion, during the time we spend on our walks, a young Protestant who has been given hospitality while being prepared for the abjuration of his former faith. Poor young man, I feel so sorry for him! He is a good youth, but for the best nine years of his life—he is now eighteen—he has been thoroughly imbued with the instruction which the Protestants are so expert at giving. . . . As for these unfortunates outside the church, we must feel sorry for them, poor children, pray hard for them."

Still, the pontificate of Leo XIII was not without significant steps toward reconciliation and reality. Leo had defended Catholic political participation in Germany and tempered Catholic

absolutism in France. He established the transcendental philosophy of Saint Thomas Aquinas as church doctrine and, with the
encyclical, *Rerum Novarum*, charted a path toward economic
liberty in modern society. And though Leo remained shut away
in his Vatican domain, though he continued the ban of Pius IX on
Catholic involvement in national politics in Italy, he did encourage Catholics to vote in municipal elections and even to serve on
local councils.

On July 20, 1903, in his ninety-fourth year, the Holy Father
died. For twenty-two-year-old Angelo Roncalli, it was a deeply
emotional time. Leo was the pope of his entire lifetime. Now after
the solemn stateliness of the funeral came the tense, rumor-ridden
days of the conclave. With fellow students, he was often in the
crowded square of Saint Peter's, watching for the swirl of white
smoke that would herald the election of a new pope. But day
after day the smoke was black, and instead of a decision the
people heard reports, which were later confirmed, that Franz
Joseph, the Austrian emperor, was attempting to exercise a veto
over the selection of the leading aspirant. He was Cardinal
Mariano Rampolla, Leo's secretary of state, a man of forward-
looking social views. Angelo was appalled. The intrusion of
power politics into the affairs of the church was inconceivable to
him and the lesson he learned was unforgettable. Whether Franz
Joseph's threat had any effect, or whether Rampolla's outlook
was also too advanced for his brother cardinals, the man who
finally appeared on the central balcony of the basilica to answer
the cheers of the crowd was Giuseppe Sarto, cardinal patriarch of
Venice, who chose to be known as Pope Pius X. One of his early
acts was to reaffirm the nonviability of the sacred conclave and to
deny again any right to a secular veto.

Early in April 1903 Angelo had written, "The more I love obscurity the greater and worthier I shall be before God and men,
and the more useful my ministry will be."

His ministry was drawing closer. On April 10, he was ordained subdeacon at Saint John Lateran in Rome. "The only words my stammering tongue can utter are those of Saint Paul: 'It is no longer I who live, but Christ who lives in me.'" Just before Christmas he was ordained deacon. His investiture as a priest was only eight months off.

"What will become of me? Shall I become a good theologian or a famous jurist, or shall I have a country parish and be just a simple priest? What does all this matter to me? I must be prepared to be none or all these, or even more than all these, as God wills. After all, it is easy for Jesus to scatter to the four winds my dream of cutting a brilliant figure in the eyes of the world."

This last continued to trouble him, that his aspirations were worldly, that even his zest for learning was a sin of pride: to do well on his examinations; to succeed in the eyes of others. "Mind and memory are gifts from God," he wrote. "Why should I lose heart if others have more of these gifts than I?"

Nor in all the long years to come was he ever wholly free of concern that he might be trying to bend circumstances to his ambition rather than accepting them as the will of God. His route to the throne of Saint Peter may appear to be a direct one, one success in the service of the church following after another. In truth, his life would be full of obstacles, frustrations, seeming failure, even humiliation. But he kept trying to face up to all these with the stoic calm of his peasant fathers: If the grapes froze in spring there would be no wine in winter, but there would always be another spring. That was God's way.

On August 1, 1904, along with ten other ordinands from various seminaries, he walked up the narrow streets that led to the top of the Caelian Hill, to the house of the Passionist Fathers of Saint John and Saint Paul "with its crown of Christian monuments," there to lock himself in retreat until the day of his consecration. He thought of the future but the past was much with him. "From my window I could see the Colosseum, the Lateran and the Appian Way." In the night, he heard the fathers as they rose for the matins, "the sound of their footsteps and the trailing of their long black habits along the dark corridors." And before the final vows, before finally and irrevocably he gave himself to God, he attuned his perspectives to the inspiration of a humble Spanish lay brother: "Good Brother Thomas who cleans my room and serves me at table gives me plenty of food for thought. He is no longer young . . . at everyone's beck and call, as simple as a creature can be who has no alluring ambitions, no glowing mirages ahead, content to be a poor lay brother for the rest of his life. Before the goodness of Brother Thomas I feel my nothingness; I ought to kiss the hem of his habit and take him for my teacher. And yet I am almost a priest, the recipient of so many graces! Ah, Brother Thomas, what a lot I am learning from you!"

On the evening of August 9, he went to Saint John Lateran to pray. Just after dawn on the tenth, the vice-rector, Father Domenico Spolverini, came to him at the monastery, and together they made their way down the long, rocky hill and crossed the city in silence to the Piazza del Popolo. There, in a little baroque church with a golden dome and pillared doorway, Santa Maria in Monte Santo, Angelo Roncalli, still three months short of the canonical age of twenty-three, was ordained a priest.

"When all was over and I raised my eyes, having sworn the oath of eternal fidelity, I saw the blessed image of Our Lady. She seemed to smile at me. She sent a gentle calm and peace into my soul which I shall never forget."

Afterward, he went back to the Apollinare, which was deserted, for the students were all on holiday at Roccantica, the summer villa of the seminary. He wrote letters to Bishop Guindani in Bergamo and to his family in Sotto il Monte, "that they should share the joy in my heart." Then he was alone with God.

In the morning he went to Saint Peter's to celebrate his first mass. "The great square had much to say to me as I crossed it. I went down into the crypt near the tomb of the Apostle. There was a group of friends invited by the vice-rector. I said the votive Mass of Saint Peter and Saint Paul. I remember that among the feelings with which my heart was overflowing, the most powerful of all was a great love for the church, for the cause of Christ, a sense of total dedication, and of an intention, indeed a sacred oath, of allegiance to the chair of Saint Peter and of unwearying work for souls."

Another great joy awaited him. Father Spolverini had arranged an audience with the pope and when Pius appeared, serene, white-haired, the good father said, "Your Holiness, here is a young priest of Bergamo who has just celebrated his first mass." Roncalli, kneeling, repeated the vows he had made over the tomb of Saint Peter. The pope placed a hand on his head. "Well done. Well done, my boy," he said. "I will ask the good Lord to grant a special blessing on these good intentions of yours."

Pius moved on and spoke to someone else. Then, for some reason, he turned back. "When shall you be back home," he said, "in Bergamo?"

"For the Feast of the Assumption, Holiness," Roncalli replied.

"Ah, what a feast that will be. And how those fine bells of Bergamo will peal out on that day!"

That evening, the young priest journeyed to Roccantica in the Sabine Hills, a compact little village that reminded him of Sotto il Monte. The students waited for him at a little bridge, and behind them the villa was beautifully lit, as in celebration. They sang *"Tu es sacerdos"* ("Thou art a priest forever") and Father Pitocchi came forward to embrace him. Later Roncalli wrote, "The father was too kind in what he said about me: his affection blinded him a little."

The day after, he started for home.

V

RETURN TO BERGAMO

Going north, bearing him home, the train seemed to crawl. On the way, he celebrated mass in Florence and the next day in Milan, at the tomb of Saint Charles Borromeo. And finally on August 15, 1904, the Feast of the Assumption, he was back in Sotto il Monte. "I count that day among the happiest of my life," he wrote, "for me, for my relatives and benefactors, for everyone."

The weathered little church where he had been baptized twenty-three years before was crowded with Roncalli relatives, expectant and proud, dressed in somber Sunday black despite the heat of the summer day. After the mass, Angelo Roncalli preached his first sermon. At the suggestion of the pastor, Father Luigi Battaglia, he had chosen for his subject the theological significance of the Assumption of the Blessed Virgin. It was said to be a sound discourse, although perhaps a bit beyond the comprehension of the brethren. (The Assumption did not become church dogma until the *ex cathedra* declaration of Pope Pius XII in 1950.)

No matter. There was open weeping, and at one point, himself a little undone, the young priest's voice broke and he said, "Dear brothers, my dear real brothers, seeing you cry this way unsettles me, though I know they are tears of joy."

Afterward, they swarmed around him with congratulations. And an elder, clinging to his hand, offered the traditional commendation to a new priest: "Now you must work hard and become pope." They both laughed.

The serene summer days at Colombera Farm passed quickly enough. In November, the start of the new academic year, he returned to the Apollinare for further study. He had already earned a doctorate in theology; now he enrolled for another in canon law. He was also appointed assistant instructor.

His exalted station in life seems not to have changed him much, nor stifled his wit. Responding to his mother's request for another photograph of himself, he wrote, "It is true that I have not yet sent my portrait to the family whereas I have sent it to the parish priest, but this is first of all because you already had it and he hadn't—and then I don't want to distribute too many of my portraits, not being a pope or cardinal or bishop but a mere humble priest. It is neither necessary nor seemly for my face to be seen here, there and everywhere."

The new priest faced some insecurities in those early days, however. In December 1904, for the Feast of the Immaculate Conception, Don Francesco Pitocchi, his spiritual director at the Apollinare, had arranged for him to preach a sermon to the Children of Mary, an association of girls and young women who met at the Chapel of the Madonna in San Gioacchino, near Roccantica. Eighteen years later, in a memoir of Don Francesco, this is how Roncalli described what happened:

> Naturally I wrote everything down. At the time I was
> quite pleased with it, but now that I am more mature I would

take care not to prepare it in that way: it was too studied, too flowery, too poetical.

The next day, complete failure! I was at once put off by the general atmosphere which to me, a country man, seemed too aristocratic. I lost my presence of mind, my fluency, my fervor; I even lost my way in my own manuscript: I confused the New Testament with the Old, the middle with the beginning and the beginning with the end: in short, a disaster! When I had finished and torn myself away from the altar, I was like a shipwrecked man cast up on shore, completely lost.

But I found myself in the arms of Father Francesco, in his little room near the sacristy, and he was doing all he could to encourage me. In the end I was content to have suffered that mortification, which he made me offer to Our Lady, with a resolve to attempt another public sermon as soon as possible.

Bishop Guindani of Bergamo, revered in his diocese and respected by the Vatican, died in October 1904, and Pope Pius X designated Msgr. Giacomo Maria Radini-Tedeschi, a patrician and progressive, who was nervously regarded by some in the curia, to be his successor. The consecration took place on January 29, 1905, in the Sistine Chapel, in the yellow light of the altar candles with the sunshine filtering through the high windows, and was in every way a splendid ceremony. The pope himself performed the sacred rite and two young priests of Bergamo, Guglielmo Carozzi and Angelo Roncalli, were chosen to assist at the mass. At the ultimate moment, it was Roncalli who held the Book of the Gospels, symbolizing the yoke of Christ, on Radini's bowed neck as Pope Pius placed his hands on the newly consecrated bishop's head and conferred on him the special gift of the Holy Spirit.

As it happened, that moment was to have a special significance for Roncalli.

Afterward, the pope raised Bishop Radini-Tedeschi to his feet and spoke to him so softly that no one else could hear the words. A look of transcendental happiness lit Radini's face.

"What did he say?" someone whispered. "What's it about?"

No one knew. But it was a secret Roncalli would some day share.

Giacomo Maria Radini-Tedeschi was born in 1857, in Piacenza, a farming center on the Po, little more than forty miles south of Bergamo. His family was of the old Emilia-Romagna nobility, elevated in spirit as well as title, and several had become priests or nuns. He himself had been Count Radini-Tedeschi when he surrendered the privileges of his rank to serve God.

Tall and regal, gifted with grace and eloquence, he soon attracted the notice of Pope Leo XIII. He was called to Rome and for the next fifteen years served as unofficial ambassador of the Holy See, furthering the movement for social action, coordinating the activities of diocesan associations throughout Italy. His quarters in Rome became a center of discussion for people of diverse stations and backgrounds who held in common a belief that the faithful must not shut their eyes to the material needs of men. Their instrument was the organization called *Opera dei Congressi*. From the time of the *non-expedit* of Pius IX forbidding Catholics to participate in national affairs, the *Opera dei Congressi* had served as a sort of clearing house, the only church body in Italy able to exchange information with the government and act on the nation's grave educational, economic, and social problems. Radini-Tedeschi became its vice-president.

He and his followers believed that the struggle for social justice was an indivisible part of the Christian ethic and they worked hard for a broad national program of Catholic Action, such as the one already developing in Bergamo. They felt it was time for Catholics to take up a responsibility for their own country, to vote and hold parliamentary office, even in the absence of an agreement between the Italian government and the Vatican. With their votes and voices they could seek, after all, not only the democratic advancement of the nation, but freedom for the church and the independence of the Holy See.

It was not to be. After the death of Pope Leo in 1903, a new secretary of state, Cardinal Raphael Merry del Val, branded the ideas of the *Opera dei Congressi* irreverent and unacceptable, and the members of its governing board resigned. Soon after, Pope Pius X dissolved the *Opera dei Congressi* altogether. Its work would be taken up again later, to be sure, but the enforced interruption did nothing to avert a future catastrophe: One wonders whether the roots of Benito Mussolini's Fascist dictatorship would have found the Italian soil so amenable if Christian Democracy could have had an unbroken evolution.

It was a devastating blow to Radini-Tedeschi. He had been totally committed to the work of the *Opera* and had invested in it all his considerable energies and emotion. But his loyalty to the Holy Father never wavered. When Pius offered him the bishopric of Bergamo, he accepted without question.

Pope Leo had been a man of the twentieth century. The church historian, Franz Xaver Seppelt, said of him, "His ability lay not in new ideas but in the applications of old ones to modern life." Pius was another sort, a pastor of souls. Refusing to involve himself in those church affairs in which he felt less than fully qualified, he left most diplomatic and political matters to Cardinal Merry del Val, on whose advice he had dissolved the *Opera dei Congressi*.

Yet it was Pius X who ultimately restored to Italian Catholics the right to take part in national politics. And it was Pius, and not his advisors, who decided that Monsignor Radini-Tedeschi should succeed Bishop Guindani in Bergamo, the very heart of social action.

"They proposed that you should be archbishop of Palermo," he told Radini, "and I said no. They proposed you for Ravenna. I said no. Then here is Bergamo, and I said yes." And he added warmly, "Go there, then. For such consolation as a bishop can find, Bergamo is Italy's first diocese."

Perhaps there was satisfaction in some quarters of the curia that the turbulent Radini-Tedeschi was being shunted from the centers of command at the Vatican. But there seems little doubt that Pius

did not share this feeling. He held Radini-Tedeschi in personal
esteem and high regard as a churchman, and proved it by perform-
ing the rite of consecration himself.

Soon after, the newly sanctified bishop called on Monsignor
Spolverini, rector of the Apollinare. He was seeking a young
priest of the Bergamo district to serve as his secretary, he said.
Was there someone the monsignor could recommend?

What happened next, with its immeasurable impact on the life
of Angelo Roncalli, on the distant future of the church and its
place in the world, is not certain. According to one version,
Spolverini promptly suggested Roncalli as one who was intelligent and easy to get on with. But another source has it that the
rector mentioned two of the seminarians who had come to the
Apollinare from Bergamo, Roncalli and his friend Guglielmo
Carozzi, and that Carozzi, interviewed first, told the bishop that
Roncalli was the right person for the job. And finally it has been
said that the bishop, an exceptional man with deeply spiritual
insight, asked no one's advice, and, instead of choosing some more
experienced priest of his acquaintance, decided upon the obscure
young man who had assisted at his consecration.

Whatever the circumstances, Angelo Roncalli accepted the
post and, instead of becoming a church historian or country
priest, was set on the long course, sometimes full of blind turnings, sometimes at a seeming dead end, that would lead him to the
throne of Saint Peter.

The new bishop and his secretary entered Bergamo on April 9,
1905. It would be hard to conceive of two men more dissimilar in
appearance. Radini-Tedeschi was striking, clearly at home in the
world, with the poise that comes easily to one of his aristocratic
heritage. "*Eccolà, Monsignore Radini*," Roncalli wrote years later.
"Look at Monsignor Radini, in his beautiful, erect, imposing
person. Nature was very generous to him." Roncalli himself was
half a head shorter, already inclining to stoutness and marked by a
rough, good-humored peasant face. The bishop spoke "with

incomparable pleasantness, seasoning his conversation with unexpected wit." The secretary's Italian still rang with the jarring accents of the Lombard country people, and sometimes he broke into the Bergamesque dialect altogether.

But Radini-Tedeschi had more than an elegant bearing and fine manners, and his young secretary had more than a warm peasant personality. The bishop, one of the most brilliant and best-loved leaders of Catholic Action, probably also knew more about pastoral organization for social and economic improvement than anyone in Italy. Not even in the face of his great disappointment was he one to abandon principle. In Roncalli's biography of the man he called "the polar star of my priesthood," a work that unwittingly tells us as much about himself as it does about the bishop during their ten years together, Roncalli wrote that there was something of the soldier in Radini-Tedeschi's spirit. "He loved a fight for the good cause, for the rights of people, for Christianity. But Radini did not like a war fought with needles. What he really liked were such battles in which one could fight like a perfect knight, a cavalier, out in the open and on a wide field."

As for the secretary, he gladly committed his energies to the whirlwind demands of his *padrone*. Soon he was known as the "bishop's shadow." And half a century later, in an otherwise insignificant aside to a Vatican audience, he revealed something of his compassion, not learned from Radini-Tedeschi, but surely reinforced in their ten years together. As pope, John had a small seat for his own secretary installed in his official automobile, which had originally come to him equipped with only one great thronelike chair. "When I served as secretary to my bishop," John explained, "I often had to run behind the noble man because there was no room for me in the carriage. I willingly puffed along, but the poor bishop never enjoyed a ride, for he kept worrying about me and looking back to see that I hadn't collapsed."

Before they were fairly settled in the episcopal palace in Bergamo, the new bishop and his secretary were off on the first of a continuing series of pilgrimages, first to the tomb of Saint Charles

Borromeo in Milan, then to Lourdes, France, where the peasant girl Bernadette Soubirous had seen a vision of the Virgin Mary half a century before, and to the holy places in Arles, Lyons, and Paray-le-Monial. It was the farthest Roncalli had ever traveled, and the first time he had left Italy. He noted that wherever they went Bishop Radini-Tedeschi made inquiries into the current workings of French Catholic Action groups. When they returned, they fell to work.

There were some 430,000 Catholics in Bergamo in 1905, 350 parishes, 512 churches, 2,000 priests, and 400 seminarians—and all were the bishop's responsibility. Radini-Tedeschi, then forty-eight years old and at the height of his powers, was determined to confine his activities to his own diocese. But he was not unaware, nor was Roncalli, that the example of what was achieved in Bergamo, the *cattolicissima città*, would have an inevitable effect on the entire Italian church.

They began with a widespread construction program. They had found the chancery in an appallingly run-down state: dark, damp, and uncomfortable. The magnificent seventeenth-century cathedral, too, suffered from decades of neglect, and some of its priceless masterpieces were in danger of irreparable damage. Radini-Tedeschi promptly moved all the curial offices to the bishop's palace and ordered construction of a new episcopal residence. At the same time, work was begun on a major renovation of the cathedral, including restoration of the bishops' tombs. Churches, monasteries, and schools began rising across the diocese. "Stones will speak of thee," wrote Roncalli, proudly, of his bishop.

The seminary, too, was modernized, with the installation of electricity, piped water, baths, and science laboratories. When it became a military hospital during World War I, a visiting general remarked, "And they tell me that priests are backward! This building is proof that they are pioneers of progress."

Radini-Tedeschi began a series of canonical visits that would eventually take him into every one of the parishes in the diocese; Roncalli accompanied him faithfully, taking notes. And hardly a year passed that the two were not off on a pilgrimage to some distant place. Before the bishop's illness and the outbreak of war curtailed their travels, they had visited France, Spain, Palestine, Germany, Austria, Hungary, Poland, and Switzerland. Between 1905 and 1913 they made five pilgrimages to Lourdes, a shrine of special meaning for both, and regularly attended social study conferences in various parts of France. Soon Roncalli was at ease in the French language and had come to know a goodly number of foreign prelates. He gained important insights into other cultures and other customs.

It is likely that no trip abroad was more memorable for him than the pilgrimage to the Holy Land in 1906. He sent back a series of dispatches to *L'Eco di Bergamo*, a newspaper for which he retained a particular affection until the day he died. The present editor, Msgr. Andrea Spada, notes that although Roncalli was only twenty-five years old at the time and preoccupied with religious obligations and his duties for Bishop Radini-Tedeschi, he made an excellent reporter. His observations were astute, his journalistic instincts sound, and he could turn a fine phrase. From Cana, on September 30, he filed this dispatch: "The road between Nazareth and Cana is something horrible. For us Italians it would hardly be acceptable as a rural path, and to think that the poor people here pay ten times what it is worth. But we are under Turks here, don't forget, and the Turkish government knows all about extortion and incredible injustice, but nothing about roads."

Next day, he reports an incident from Tiberias: "Because of the salvos that these Arabs fired under our noses in honor of the occasion, the horse of Don Soldini reared up and fell with the unfortunate priest directly under the hooves of the horses that were drawing one of the coaches. I saw our bishop leap from the coach and return holding up good Don Soldini with one hand and stanching the blood flowing in great quantities from his cheek with the other. Fortunately, the wound was not too serious. . . ."

And from the Lake of Tiberias, he writes with that ineffable sense of the real and the mystical that was the fabric of his faith, the clear vision of what we are and the shining aspiration of what we might be:

> At 4:30 A.M. nearly all the pilgrims were up. The indescribable racket of the boatmen, young Moslems all, who had been waiting a long time with their boats, had roused even those who were dog-tired. And now we were in their hands. The boats were not by the shore so boarding required a special procedure. Two of these big rascals, shouting like a hundred, took each of us by the legs and, with singular ease and speed, they carried us gently to the boats. . . .
>
> But I shall never forget the enchantment, the heart's ease, the spiritual flavor I discovered this morning floating upon these waters. Little by little, as our small boat stood out into the lake, the first light of dawn gave color to the water, the houses and the surrounding hills. We did not speak, but our hearts were stirred. It was as though we could see Jesus crossing this same lake in Peter's boat. Jesus was before us and we could see him: unworthy though we were, we sailed toward him on the water, and our prayer was silent, but spontaneous and eloquent . . . as we touched the shore the sun appeared.

In the company of his bishop, Roncalli found himself in the very mainstream of the church. Radini-Tedeschi moved in a circle of ranking prelates, cardinals, and diplomats, and where he went his secretary went. Giacomo della Chiesa was one of Radini's closest friends, and Achille Ratti had been his classmate at the Lombard College in Rome, and both would attain the papal throne.

To the ecclesiastical palace in Bergamo, to confer with the bishop, came the churchmen and lay leaders of a reanimated Catholic social movement that Roncalli had long admired from a distance, whose works he had studied: Professor Guiseppe Toniolo, president and intellectual driving force of the *Unione*

Populare, advance guard of the new Catholic Action; Count Stanislao Medolago Albani, director of the economic and social unions that founded a series of Catholic cooperatives; Nicolò Rezzara, who spent forty years in the service of Catholic Action; and Don Luigi Sturzo, a young priest of Sicily, whose *Partito Populare,* founded in 1919, eventually became the Italian Christian Democratic party. It was at this crucial time of his life, in the very beginning of his priesthood, that Roncalli was exposed not only to a stimulating ferment of ideas, but to their practical applications, the ways and means of administering Christian principles to the worldly needs of the people. It was a ripening experience, that part of a man's education that cannot be learned until it is lived.

The bishop quickly perceived that young Roncalli's spiritual and intellectual energies would not be contained by purely secretarial or diocesan duties. He encouraged him to accept a teaching post at the seminary where, from October 1906, he lectured in ecclesiastical history, later taking on courses in patrology, the study of the church fathers, and apologetics, the defense of the Christian doctrine. "You must be prepared," Roncalli would say, "to answer anyone who asks a reason for your faith."

We have it on the evidence of several of his onetime students that Roncalli was a popular teacher. His manner was informal, almost conversational, the natural expression of his easy and outgoing character, so that his enthusiasm for the material at hand was naturally conveyed. One of those former students, Msgr. Giuseppe Angiolini, now rector of the Bergamo seminary, remembers the stocky young priest bursting into the classroom, sometimes a little late, invariably puffing as though he had run the last hundred yards. "He would look around in the manner of a man surprised to see us all there. He would ask after one or another of us. Perhaps he would tell us of something amusing that happened to him that morning. Then he would begin."

The range of his duties kept broadening. Early in 1909, a new diocesan newspaper, *La Vita Diocesana* (Diocesan Life), was launched and Bishop Radini-Tedeschi named Roncalli's friend

Carozzi managing director, with Roncalli himself as editor. At the same time he was teaching catechism to the children at the Church of San Michele del Arco and regularly substituting at mass or hearing confessions for some local pastor who was ill or away. And should there be a wedding or a baptism in the still-growing Roncalli family, he had only to walk over the mountain to be back home in Sotto il Monte to officiate.

He was never long out of touch with his family, sending letters when he was unable to visit, and assuming responsibility for its welfare. When he heard that his sisters Ancilla and Assunta had gone to work in a silk factory where "disreputable" newspapers were distributed, he wrote his mother, "I beg you to be very watchful and, if you think there is any danger, to remove my sisters at once: the Lord will see that you do not go short of bread." Actually, Assunta soon married and in time Ancilla and another sister, Maria, would come to Bergamo to keep house for their brother, the young priest.

When the wife of his brother Zaverio fell ill, he wrote from Bergamo to assure her, "Today I have spoken with a very good and clever doctor up here; when I let you know, and it will be quite soon, you will come here with your husband and undergo a thorough examination: I will see to the expense."

And to his father, who was perhaps feeling the irritations of advancing years, he wrote, "The only comfort there is is the consciousness of having lived a good life. You must forgive me if I am preaching to you, but it is my love for you that makes me say these things; and remember, I am a priest for this very purpose, not in order to enable you to become rich and blessed with this world's goods but to help you to be spiritually content in this life and happy in the life to come."

He was even harder on himself, as the journal entries for this period make plain:

> One of my chief faults consists in not having learned to make the right use of my time. I must find a way of doing much in a short time, and with this in mind I must be most

careful not to waste a single moment in useless things, idle chatter, etc.

I promise to practice self-denial, especially in food. Eating a little less than usual will certainly do me good. So I will cut down my portions by half, and in general drink little wine, and that mixed with water. On second thought, it seems to me I am promising too much. However, I hope the Lord will help me to keep my resolves. . . . .

My set time for getting up in the morning must be regulated according to the circumstances, so as to leave time for everything. As a general rule I will get up at half past five.

(As his notes, year after year, make fresh reference to this need for an early wakening, we must conclude that he was not always able to manage it.)

Late in 1906, accompanying the bishop on a visit to Cardinal Ferrari in Milan, Roncalli wandered off to browse through the archives of the archbishop while the two older men talked. And there, buried amidst a stack of ancient tomes and manuscripts that hadn't been dusted, let alone examined, for many years, he found thirty-nine volumes of parchment documents relating to the pastoral visitations of Saint Charles Borromeo to the diocese of Bergamo in 1575. He recognized at once the historical significance of his discovery: Here was a detailed, first-hand account of what church life was like in the Bergamo district as it moved from the Middle Ages to the Renaissance, as it worked to accommodate itself to the great Catholic Counter-Reformation mandated by the Council of Trent. "I decided then," he wrote, "to publish these papers, edited, of course, provided with notes, using modern scientific methods for the explanations and critical notes." It was to be a lifetime's work.

For more than a year, whenever he and the bishop happened to be in Milan, he closeted himself with the documents. Finally his enthusiasm touched Radini-Tedeschi, who arranged for a meeting between his young secretary and his old friend, Msgr. Achille Ratti, prefect of Milan's prestigious Ambrosian Library. Long after, Roncalli wrote of this first encounter with the future Pope Pius XI:

> I still vividly remember our first meeting at the Ambrosiana on the ground floor in the great reading room when I was so full of fear and uncertainty. Sitting at his desk at the right end of the hall, he received me with dignified yet cordial amiability. I can still see his broad and open-browed head inclined toward me while he listened and formed his first impression about the plan that I explained to him. He found it attractive and interesting immediately, but he reserved judgment until he examined the material. When I returned a few days after this meeting, Monsignor Ratti had already gone through the voluminous documentation in the archbishop's archives. He said that the sixth and seventh volumes seemed to contain the most detailed notes and decrees concerning Saint Charles Borromeo's visits to the city of Bergamo and the diocese, and that these volumes should serve as a basis for the outline of the rest of the study. These documents were already on Monsignor Ratti's table, ready to be photographed. . . . The copies of the sixth and seventh volumes were then made under Ratti's supervision and he personally put the negatives in sequence.

It would be an overstatement to say that the two men actually became friends. Ratti was twenty-five years older than Roncalli and a prelate of considerable consequence. Nonetheless he was an unfailing source of inspiration and help, in fact the only tangible help Roncalli could count on in the first years of his monumental work. Radini-Tedeschi organized two committees to aid in the research, but in a preface to the first volume, published in 1936, Roncalli whimsically notes, "As often happens, so it happened in this case too: A project begins with the naming of committees, but the work has to be done by a single person."

He didn't begrudge it. Over the next fifty years, devoting himself to it whenever he could, he would lose himself in the history of his beloved Bergamo. when Borromeo, a giant of the church, walked its streets, visited its parishes, and introduced the reforms that shaped the life of northern Italy. Except for a brief period when he had a collaborator. Father Pietro Forno, Roncalli worked on alone. Not until 1958, the year he became pope, was the last of the five-volume study. *Records of the Apostolic Visit of Saint Charles Borromeo to Bergamo, 1575,* finally completed. It is a monument to a man and a place, both of which Roncalli revered, and a testament to the level of scholarship attained by the peasant's son from Sotto il Monte.

The conflict between church and state raged on. Within the church there were clashes between those who saw God's will in widespread poverty and deprivation, and those—called activists, liberals, and, most damning of all, Modernists—who strove to involve the church in the social welfare of the brethren. So bitter and unforgiving was the struggle that long after he became pope, John XXIII revealed that the Holy Office still held a postcard he had written forty years before to a friend with Modernist views, a former classmate at the Apollinare named Ernesto Buonaiuto. But he also recalled, in his biography of Radini-Tedeschi, that there were always two texts lying open on the bishop's desk, the Holy Gospels and Leo XIII's lofty social encyclical, *Rerum Novarum.* "These two texts were sufficient for him. In them, his own great heart throbbed. He engaged himself in work with the poor precisely because he was moved by religious concerns. 'It is the workers,' he said, 'who are most tempted by sects. Through their work and their day-to-day economic conditions, they are most driven to rise against God, the government and the laws.' "

This is hardly revolutionary doctrine. The fact is that even in terms of the definitions that prevailed around 1910, neither the bishop nor his secretary could be called Modernists. But Roncalli was beginning to see that, apart from the merits of the separate sides, the raucous hue and cry sometimes raised by both served nobody's best interest. Radical demagogues cursed the church as a bloated, inflexible vested interest, and overheated ecclesiastical apologists fervently condemned any divergence from the most relentless orthodoxy.

In the summer of 1911, the seminary at Bergamo was the scene of such a conflict. A certain priest, whom Roncalli tactfully identified only as Padre M., had come to the summer school, ostensibly to teach a course in social science, but in fact to denounce Modernist fallacy. This he proceeded to do with arm-thrashing gusto, though it had little to do with the subject at hand, going so far as to make critical references to Cardinal Mercier of Belgium and the late Pope Leo XIII. Roncalli, who had audited many of Padre M.'s lectures, made his own position plain in an article written for the September 29 issue of *La Vita Diocesana* which was signed with his name and seminary title, professor of apologetics: "I must express my disappointment and consternation at the impulsiveness and habitual sharp tone, to put it gently, which the lecturer employed in his reference to specific persons, confusing his valid views with those that were unsupported and even exaggerated. I do not see how such controversial arguments can be made to fit into the calm of a seminary summer school. Certainly Padre M. correctly stated many hard and burning truths, especially against those who in particular ways favor Modernist ideas: but are there any of these in the school for social studies?"

He went on to question whether the good padre was aiming his accusations at his pious young students, or at the priests who had seen to their education. And, finally, he concluded with a gentle dig at the padre's classroom dramatics: "If the truth and the whole truth were to be told, I do not believe it would be accompanied by the thunders and lightnings of Sinai, but by the calm and serenity of Jesus on the lake and on the mount."

It was a time curiously like our own. The pope felt obliged to caution young clerics against a sort of restlessness with ecclesiastical authority, to urge upon his bishops stricter standards in the selection of postulants. Yet in Bergamo, a city characterized by ruggedly independent thought, Bishop Radini-Tedeschi had no embarrassments with insurgent priests or parishioners. In fact, there was a comforting saying among Italian Catholics in those difficult days: "No matter what evil strikes, we have only to go four paces and we are in Bergamo."

The reason was plain: Under the bishop's ministry, every parish in the diocese was committed to social as well as religious leadership; the priests felt wholly involved and the people were grateful. From the episcopal palace there came a rhythmic stream of innovations aimed at tempering the adversities of those trying times, and Roncalli had a hand in most of them. Together they organized an emigration office for those tens of thousands of Italians who were then bound for America or other European countries in search of employment. Then Radini-Tedeschi turned his attention to the special needs of working women, the first bishop in all Italy to do so. He created three organizations: the League of Women Workers, the Association for the Protection of Young Women, and the *Casa di Maternità*, which provided a broad range of assistance to expectant mothers and the newborn.

It was Roncalli who became ecclesiastical advisor to these groups and, later, president of the women's section of the diocesan Catholic Action. So, at twenty-eight, he had a seat on the central coordinating committee, a mark of the bishop's reliance on his secretary's good sense. Naturally his energy and organizing ability also attracted the notice of Bergamo's burgher class, who found a priest in politics as suspicious as a politician in church. One of them said, and the remark gained some currency, "Our fine Don Roncalli has tried to organize even the telephone operators. Would that he were satisfied just to organize the sacristans!"

Radini and his secretary further unsettled conservative Catholics by maintaining a working liaison with the civil authorities, despite the government's antichurch bias. "The bishop," Roncalli succinctly wrote, "had a saintly terror of cheap popularity." Radini-Tedeschi instituted a custom of New Year's Day visits to exchange greetings with the mayor and city council, and in other ways acknowledged the realities of life. When it was announced that Margherita, the queen mother, would make a trip to Bergamo, there were those who wondered aloud whether, in view of the rift between church and state, Radini-Tedeschi would call on ner. To anyone with perception, the answer was obvious. "He acted like an Italian bishop and a gentleman," Roncalli recorded, "and went to pay the queen a visit."

But no event of those years so sharply drew the line between the bishop's supporters and his antagonists as did the bitter strike at the iron works in Ranica, a small community just outside Bergamo. In the late summer of 1909, the shop foreman, Pietro Scarpellini, on behalf of the eight hundred employees, requested a labor contract. It called for a reduction in the work week, which was then six days of ten and a half hours each, and some increase in wages. Infuriated, the employers countered by declaring that Scarpellini had "compromised his position" and dismissed him on the spot. On September 21, the workers, led to action by Bishop Radini-Tedeschi's good friend Nicolò Rezzara, affirmed their inherent right to organize on their own behalf and went on strike.

There were, of course, no benefits or organized aid for strikers in those days, nor, in truth, very much public sympathy. Without wages, they were completely dependent on charity for the welfare of their wives and children. Radini-Tedeschi and Roncalli were among a handful of outsiders who pledged money to a relief fund. They visited the workers in their homes, bringing gifts of food and yet a greater gift, moral support. And as the days of the strike stretched into weeks and the hard winter came on, they organized soup kitchens and saw to it that no striker's family went without food or clothing or shelter. But it was less Radini-Tedeschi's cash contributions than his open advocacy of the iron workers' cause that most inflamed his critics, as it most heartened the striking men, and Roncalli noted with wry understatement, "Less than benevolent reports were sent off to his superiors in Rome." In his biography of Radini-Tedeschi, he points out that unlike France, Germany, and Belgium, there was neither law nor any administrative provision for negotiating labor disputes in Italy, and reveals his own attitude about the Ranica strike:

> It was good to see that the cause of the workers was defended by the bishop, not only from the heights of the episcopal pulpit but openly in the public square, in capital-labor conflicts, and in the workshops. Monsignor Radini felt that it was his duty to give an example and he had the courage to do it.
>
> When the strike began, Radini was among the first to put his name down on a list to help the workers; and he was among those who gave generous sums to assure the daily bread of the striking workers. Then from all sides this was called a scandal; unfriendly reports were sent to higher authorities. . . .
>
> At Ranica it was not the problem of wages or persons that was at stake, but a principle: the fundamental question of freedom of the Christian organization of labor, as opposed to the powerful organization of capital. He resolutely took the side of the striking workers because in doing so he fulfilled a highly Christian duty and acted for justice, charity and social peace. He let the shouters go on shouting and went calmly on his own way, taking an active part on behalf of the striking workers.

On November 8, fifty days after it had begun, the strike ended with the employers acknowledging defeat by agreeing to the formation of an iron workers' union. And Bishop Radini-Tedeschi was vindicated. When it was all over, and the dust had settled, he received a handwritten letter from Pope Pius. "We cannot disapprove of what you have thought prudent to do," said the Holy Father, "since you were fully acquainted with the place, with the persons involved, and with the circumstances."

Prudent. It was a word greatly emphasized among the Catholic clergy and, by them, to the laity, and now Angelo Roncalli understood it more clearly. "There is so much talk about prudence," Radini-Tedeschi told him, holding out the pope's letter for emphasis. "But I have told you many times that prudence does not consist in doing nothing. It means to act, and to act well."

Early in May 1912, Roncalli wrote to his father, "I hear from Giovanni [his brother] that Great-Uncle Zaverio is unwell. This very day I had ordered the carriage in order to come to see him, but the continual rain has prevented me from setting out. Unless the news from you is more serious, I plan to come on Sunday. . . ."

He arrived in Sotto il Monte on May 21, and next day, Zaverio Roncalli, his cherished Barba, died at the age of eighty-eight. Angelo Roncalli wrote the memorial card, and in it tried to tell something of his great-uncle's lasting influence on his own life: "He was the just man of Sacred Scripture. Simple, honest, God fearing, humble of birth and occupied with the humble labors of the fields, he had a lively and profound *sense of Christ*. . . . In a century full of agitation he never lost his youthful, fervent and loving devotion to the Sacred Heart of Jesus. When he died he left no wealth or land, but to his family and parish the shining and unforgettable example of a pure, hardworking life."

The curtain was ringing down on an epoch of Roncalli's life. With the death of Zaverio, that kindly, questing old man with a reverence for history and church who had once read to him from the Bible and the Catholic newspapers, there passed into an irretrievable yesterday the first teacher of his boyhood. Soon he would lose the shining light of his young priesthood. The end of the beginning was at hand.

Bishop Radini-Tedeschi was now a troubled man. The first faint clouds of war were on the far horizon, still only a trace—a bellicose speech, a blandishment of armaments—but to someone of Radini-Tedeschi's perception the promise was of disaster. And hardest for him to bear, as he sadly revealed to his secretary, he believed he had lost the confidence of the pope.

Roncalli tried to dissuade him from these depressing feelings. Did not His Holiness write often to the bishop, and in his own hand? Surely this was a sign that he returned monsignor's regard and affections.

But Radini well knew that there were those in Bergamo who damned him to Rome as a Modernist, and others in Rome whose counsel about the direction of the Bergamo diocese Pius heeded more readily than that of the bishop himself. "Sometimes," Roncalli wrote in the biography, "particularly during the last years of his life, Radini found himself in a state of uncertitude and doubt as to whether he still deserved the complete confidence of the Holy Father. This was the hardest test of his goodness. Though it is still too delicate a matter to discuss fully, to remain silent about it would be to risk grave untruthfulness and injustice regarding the real virtue of Monsignor Radini."

This much is known: During a visit to the Vatican in November 1911, Radini-Tedeschi addressed himself directly to the pope in a memorandum notable for its candor.

> I wish to be a pastor and a father, to try to win the people with affection, with much affection, without giving way to weakness. Perhaps all this, if judged by someone who is not enlightened by the Holy Spirit, or who does not feel the pains of being father to all, might appear to be remissiveness, or excessive goodness, or an inclination to see everything in a rosy color. Rosy views and remissiveness were perhaps those sins, Holy Father, which brought upon me the accusations of being intransigent. . . . I beg your forgiveness. I spoke too much about myself, but it seems to me that it was my duty to assure Your Holiness about my best intentions in asking that, in blessing me, you should confirm your humble brother.

Whether Pius ever responded to this remarkable document is not known. Roncalli concludes by asking whether the bishop perhaps exaggerated the assumption that the pope did not fully trust him. "Did the delicate love he felt for the pope, which he felt was damaged now, make him see things blacker than they actually were? It could be."

It could also have been that the bishop's unhappy instinct was correct. In any event, as Roncalli relates, "This suspicion became a crown of thorns for him and created pressing anxiety around his heart," and all this at a time when the bishop could see ahead to the end of his life, and was terrified by the enormity of what he had to leave undone.

He had been ill, in greater or lesser pain, for four years. The doctors suggested he work at a less intense pace, and he did indeed seem to win back his strength during summer holidays with Roncalli at Einsiedeln, the Marian Shrine in the Swiss Alps, and in the Italian Piedmont. But by early 1914, the change in his appearance, the wasting, wan look, was shocking. Seeing him so, his secretary's heart was torn. He wrote, "Radini sensed the awful menace hanging over his head." That summer, unable to travel, the bishop remained in bed in his little villa in the hills outside Bergamo, the faithful Roncalli in attendance.

It was there, late in June, that they learned the Austrian archduke, Franz Ferdinand, and his wife Sophie had been assassinated at Sarajevo. The tinderbox was lit. A few weeks later Europe exploded into war. Germany invaded Belgium and, together with Austria, was soon locked in mortal combat with Russia, France, and England.

Roncalli left a moving account of those hot August days when Radini-Tedeschi's life dwindled away and the world he knew fell into ruin: "He gave the most disciplined example of calm and patience, even in moments of the greatest pain. . . . At times, all alone in the silence of the night, he was heard to moan, '*O Madonna mia*, give me strength.' The outbreak of the European war had veiled his brow and spirit with profound sadness. He was anxious to have read to him all the news, which gradually became more and more bloody and saddening. He thought continually about the war and brooded for entire nights almost in a state of terror, saying: 'Who knows what the future holds for Europe? Poor Belgium! Poor Cardinal Mercier. . . .' "

On the evening of August 11, the pain worsened and the doctors came again. After a brief consultation with Roncalli, they decided they had to tell the bishop exactly how serious his condition was, and that he must return to Bergamo for exploratory surgery. That night he did not sleep and in the morning, drained of strength, was momentarily unequal to his trial. When Roncalli came to his room, he said, "Last night all of you were a bit cruel, although with the best intentions, in giving me the news in such a sharp way. After all, what do you expect? I am human, too." He sighed. "But now I am prepared for everything. The will of God—that is all."

Later he mused, "We must trust in God, not men. Men do what they can, but that is very little. They want to operate and will undoubtedly be successful. Nevertheless I will go to the other world."

They returned to Bergamo by automobile. Roncalli recalled that as they began the long descent, the blazing summer sun, "shooting its rays over the crests and peaks of Alban in a glory of gaiety and color, and all the mountains around us, like a magnificent stage setting, appeared to be giving the final salute to their pastor."

The operation revealed a massive intestinal malignancy. His life could not be saved. It was a matter of days, the doctors told Roncalli, no more. And Radini, who immediately read the truth in their eyes, was facing his darkest hour. Alone with Roncalli, he broke down and sobbed. "I had never seen him cry that way," Roncalli wrote.

" 'Take heart, Monsignor,' I said. 'Are we not all in the hands of God who gives strength and life?' "

" 'Oh, my son, I am not a hero in the face of death, but I am not a coward, either. It is the thought of my responsibilities that frightens me. I am a bishop. I am a bishop with great power to do good and I have not done enough. And now God is to judge me.' "

The secretary comforted him with assurances that he had done God's work truly and well, and Radini reconciled himself to what had to be and faced the final days with calm and steady courage.

The great world war raged on. As Radini lay on his deathbed, Pope Pius X, who had pleaded with the nations to find some peaceful settlement of their differences, received in audience the Austrian ambassador to the Vatican. "Holy Father," the diplomat said, "thousands of Catholics march in the armies of Austria and Germany. His Majesty, the emperor of Austria, has asked you to bless his armies in the struggle."

Good Pius, also at the very end of his life, tautened with anger. "I bless peace," said this militant Christian, "not war." And the interview was over.

A few days later, worn out by his efforts to end the war and appalled by its slaughter, Pius X died. When the news was brought to Radini on the morning of August 20, he closed his eyes and murmured, "Then I shall not linger much longer. The Holy Father is calling me."

Then he revealed to Roncalli the secret of his consecration, the whispered words of nearly ten years before, unheard by any but the pope and his new bishop, "When the Holy Father raised me to my feet that day, he promised that when I died he would come for me and that we should be together in paradise. Now he is there and calling me. I will see him soon."

On the evening of August 22, the time was clearly at hand. "Well, is it my last hour?" he said to the doctors. "I thank you for your skilled and dedicated care in these days, but I ask you, dear doctors, to hear the last memory that the bishop who dies leaves for you. Oh, the faith! What a great gift faith is, and especially in this moment when I stand before the gates of eternity. Now I go, and I am happy."

For a little while Roncalli consoled him with prayer, Radini responding feebly. Then his voice faded and the secretary, thinking him unconscious, was silent. But the bishop spoke one last time. "Courage, my dear Don Angelo," he muttered, "it goes well. Continue, for I understand every word you say." Then, just before midnight, at age fifty-seven, Giacomo Maria Count Radini-Tedeschi died.

The new pope was elected on September 4, and took the name Benedict XV. He was Giacomo della Chiesa, cardinal-archbishop of Bologna, who had been a close friend of Radini-Tedeschi and, like Radini, was once banished from the Vatican for alleged Modernist leanings. Angelo Roncalli would have been less than human if he were not particulary pleased at the choice of a man who shared his beloved bishop's spiritual and social views.

But these were difficult days for Roncalli. Just past the tenth anniversary of his ordination as a priest, thirty-three years old, he suddenly felt cut loose and adrift. Others, he knew, had moved on, advanced. So long as Radini had lived he never gave a thought to his own future prospects. But now Radini-Tedeschi, the "polar star" of his priesthood, was dead and he could not shake his grief, the sense of irreparable loss. No doubt the new bishop, whoever he was to be, would have found a place for him, but he did not want to presume this. He moved out of the episcopal palace and took an apartment with his old friend Carozzi. And of course he had plenty to keep him busy: his classes at the seminary, editing *La Vita Diocesana*, and the work with the women's section of Catholic Action. He went often to Sotto il Monte during this period, and spent long hours on the Saint Charles Borromeo work. He also began the biography of Radini-Tedeschi.

Then, on May 23, 1915, Italy declared war on Austria and Germany. Next day Angelo Roncalli was called up with the reserves.

VI

A WORLD IN TURMOIL

The question of whether Italy should involve itself in the war had racked the nation. Over long and bitter months, violent campaigns and bullyragging rhetoric had divided the people, blurring every other issue, even the matter of a Catholic entry into national politics, and the faint voice of reason was shouted down and mocked. No matter that the country had no honorable interest in the war, that the military was wretchedly prepared, even that the government was signatory to an alliance with Germany and Austria. The swell of nationalism ran too strong. Secret promises of territorial gain were too intriguing. So with brave speeches and proud banners, Italy committed its army and navy to disaster, its people to harrowing years of bloodshed and bereavement, and the nation to a generation of shame.

On May 23, 1915, Angelo Roncalli made this entry in his journal, "Tomorrow I leave to take up my military service in the medical corps. Where will they send me? To the front perhaps? Shall I ever return to Bergamo, or has the Lord decreed that my last hour shall be on the battlefield? I know nothing: all I want is the will of God in all things and at all times."

The next day he reported to the headquarters of the military district in Milan. One of his former students from Bergamo, who met him there and helped guide him through the bureaucratic maze, later said that he seemed bewildered by the bustle and thoroughly ill at ease in nonclerical garb. Roncalli gave the young man the few lire that made up his first day's soldier's pay to buy a glass of wine and wished him a safe return to his family. Once more he was Sergeant Roncalli, assigned this time to the medical corps and sent back to Bergamo for duty.

To the north, Italian divisions, already massed on the Venetian plain, commenced a drive against the Austrians on a narrow front that gave onto the southern slopes of the Alps. It was back-breaking terrain, the way always upward, with mud and rock underfoot, and later snow, with the Austrian artillery spouting death from above. Eleven times in the next twenty-seven months the Italians threw themselves forward and, at a cost of 66,000 killed and 190,000 wounded, managed to wrest from the enemy a pathetic gain of ten miles.

Meanwhile, Bergamo, less than two hundred miles from the front lines, became a major receiving center for the unending stream of casualties. Sergeant Roncalli, who rarely slept more than five hours a night during this convulsive time, served as both medical orderly and priest, nursing wounds, fighting death and, when the battle was lost, as he later put it, "offering to the dying the last consolations of friendship and the reconciliation of final absolution."

He had grown a bristling black mustache. At the time it must have seemed the thing to do, a declaration of his oneness with the ordinary soldier. But years later, looking at a photograph of himself in those early wartime days, he said, "The mustache was a mistake. I grew it in a moment of weakness."

There were those assigned to Roncalli's hospital, officers and a few doctors, whose anticlerical prejudices were undisturbed by the selfless concern he brought to the wards and the long, wearying hours he spent there. He was a priest—nothing could erase *that* black mark. One officer especially heaped so much sarcasm and abuse on his head that Roncalli, afraid that he might lose control over the men in his little unit, submitted a written complaint. This wrung a strangely prescient apology from the officer. "I am only a poor lieutenant colonel, sergeant, and unlikely to rise higher," he said with a smile of questionable sincerity, "whereas you are only at the beginning and shall probably become a cardinal."

It was clear that he did not fit the military mold, this bulky, balding sergeant of thirty-four years—mustache or not. Missing, among other things, was that fine, dispassionate hardheartedness with which successful noncommissioned officers dealt with subordinates. He had occasion once to confine one of his men to the barracks. Next day, with the rest of the platoon off on leave, Sergeant Roncalli was dismayed to find the offender still in camp. "What are you doing here?" he asked. "Why didn't you go into town with the others?"

"But sergeant," the man replied, "you gave me three days' confinement."

"Yes, yes," said Roncalli, contrite, "but I only meant at night. In the daytime you are free to go."

He organized a special soldiers' mass in Bergamo and a Catholic association to assist the district troops. Whenever he could find a half day's respite from his duties, he made his way over the mountain to Sotto il Monte where he found the dearly familiar village of his childhood changed, like everything else, by the insatiable demands of the war. All the men of military age, including all four of his brothers, had been called into service. Working the land had fallen to the women and the old men, and the centuries-old rhythms of life—toil and prayer and gratitude to God for a full stomach—were upset. Now the people of his village waited for letters, for news from some far battlefield, for the posting of the latest casualty lists, and fashioned their lives around those anxious moments.

In the early spring of 1916, by special dispensation of the

government, all priests in the Italian army were designated chaplains and given officers' rank. Sergeant Roncalli was promoted to lieutenant on March 28 and promptly shaved off his mustache. His duties multiplied. Now he had spiritual responsibility for Bergamo's great reserve hospital, the New Shelter, as well as for the smaller hospitals, schools, and other improvised wards of the district in which the flow of wounded from the north had to be accommodated. He was appointed clerical adviser to the civil defense organization and in the months ahead would set up a convalescent home for soldiers and an association for the aid of the mothers and widows of those who had fallen in battle.

He was also teaching at the seminary. On his first day of class there was a great deal of speculation about this man who could be a military chaplain and a professor of apologetics at the same time. But when he entered the classroom, recalled one of his students, Simone Bottani, he was dressed just as any priest, except that on his sleeves and the flat crown of his clerical hat there were two gold stripes denoting his military rank. He put down his hat, smiled at the students, made the sign of the cross and began with a quotation from Saint Peter that seemed poignantly apt in those discordant days: "Let none of you suffer as a murderer, or a thief, or a slanderer, or as one coveting what belongs to others. But if he suffers as a Christian let him not be ashamed. Let him glorify God under this name."

Because of the war, the usual two-semester course had to be crammed into a single term. "At the end of that one semester," recalls Bottani, "we all left, but it remains unforgettable because of Don Roncalli's teaching. And we all knew that in order to give us the lectures he had to study night after night."

Despite his busy schedule, Roncalli managed to complete the biography of Radini-Tedeschi, and in an introduction to the first edition, published in 1916, he noted, "These pages were written while in Europe the war went on, the horrible war that caused so much bloodshed and tears. I have written these lines and worked on this book not in the sweet quietness of the life of studies but amidst the most varied occupations, following the teachings and examples of Monsignor Radini, first for several months as a simple soldier, then as a noncommissioned officer of the lowest rank, and finally more directly as a priest."

He traveled to Rome to present a copy of the book to the pope but otherwise held to the demanding work routine he had set for himself. Explaining to his brother Zaverio why he had not written sooner, he said, "I have my sermons to prepare, and some classes to give, and so many other duties that sometimes I feel quite breathless. When I go to bed, about midnight, I am dead tired. But after a little rest I feel better and take up my work once more."

The war pressed in on Roncalli ever more closely. In a letter to Zaverio dated September 1, 1916, he wrote, "This morning I have been told that our cousin Battista Mazzola has died at the hospital of Verona, of wounds, it appears, caused by an Austrian grenade." And in his own hospitals the casualties mounted daily

But the worst was yet to come. In October 1917, the Austrians, reinforced by seven German divisions, launched an offensive at Caporetto that was intended to break the bitter stalemate and drive Italy to surrender. It was one of the most devastating Allied defeats of the war. Within days the powerful Austro-German force tore open the front and shattered the Italian armies. Unable to regroup and make a stand, they began a hellish, headlong retreat down out of the mountains under murderous enemy artillery, not stopping until they had reached the Piave River north of Venice, seventy miles behind the trenches where the battle began. Only the frantic dispatch of French and British reinforcements from the western front enabled the gutted Italian forces to hold here, and Caporetto took its place as one of the greatest disasters in the annals of war. The Italians suffered 45,000 killed and wounded, and 275,000 taken prisoner.

For Angelo Roncalli those days when autumn turned to disconsolate winter were a time of desolation and agony of soul. In December, a letter to his youngest brother, Giuseppe, was returned stamped "Addressee Missing in Action," and on January 6, he wrote again to Zaverio, who was also at the front, "I have just returned from Sotto il Monte. . . . They are all very anxious about Giuseppino, and now they begin to worry about you too. I cannot tell you what I feel, or what I suffer. I have always been fond of all my brothers and sisters, but now, especially when I think of you two, I am so moved that at times, when I am alone with the Lord, my eyes fill with tears and I cannot resist the emotion that overwhelms me."

In Bergamo the battle's victims overflowed every prepared facility and had to be carried to the churches and other public buildings. There they lay in their stretchers on the floor, waiting for one of a meager number of doctors and nurses already overwhelmed by the torrent of mangled men. Lieutenant-Chaplain Roncalli and his little cluster of aides went among them. Often the long nights slipped into dawn, and still they worked on, bringing what medical sustenance and comfort they could to the wounded, and to those for whom the struggle was lost, absolution.

Years later, Roncalli would say, "I thank God that I served as a sergeant and army chaplain in the First World War. How much I learned about the human heart during this time, how much experience I gained, what grace I received." But at the time he lived through it, his sensitive spirit was sickened by the brutality and waste of war. Kneeling on the cold floor beside a stricken soldier, he could be brave and consoling. But afterward, alone in his room, a great bleakness overtook him and, as he wrote, "Many times it happened that I had to throw myself on my knees and weep like a boy, unable any longer to contain the emotion aroused by the spectacle of the simple holy deaths of so many poor sons of our people."

Early in 1918, he learned that his brother Giuseppe was alive and a prisoner of the Austrians. He promptly sent this good word to Zaverio, enclosing, as was his habit, twenty lire for such small comforts as a soldier could buy. For the moment the front was stabilized along the Piave. There would be further offensives, more casualties, but as spring came to the war-weary continent, there were those who dared to look forward to peace. Roncalli was one, and on April 17, he wrote to Zaverio with some excitement, "When you return to Bergamo you will find something new. I shall be no longer living at the Seminary but in a palazzo not far away in which the bishop has asked me to open a 'Home for Students' and where, after the war, I shall live permanently with our two sisters Ancilla and Maria. After all, they have worked so hard, they have the right now to live with a little more comfort, and they will be most useful to me in my various activities. . . . Meantime I am getting the necessary furniture and as I am short of money I am borrowing from our father two thousand lire—paying an interest of 5 percent—I hope that by the end of next year I shall be able to pay him back."

Two years after Italy's entry into the war, in May 1917, Pope Benedict had consecrated Eugenio Pacelli an archbishop and sent him to Germany to press for a peaceful settlement. But Kaiser Wilhelm II was unwilling to discuss peace, and instead lectured Pacelli on how the Vatican should deploy its soldiers to fight in the event of an attack. Disheartened but not defeated, Benedict, in August, sent to all the belligerent nations a peace plan based on the "moral force of right," international arbitration, and restoration of occupied territory. This effort failed as well, and the war ground remorselessly on.

But there remained broad areas of humanitarian endeavor in which the efforts of the church meant the difference between hope and despair, life and death. Into the Vatican poured thousands of letters from the bereft families of missing soldiers, and although the names and nations differed, the question was always the same: Can you help us find him? In response, the pope established the Vatican Prisoners of War Office. It was staffed by dozens of clerks and four orders of nuns who, by searching out the names of prisoners in internment camps of both the Allies and Central powers and matching them against their mountains of letters, could often send on some precious scrap of news—"Your son is alive and a prisoner in Germany"—thus easing the terrible anxieties of those who grieved.

Benedict worked ceaselessly for the exchange of wounded prisoners. Nearly twenty-five thousand soldiers of both sides who had contracted tuberculosis in the trenches were conveyed to convalescent retreats in northern Italy aboard a special train that came to be known as *Il treno del Papa* (the Pope's train). To feed and shelter war-ravaged millions across Europe and Russia, some 30 million lire was collected in Catholic churches, with another 5.5 million coming from the pope's own resources. So drastically did this great effort deplete the papal treasury that when Benedict died in 1922 the Vatican had to borrow money to pay for his funeral and the ensuing conclave.

But at last, in November 1918, there was peace. It came not as a result of reason and good will, but by force of arms, attrition, and a final surfeit of bloodshed. And it brought not Woodrow Wilson's world made safe for democracy, but a world of old wounds unhealed and new ones festering, marking time for the next eruption. In Russia, the blind and brutish Romanov dynasty was overthrown, with Czar Nicholas and his Czarina and all their children brutishly murdered. And the new regime promised not tranquility but a reign of terror and worldwide revolution. In Germany, a soldier named Hitler came out of the army seething with hatred, and matching his hatred to the turmoil and outrage of the defeated nation, turned his warped mind to politics. And in Italy, left-wing radicals demonstrated and fomented strikes, and bands of black-shirted Fascists under the leadership of Benito Mussolini roamed the streets and cracked the skulls of any who opposed them.

The war was over and there was a new day dawning. But it would be dark.

On October 15, 1918, Roncalli's sister Enrica died of cancer at the age of twenty-five. He made the journey to Sotto il Monte for the funeral and a few days later, from Bergamo, he wrote to his grieving parents, "We must honor the memory of our poor dear Enrica and not be downhearted." Then the family had happier news: Giuseppe, so long a prisoner in Austria, had been moved to an Italian field hospital near Padua and, although seriously ill, would soon be coming home. Thankful but still concerned, Roncalli wrote to his brother Giovanni, "When Giuseppino is fit to be moved let me know so that I may come at once to fetch him. We have been granted such a great blessing; we must not make a mistake now. Giuseppino must be very careful even in small matters; he must avoid catching cold, getting overtired, etc., and not be impatient. I am sending you some socks and a jersey. Let me know if you need any money. . . ."

In November, a few weeks before he was mustered out of the army, Don Roncalli opened his students' hostel at the Palazzo Marenzi on the Via San Salvatore in Bergamo's old city. Though the new bishop, Msgr. Luigi Marelli, enthusiastically supported the idea, seeing it as a Christian haven for young people in the nihilistic storm, he was unable to give it much financial support and Roncalli used borrowed money and his own demobilization pay to freshen and furnish the venerable and long-unused palazzo. It was intended not for seminarians but mainly for lay students who found there wholesome, inexpensive meals, a quiet place to study, and a large recreation room. Sleeping quarters were on the second floor. On the stairway landing, amid some tattered tapestries and ancient portraits, Roncalli hung a full-length mirror and above it lettered in Latin, the injunction, "Know Thyself." To those who found the message too subtle, there was a more direct approach. "What does that mean?" asked a rather unkempt student squinting at the sign.

From behind him on the landing came Roncalli's brisk reply, "You need a haircut."

The hostel quickly gained popularity. Students from out of town much preferred it to lodging with strangers, and those who lived at home came to the recreation room for fellowship and a lively exchange of ideas. It may have been the first such student hostel in Italy and its success soon led to others, first in Bergamo, then in other Italian university cities.

Inevitably, perhaps, the very success of the Casa della Studente generated criticism in certain circles. There was too much coming and going, some said, and not enough piety or discipline. Don Roncalli was too simple-hearted for those young knaves; they took advantage of him. This was hardly the case. True, Roncalli tempered the rigidity and stern discipline that marked the seminary with a warm-heartedness that enabled him to establish a personal relationship with his students; he helped with their studies, loaned them small sums, eased the loneliness of newcomers with his friendship. But there was daily mass and never any question about the high Christian morality that animated the hostel. It was not until Roncalli left Bergamo, some two years later, that the Casa della Studente ran into difficulty and was finally closed. But by then the idea had taken root and student hostels had sprung up elsewhere in Italy.

Meanwhile Roncalli spent all his free time at the converted palazzo and thought he had found his true calling. In the spring of 1919, he set down these paragraphs in his journal:

> During these last years there have been days when I wondered what God would require of me after the war. Now there is no more cause for uncertainty, or for looking for something else; my main task is here, and here is my burden, the apostolate among students. . . .
>
> I shall be particularly careful always to maintain in my house a fragrant atmosphere of purity which may influence my young men and make such a profound impression on them that it will survive in later years, even in the future conflicts of their lives. . . . Lord, help me to follow, if only from afar and in my humble way, those shining examples of great teachers of the young.
>
> The work I have set my hand to is enormous; the corn is already golden in the fields, but alas! The reapers are few.

Nonetheless, Roncalli undertook a multitude of other duties. He was again spiritual adviser for the women's section of Catholic Action at a time when women were venturing into new fields of commerce and education and needed guidance and the strength of their organized numbers. He was one of the principal organizers of the first postwar Eucharist Congress, a labor of love, for Bishop Radini-Tedeschi had once planned such a congress for Bergamo. And Bishop Marelli appointed him spiritual director of the seminary, a position of considerable importance in a period when young clerics were returning from the front lines and the rough life of the barracks. But it is worth noting that though his scholarship was unquestioned, and though he had published the biography of Radini-Tedeschi and remained steadily at work on the Borromeo volumes, he was given no teaching post. In view of later developments, it may well be that he was already suspected of Modernist tendencies.

Rarely did a month pass that he did not seek the spiritual refreshment of a few days at Sotto il Monte. The little village seemed unaffected by the tuggings and haulings of the world beyond the mountain, its people marked by a peasant calm that recognized the inevitability of some things and the unimportance of most others. And especially as the years passed—Roncalli was now nearly forty—he cherished the long evening talks with his father. Giovanni's essential faith was undimmed, his piety absolute, and he spoke with the rough eloquence and dignity of his old age—and sometimes with painful honesty. He had not been happy, long before, to learn that his eldest son felt called to the priesthood, he confessed, and he had sent him off to the seminary with some reluctance, for they could surely have used another pair of strong arms in the field. And even now, even with greatest respect for Don Angelo's office, he often asked himself whether he had done the right thing: a peasant's life was hard but simple, and the burdens of a priest were heavy. Another time, speaking of his dead daughter, Enrica, he said that though he was old and poor he would gladly accept the struggle of raising another ten children in place of losing one.

Did Roncalli himself ever wonder what his life would have been like if he had never left Sotto il Monte, if, like his father and his brothers, he had devoted himself to a family and the fixed and elemental demands of the field? There is no evidence. The only thing clear is that self-questioning never deterred him from his course, and that doubt never weakened his priestly resolve. And, in fact, throughout those postwar years, he seemed not only convinced of the rightness of his calling but happily set on the path of his life's work.

He liked young people and had a way with them. And especially in those troubled times, when the old verities were scorned and the violent extremes of the Left and the Right lured youth into the streets, he felt his mission to be worthy and important. How far his concern for modern youth might have taken him in their behalf, however, cannot be known. On December 10, 1920, he was summoned to Rome, and thereafter his life was directed away from pastoral duties and toward the world outside.

When Cardinal Giacomo della Chiesa, the archbishop of Bologna, became Pope Benedict XV in 1914, a young prelate noted, "He strikes me as a man who has been treated by nature in rather a stepmotherly fashion." Small and stooped, he walked with a limp, and the eyes that gazed luminously out from behind rimless glasses seemed somehow unaligned. Benedict himself once said, "I am but an ugly gargoyle on the beauties of Rome."

But he was also a compelling force leading the church into the mainstream of twentieth-century life. His plan for peace had been rejected, but President Wilson's famous Fourteen Points, which formed the framework for the peace conference at Versailles, bore a striking resemblance to that plan. Acknowledging the pope's effort, Wilson himself called on Benedict early in 1919, the first Vatican visit by an American president in office.

Nations that had shunned diplomatic ties with the Holy See, such as Holland, Poland, Yugoslavia, Finland, Czechoslovakia, and Japan, now, in the more accommodating atmosphere of Benedict's reign, sent official representatives. A long-troubled relationship with the French was smoothed. And inside Italy, recognition of political realities and a more benign approach to the political leadership promised to raise the church from the limbo of its self-inflicted isolation. At last the Vatican stopped referring to the king as the Duke of Savoy. The pope himself encouraged the Sicilian priest Don Luigi Sturzo in the formation of the *Partito Populare* (the People's Party), which promptly won more than a hundred parliamentary seats.

Nor did Benedict ignore the inner mechanisms of Catholicism. In particular, he believed that the century-old administration of the Sacred Congregation for the Propagation of the Faith needed to be modernized. The missionary arm of the church, *Propaganda Fide*, had been started as a fund-collecting society in France in 1822, and the money raised was used to send food, medicine, and instructional materials to the mission lands, particularly to Africa. Throughout the years similar societies grew up in other European nations with only nominal direction from Rome. Now all were in disarray. Parochial authority had produced conflicting jurisdictions and stagnant, outmoded administration. During the war, colonial populations who had been taught the superiority of Western civilization had a disillusioning new view of it when called upon to fight in the service of one Christian land against another. There were stirrings of discontent against the white man's plundering of the African nations, against his cruelty to black people.

Now, faced with the need to head off a great spiritual disaffection, Pope Benedict decided to truly internationalize the work of the mission societies by bringing them together under a single Vatican headquarters. It would be a prickly job, for not one would willingly give up its national prerogatives and treasury. To persuade them to do it, Benedict sought a man of particular resourcefulness and organizational skill. On the list of possibilities presented to him for consideration, he saw the name of Don Angelo Roncalli, one-time secretary to his dear friend, Bishop Radini-Tedeschi. Perhaps he remembered Roncalli's book about the bishop, or his work in organizing the recent Eucharist Congress in Bergamo. Whatever the motivation, Benedict pointed to Roncalli's name and said, "That one, that one." And a few days later, the summons went out from Cardinal Wilhelm van Rossum, prefect of the congregation of *Propaganda Fide*, so powerful a figure in the curia that he was often referred to as the "Red Pope."

Roncalli was not happy to receive Rossum's letter. He recognized it as a signal honor: He had been noticed by the Holy Father himself, and invited to take a post close to the very power center of the church. But it was precisely the sort of honor that dismayed and embarrassed him. In Bergamo he was doing pastoral work. Obscure though his office was, he could respond directly to the needs of his people. In Rome, charged with the administration of far-flung fund-raising societies, he would be thrust into the labyrinth of Vatican bureaucracy, which he deplored, and exposed to the temptations of ambition, which he feared.

Uncertain, Roncalli turned for advice to old Cardinal Ferrari, metropolitan of Milan and a long-time friend of Radini-Tedeschi. Where did duty call him? he wrote to ask the archbishop. What should he do? And Ferrari, his voice stilled by cancer of the throat and at the very end of his days, summed up Roncalli's responsibility in a warm and unequivocal letter of reply, "My dear Professor, you know how fond of you I am and, too, this is an obligation to Monsignor Radini. For this reason here is my frank, unhesitant opinion. The will of God is perfectly clear. The Red Pope is the echo of the White Pope and the White Pope is the echo of God. Relinquish everything else and go, and a great blessing will go with you."

He arrived in Rome on January 18, 1921, presenting himself at the splendid Renaissance palace of *Propaganda Fide* at the foot of the Spanish steps. Typically, no one seemed to expect him or to know quite what to do with him. Without instructions, without even a place to stay or set down his suitcase, Roncalli wandered back out to the piazza. In the street he ran into Msgr. Vincenzo Bugarini, his old rector at the Roman seminary, who insisted that the bewildered priest at least share his room until he was more permanently settled.

At fault were the vagaries of bureaucracy, not the status of Roncalli's new post, for soon enough, Pope Benedict himself sent for him. He had never been in the papal apartments on the fourth floor of the apostolic palace, and after kneeling to kiss the Fisherman's ring, he gazed enthralled through the tall window that overlooked the immense piazza of Saint Peter's, the graceful curve of its colonnade, and the low hills of Rome beyond. Caught up in the splendor of his surroundings and the exaltation of the moment—he, Angelo Roncalli, in private audience with the pope!—he had to force himself to sort out Benedict's words to understand their full significance. And for the task they set before him, they were significant indeed.

The missionary societies had to be freshly inspired, the wizened pontiff said. The narrow, nationalistic approach of the past no longer served well in a world grown smaller, interdependent, sensitive to reverberations in its farthest reaches. His plan was to elevate the separate societies to the dignity of a papal institution with direction from the Vatican, but how to do it, when to do it, that would depend on the information Don Roncalli brought him. He was to visit the mission centers abroad, in France, Belgium, and Germany, and prepare the way.

"You will be God's traveler," he told Roncalli, and dismissed him with a blessing.

Novice though he was in Vatican affairs, Roncalli knew he had been given a thorny assignment. How was he to convince far-off prelates and prominent laymen that things they had been doing for years must now be done differently, perhaps even undone? He was further handicapped by his subaltern ranking within the Vatican. He had been given a florid title—president of the Central Council for Italy of the Pontifical Missionary Works—but he was, in fact, inexperienced, a novitiate among the crusty veterans of the papal court, and an outlander at that, a poor peasant's son from an obscure diocese in the country. But he did have a commission from the pope, and his own determination, and these would have to do.

His first journeys were to Piacenza and Bolzano in the north of Italy. Soon after he returned, on May 7, he was named a domestic prelate of His Holiness, a designation that entitled him to wear monsignorial purple. Roncalli took the distinction seriously enough, but in relaying the news to his family, he cautioned them, as always, against unwarranted pride, ". . . The Holy Father has appointed me a domestic prelate. This is a great honor for me, and for you. But we must not be boastful . . . the man who rises to a certain height is more likely to fall than the man who stays on the ground."

Still, when he returned to Sotto il Monte for the Feast of Saint John in June, the women of the village, who had once chucked him under the chin and called him Angelino, were awed by his new cassock with the purple cape and belt. Finally one said to his mother, "What does it mean? Why is he all dressed up like a bishop?"

And Marianna who, in truth, did not really know what it meant, shrugged eloquently nonetheless, "Oh, you know how it is. Priests arrange these things among themselves."

Now—and later as bishop and cardinal—he set aside time to receive the priests of his native region. They tended to be unworldly men who often felt themselves lost in a backwater and forgotten. Monsignor Roncalli, by his presence, by his interest, sought to rekindle their original sense of mission, and sometimes had to begin by rekindling their sense of themselves. To one whose face had obviously gone long unshaven, he handed a razor, remarking, "It's an extra one—I just happen to have come across it. Perhaps you can use it, *Reverendo*." To another whose collar was nearly as dark as his habit, he gave some collars of his own, saying, "They've gotten too tight for me, *Reverendo*, but ought to fit you nicely." Rarely was the unspoken message lost.

He passed the summer and autumn traveling through Italy— Venice, Turin, Bologna, Genoa, Monte Cassino—in the difficult, delicate work of *Propaganda Fide*. Between times, he was searching for a suitable house in Rome so that he could settle down and send for his sisters. He had decided that he would also invite Monsignor Bugarini to live with him, for his old friend was nearly seventy and ailing. His modest finances limited his choices, but finally, in late October, he found a roomy house within his means at Santa Maria on the Via Lata and soon after went to Sotto il Monte to bring Ancilla and Maria to Rome. On November 13, he wrote to their parents, "We are happily installed in our fine

house . . . today for the first time Ancilla prepared a fine little
dinner which gave great pleasure to Monsignor Bugarini. She
grumbles a little because she finds everything here costs more
than at Bergamo. Let us hope that Providence will help us to
make ends meet. And indeed you will see that He will. . . ."

In December, he was off on his longest trip yet, visiting mission
offices in France, Belgium, Holland, and Germany. Not long after
his return, barely three weeks into the new year, Pope Benedict,
who liked to say that he had spent only two and a half lire on
doctors and medicine throughout his lifetime, contracted acute
pneumonia and early on January 22, 1922, as the Vatican bulletin
put it, "with great holiness fell asleep in the Lord."

It is known that the assemblage of the church's princes, soon
afterward gathered together in solemn conclave in the Sistine
Chapel, first offered the white robe to Cardinal Laurenti, head of
Propaganda Fide. This good and humble servant of God was so
appalled by the prospect of becoming the pope that he fell to his
knees before his brother cardinals and pleaded that "this exalted
office be given to another who is stronger and better able to carry
the burden." There then ensued a deadlock between conservative
and progressive factions lasting thirteen ballots and when, following the fourteenth ballot, white smoke finally issued from the
stovepipe above the Sistine Chapel, it signaled the election of a
compromise candidate. He was Cardinal Achille Ratti, the recent
successor to Cardinal Ferrari as archbishop of Milan and, only
four years before, director of the Vatican Library. A reflective
man, a humanist, he might have become one of the eminent
scholars of the time. Instead, as Pope Pius XI, he would be called
upon to shepherd his fold through the ravages of a second great
war.

Roncalli's work went forward. The new pope had a deep personal interest in the mission societies, and one of his first acts was
to commence the business of transferring the headquarters to
Rome. Roncalli prepared the *Motu Proprio*, the papal decree

embodying the change, and became a member of the reorganized superior council.

His travels continued. And wherever he went, he was faced with older, dedicated men who had long labored in the service of the missions and who now had to be convinced that while their dedication was appreciated, their methods had been outpaced by events. Patience and charity, he kept reminding himself, and gradually won the old hands over. His felicity of expression helped, too. At one point an aged mission director in Lyons, head of the oldest of the associations for the propagation of the faith, complained, "For a hundred years we have faithfully carried on this work here. Now you want to boss us from Rome. Why?" And in his best French, Roncalli replied, "To offer your example to the other societies. To raise all to the level of the best."

He launched a magazine, *The Propagation of the Faith in the World*, that told the stories of the mission founders and urged the organization of lay groups to support the mission work. In May 1922, in commemoration of *Propaganda Fide*'s centenary, he addressed a distinguished assemblage in the great hall of the apostolic chancery, describing the work of the missions as "the greatest opportunity for the Catholic religion in the twentieth century." Several cardinals congratulated him, not only for his speech, but for the progress he had made since coming to Rome. And indeed he had. Apart from smoothing the transfer of the missions' administration, he had doubled their income in 1921, and would almost double it again in 1922.

But these were bitter days for Italy, plagued by economic distress and a government that seemed incapable of decisive action, and Roncalli, in Rome, was witness to the crucial turnings that would change the nation and shake the world. It was a time of rampant unemployment and paralyzing strikes, and the threat of the black-clad Fascist bands grew ominously. They had only meager representation in Parliament but swelling strength in the streets and, in Mussolini, a raucous demagogue for a leader. On October 28, 1922, after a crisis-ridden week during which he waited in Milan while his Blackshirts terrorized the populace of

Rome and intimidated the press, Mussolini was asked by an irreso-
lute King Victor Emmanuel III to form a new cabinet. That
night, the *Duce*-to-be took a train to Rome to begin two decades
of ruthless dictatorship, consolidating his power by violence and
murder.

There can be no serious argument that the church did not, in
the beginning, harbor some illusion that Mussolini's Fascist state
might be a bulwark against the radical left and perhaps an acceptable alternative to a democracy too anemic to stand against the
revolutionary tide. It was not hard to be so deceived. As apostolic
visitor in Poland, Pius XI had seen communism in action and
dreaded it. Eminent statesmen, Winston Churchill and Herbert
Hoover among them, found much to admire in Mussolini's early
bombast. King George of England knighted him. And once in
power, Mussolini, onetime socialist, lifelong atheist, devoted considerable effort to coming to terms with the church for the most
cynical of political reasons. "Since the Italian people is all but
completely Catholic," he said, "and Catholicism is the ancient
glory of Italy, the Italian nation can be nothing less than
Catholic."

What this convoluted rhetoric actually meant was that Mussolini recognized that the presence of the Holy See in Rome lent the
city a particular aura and importance. Also unspoken, at least
publicly, was his conviction that he could more easily bend the
people to his will by feigning deference to their faith. Why risk
the enmity of millions of good Catholics when, with a few gestures, he could have them cheering wildly in the Piazza Venezia?
So he allowed a semblance of Catholic education in the public
schools and sanctioned negotiations between church and state that
would culminate in the concordat signed in the Lateran Palace in
1929. By its terms, the pope renounced any claim to the one-time
Papal States, and the Italian government recognized and guaran-
teed the independence of the 108-acre state to be called Vatican
City. The burning Roman question was settled at last by acknowledging the reality of circumstances that both sides had lived
with for sixty years.

Meanwhile, Don Luigi Sturzo, the Sicilian priest who founded the *Partito Populare*, reacted to the Fascist version of coalition government by proclaiming, "One collaborates standing, not kneeling." Such pronouncements were not healthy in the prevailing atmosphere, and eventually he was forced to flee Italy. His successor, Alcide de Gasperi, led a last stand in the elections of April 1924, marked by deadly street brawls, including a Fascist attack on the offices of the *Partito Populare*. Not long after, de Gasperi was imprisoned by the government. Released after four years, he was soon in trouble with the Fascist authorities again and once more a hunted man. He found shelter in the Vatican, where he was given a job in the library and hidden, to emerge after World War II as the leader of the Christian Democrats and premier of Italy during the throes of reconstruction.

What did Roncalli think of all this? His journals reveal nothing. But in some recently published letters written to his family during the political campaign of 1924, he made clear his distaste for the Fascist turmoil and the feelings he was forced to mask because of the sensitivity of his position: "I advise you not to get excited about the elections. You will give your votes when the time comes. Now it is better to stay put. Stay quietly at home, and think your own thoughts. Let others do as they deem best. I, for my part, shall remain faithful to the *Partito Populare*, but, because of the post I hold in the service of the Holy See, I cannot and must not publicly state my opinions. For this reason I shall not come to Bergamo to vote."

In a letter written April 4, only two days before the elections, he was even more explicit:

> I cannot find it in my conscience as a Christian and priest to vote for the Fascists. Everyone has the right to vote as he thinks best. In the end we shall see who was right. You must do as you wish. My advice would be as follows: to vote for the "Popular" list, if there is a free vote. If instead there is a risk of reprisals, then stay at home and leave things alone.
>
> Of one thing you can be sure, that the salvation of Italy

cannot come about through Mussolini, clever man as he is. His aims may be good and honest, but the means he employs are wicked and contrary to the laws of the Gospel. So, as *barba* Zaverio would have said, "If we live long enough we shall see. . . ."

Earlier that year, Roncalli had set down in the journal some thoughts about his work:

> Today, January 18, the Feast of Saint Peter's Chair, it is three years since I began, under obedience, my task as president for Italy of the Propagation of the Faith in the World. . . . To my sorrow, I left behind in Bergamo what I loved so much: the seminary, where the bishop had appointed my most unworthy self as spiritual director, and the students' hostel, the darling of my heart. I have thrown myself, heart and soul, into my new work. Here I must and will stay, without a thought, a glance or a desire for anything else. . . .
>
> I am here . . . to set my life in order, that is, to overcome my sluggishness which still hampers me, and to increase my activity and output, but I know that I really do very little, compared with so much more that I could do for my principal ministry, which is my work for the Propagation of the Faith.

But even as Roncalli set himself for greater efforts in what he took to be a permanent assignment, the train of circumstances that would lead to his next post was already in motion. Pope Pius had declared 1925 to be a Holy Year and appointed Monsignor Roncalli to organize a missionary exhibition of artifacts, charts, and pictures illustrating the work of the missions in Africa and Latin America. The material he gathered had anthropological as well as religious significance and therefore entailed considerable dealings with scholars and the press. He was also called upon to cope with the logistical details of caring for the hundreds of thousands of pilgrims expected in Rome. It was a fairly large task, and Pius was obviously pleased with his work. Roncalli even dared to wonder whether "the Holy Father had transferred to me the friendship he felt for my late Bishop Radini."

In the midst of these Holy Year preparations, he suffered an emotional wrench. Early in February 1924, Monsignor Bugarini fell ill with a bronchial ailment that developed into pneumonia. On February 14, Roncalli administered the last rites and then, as he wrote to his family, "accompanied him to the Lord in prayer." It was a deeply felt loss. The old priest had been a staunch friend and Roncalli had gained considerable solace from their late evening talks, when he could vent the small disappointments and occasional discouragement to which all men are subject. Now, as keepsake, he had the silver chalice with which Bugarini had celebrated his first mass half a century before, and a worldly legacy as well. Bugarini had left him his typewriter, and thereafter nearly all Roncalli's letters were typewritten.

In November, he was named professor of patristics, the study of the church fathers, at the Pontifical Athenaeum of the Lateran. It was an important appointment. His students were young clerics from different nations, and the university was among the most eminent in Europe. After only three months, however, he was relieved of his teaching duties, as well as of his post with *Propaganda Fide,* and notified that he was being sent to Bulgaria as apostolic visitor. He was to be made a bishop and, as the pope's envoy, given the rank of archbishop.

Was it really an advancement? Roncalli seems to have thought so, perhaps because he was also told he would remain only a short time in Bulgaria, where there were a scant fifty thousand Catholics and where he would have no diplomatic standing, before being sent to South America in the service of the Holy See. But nothing would ever come of this latter assignment and Roncalli was to spend the next two decades in the remote Balkans, seemingly forgotten by the Vatican.

In any case, when he sent the news to his family on February 19, 1925, he expressed no reservations, except for brotherly concern about Ancilla and Maria:

Before you hear about it from other people I wish to tell you confidentially something that will make your Christian hearts rejoice. . . . The Holy Father is about to make me a bishop because he intends to send me as his representative, first of all for some months to a European country which I cannot yet name, and then to a country in South America. . . .

As you see, this is a great honor for me, of which I feel most unworthy. . . . But it is also a sacrifice, because of the enforced separation which we must suffer for a time. . . .

As for my sisters, although we must give up the house in Rome, it is by no means my intention that they should return to live permanently in the family to increase the number of women who would then be too numerous, even if they are all good and God-fearing women. . . . They have been with me for six years; in five years time, or perhaps even sooner, they will come to live with me again, God willing. So they are still my responsibility. . . .

The question remains: Why was Roncalli chosen for a diplomatic post in Bulgaria, a job for which he had no experience, in a place of which he had no special knowledge? The circumstances and timing of the unexpected appointment strongly suggest that certain negative reasons may have played a part.

The Lateran Seminary had always been a stronghold of Catholic conservatism. That Roncalli, given his long association with a social activist like Radini-Tedeschi, should have been invited to lecture its impressionable young clerics and seminarians is curious. That he should then have been removed even before the end of the first term suggests that his teaching only confirmed Holy Office doubts about his orthodoxy. Certainly he led his class into wide-ranging discussions that sought to relate the inspiration of the Christian fathers to the present age. Some of his pastoral notions must have seemed revolutionary. "In certain cases, it may be quite all right to sanction a mixed marriage," he is reported to have told a class, and one can imagine some shocked student speeding word of this heresy to the Holy Office.

And there was the matter of Ernesto Buonaiuti. Roncalli's old

classmate had become a brilliant priest and gifted teacher, but his
books and articles, marked by sweeping new concepts, soon alienated the Holy Office guardians of Orthodoxy. Buonaiuti was
dismissed from his teaching post in 1915, and when he continued
to proclaim ideas at variance with established doctrine, he was
defrocked and, in 1926, excommunicated.

Roncalli, who was painfully aware of all this, continued to
correspond with his friend, with the inevitable result that the
Holy Office began to worry that he, too, might have become
contaminated by the scourge of Modernism. He himself was to
learn nothing of this until 1958, when he became pope, and visiting a certain congregational office, asked to see his own file. There
he found, marked alongside his name, the charge, "Suspected of
Modernism." As evidence, the file contained a postcard addressed
to him by Ernesto Buonaiuti. Then the rarely manifested Roncalli
anger erupted. Demanding a pen, he wrote beneath the condem-
natory words, "I, John XXIII, Pope, declare that I was never a
Modernist!"

Some time later, when his innate good humor had put the episode in cooler perspective, he was talking with a group of seminarians. Discussing first the importance of doctrinal principles, he
then urged them to strive against timidity. "I am the living example," he said smiling, "that a priest who has been placed under
observation by the Holy Office can still become pope."

The date for his consecration as bishop was fixed for March 19,
1925. Amid the preparations, Sotto il Monte and his family were
much on his mind. He arranged to rent the stone villa that his
ancestor Martino Roncalli, had built nearly five hundred years
before, thus assuring a home to which he could return for respite
on holidays, and a place for Ancilla and Maria to live.

Told that the villagers were preparing a celebration for him, he
wrote his father, "If you are asked, say that the more modest the
celebration the better I shall be pleased, especially if they avoid

spending too much money, which would be better spent for the church."

The smallest family matter was not beyond his concern. Anxious about accommodating all who wanted to be present at the consecration, he asked his father to dissuade his married sister Teresa from coming to Rome: "The reason is that I cannot ask a sister to sleep away from my house. . . . And the house is already chock full, so that even Ancilla and Maria will have to make do as best they can for a few days. And to ask a sister to sleep on a chair in her brother's house—and when that brother is an archbishop!—is one of those things which are easy to say but impossible to do. But I shall go to La Corna to see her in her own home. . . ."

Still, there was a considerable representation of family and friends at the solemn consecration ceremony in Rome. The lovely Spanish church of San Carlo al Corso was full. And as the consecrator, Cardinal Giovanni Tacci, intoned the ancient rite, there were those who keenly understood, as did Angelo Roncalli, that all that had gone before in his life was prologue, that the bishop's robe was a mantle of responsibility such as he had never worn, and that, for better or worse, it would remake his personal history.

During his retreat in preparation for the episcopal consecration, he had written in his journal:

> I have not sought or desired this new ministry: the Lord has chosen me, making it so clear that it is his will that it would be a grave sin for me to refuse. . . . The church is making me a bishop in order to send me to Bulgaria, to fulfill there, as apostolic visitor, a mission of peace. Perhaps I shall find many difficulties awaiting me. With the Lord's help, I feel ready for everything. I do not seek, I do not desire, the glory of this world; I look forward to greater glory in heaven. . . .
>
> I insert in my coat of arms the words "*Obedientia et Pax*" ["Obedience and Peace"] which Cesare Baronius used to say

every day, when he kissed the Apostle's foot in St. Peter's. These words are in a way my own history and my life. O may they be the glorification of my humble name through the centuries!

The morning after his consecration, Bishop Roncalli, apostolic visitor to Bulgaria and titular archbishop of Areopolis, an ancient diocese in Palestine long lost to the church, went with his parents to pray at the tomb of Saint Peter, where he had celebrated his first mass as a priest. Then they were received in audience by the Holy Father, who blessed the new bishop and his mission. And on April 23, 1925, in company with a Belgian Benedictine, Don Constantine Bosschaerts, who was to be his secretary, Roncalli left Milan aboard the Simplon-Orient Express for Sofia.

VII

EMISSARY OF THE POPE

A week before Roncalli arrived at his post in Sofia, Pope Pius received a contingent of Catholics from Bulgaria and told them, "I am sending an emissary to represent my person among you. He will have my ears that I should hear you, my lips that I should talk to you, and my heart that you should feel how much I love you."

Defined in more pragmatic terms, Archbishop Roncalli's mission was to report on the region's scattering of Catholics, to seek out possibilities for improving their lot among a people overwhelmingly committed to the Eastern Orthodox church, and to establish a more agreeable relationship with a hierarchy that had always been stonily suspicious of Rome. He was the first such envoy to Bulgaria in six hundred years—and arrived at a moment when the nation hovered on the brink of civil war.

Bulgaria had fought on the German side in World War I and lost much of its Macedonian territory to Greece and Serbia. Waves of refugees flooded the country. Now terrorists embarked on a wave of murder and bombing to underscore their demands for an independent Macedonia. There were some two hundred political assassinations in 1924, to which the government of King Boris III responded with its own reign of terror, mass arrests and wholesale executions. Even as *L'Osservatore Romano* was extolling the formidable learning and judgment that Archbishop Roncalli would bring to Bulgaria, assassins were trying to murder Bulgaria's king. They ambushed his automobile, and although Boris escaped, his chauffeur and an aide were killed. The very next day, the prime minister, Gen. Kimon Gheorgiev, was assassinated. In the midst of the funeral services on April 16, only nine days before Roncalli reached Sofia, a bomb exploded high in the great dome of the Orthodox cathedral, Svate Nedelja, sending it crashing down on the tightly packed congregation below. Although the king again escaped, 150 mourners were killed and 300 injured.

Commenting on Roncalli's arrival in the wake of the tragedy, the Bulgarian Catholic newspaper, *Iskra*, said, "At the time, one could still smell the smoke. . . . Yes, one could almost say that smoke lay over the entire country and nobody could see the way out. The blood of the victims and the tears of the afflicted are still fresh."

Roncalli's first official act was to visit the wounded. Most were cared for in Saint Clementine's, a Catholic hospital administered by Swiss nuns. That medical care was freely extended to all in this emergency, and that the Roman archbishop expressed his sympathy and concern to Orthodox and Catholic alike, did not go unnoticed in Sofia. So Roncalli, who was only heeding the instincts of his heart, had begun well.

Four days later he was received by King Boris. The meeting was especially significant, both because Roncalli had no diplomatic standing—he was the pope's personal representative, no more—and because of the stormy encounters, not long past, between the Vatican and the Bulgarian royal family. Boris's father, Czar Ferdinand, had been born a Catholic, but the fact that his people were preponderantly Orthodox made it politically expedient to have his son and heir baptized in that faith. Later,

Ferdinand traveled to Rome in an attempt to justify his decision to Pope Leo XIII, but the discussion had not gone well. In the midst of the session the frail old pope had risen in fury and pointed a majestic finger at the door. Relations between the Holy See and the Bulgarian monarchy had been cool ever since.

Now Boris was king, a balding, beak-nosed young man just past thirty, who welcomed Roncalli and remarked that the archbishop's visit was an honor to his country. They talked for three hours. Boris was to bring Roncalli great personal grief, but never did the envoy say anything more damning than that the king had been misguided.

On May 3, Roncalli celebrated mass and delivered his inaugural sermon in Sofia's Church of the Latins. His mission was to the Catholics of Bulgaria, he said, but he hoped to lead them to a new spirit of friendliness with their Orthodox countrymen. "It is not enough to have the kindest feelings for our separated Christian brethren. If we really love them we must give them a good example and translate love into action." He spoke in Italian, and apologized, promising to learn Bulgarian. Toward that end, he engaged Father Methodius Ustichkoff, a Bulgarian Assumptionist, and began his lessons at once.

Meanwhile, he was settling into his new quarters. At the invitation of Msgr. Stefan Kurteff, a Catholic priest of the Eastern rite, he was staying temporarily in the small white rectory of the Church of the Holy Mother of God. Kurteff's congregation, a splinter of Bulgaria's Catholic minority numbering only five thousand, acknowledged the pope as supreme pontiff but used a Byzantine liturgy nearly identical to the Orthodox. Roncalli's acceptance of Monsignor Kurteff's hospitality was a gesture to this little group, an indication that the Mother Church had not forgotten them. Later he would move to a small house of his own at No. 2, Ulitza Massalà.

One day shortly after his arrival, he was interviewed in his study for an article in *La Bulgarie*, a French-language paper. The reporter noted, "The Monsignor is still quite young and there is in his face a striking energy, sincerity and sweetness. His welcome to us was friendly and without fuss. He explained with the liveliness typical of his countrymen the objects of his journey to Bulgaria and his first impressions of the country. He said he had come to transmit the pope's blessing to the noble Bulgarian people and to organize the affairs of the Catholics. He praised the country, the people's industry and their hospitality."

But Roncalli would not be satisfied with his understanding of the land and its problems until he had seen it at first hand. On May 19, when he had been scarcely three weeks in the country, he set out on a tour that would take him to each of the far-flung Catholic enclaves and return him to Sofia with a somber appraisal of their situation, and of the prospects for unity.

The schism between East and West, originating in religious differences and exacerbated by political conflict, had widened during a thousand years of bitterness and blunder. Although the Orthodox faithful denied the authority of the pope, the papacy recognized the validity of Orthodox sacraments and had consistently striven for reconciliation, sometimes unwisely. Thus, although Catholic schools and hospitals were welcomed in anguished postwar Bulgaria, the proselytizing and Roman propaganda that often went with them were not. As for the country's fifty thousand Catholics, loyal Bulgarians as well, they were troubled both by the government's haughty disinterest in their religious well-being and, as they were often patronized by French nuns and missionaries, by the sense that they constituted little more than a French colony in the Near East.

One of the new archbishop's early directives was aimed at ending this aggravating indignity. Henceforth, he ordered, prayers after mass would no longer be said in French but in Bulgarian. His ultimate goal was twofold: to respond to the needs of Bulgarian Catholics for new churches, schools and an educated clergy; and, without proselytizing, to demonstrate to the Orthodox majority that in the eyes of the Holy See they were true brothers.

Toward these ends, he journeyed through the land all that spring and summer, from the Black Sea to Turkey and through the mountainous country bordering Thrace and Macedonia. He bounced along sun-seared tracks meant for goats and when his auto could go no further, climbed atop a spavined old mare and rode on. He traveled by springless carriage and leaky scow, sometimes through torrential summer rains, but he went where the people were.

He was now nearly forty-five years old and accustomed to a less rigorous life, but there was no other way for him to see the Catholic communities and come to know the local priests. So he and his traveling companion, Father Privat Bélard, moved along as best they could, sharing the open fire of country priests and sleeping on straw in remote village chapels. They heard blood-chilling stories of bandits and terrorist massacres and once, returning on horseback to a place where they had had to leave their car, they found that the chauffeur had taken fright and fled back to Sofia without them. They were sheltered that night in a frontier post and when, eventually, an ox-drawn cart was summoned to carry them on, Roncalli was cautioned to hide his ring and pectoral cross. But crossing the bare brown hills to the town of Pocrovan the two priests saw only a sad file of refugees in the rain. The bandits, it turned out, were engrossed in robbing the mail carriage that day.

He had been warned to stay away from Malko Tirnovo, a Black Sea town where smoldering feelings against the small Catholic colony had recently burst into violence. He went anyway, in mid-July. On his way to the church, sensing the menace all around, he returned glares of hostility with smiles. Then he preached a sermon of such friendship and unqualified good will that afterward, the Orthodox vice-prefect, a wild-eyed anti-Catholic, came to pay his respects.

Exhausting as they were, the travels strengthened him. The land reminded him of Lombardy and the peasant villages of his own Sotto il Monte. He felt at home. And though he saw everywhere ruined, vandalized churches, he saw, too, the open-hearted response of the people. Wherever he went, they poured from huts and simple stone houses to see this emissary of the Holy

Father, sheepherders, peasants, refugees, all astonished that so exalted a personage—an archbishop!—would have crossed the mountains to see them. Not in their lifetime, nor in their fathers', had such a thing happened. Not in six centuries had Rome sent to inquire after this isolated handful who clung to the faith in the face of their neighbors' scorn.

In their churches, Roncalli celebrated mass and administered the sacraments. He spoke to the tiny congregations through an interpreter, heartening them with his words as he had by his presence, assuring them that they were not forgotten. It was this, the simple pastoral duties, and not the hardships and dangers of the journey, that he would remember. For he thought of himself as a priest first and only incidentally as a diplomat or teacher.

But he did not forget the worldly needs of his flock. He knew that the Thracian refugees around Svilengrad were in desperate straits, and helped them with a special fund from the pope. He remembered that Sekirovo needed a new church, that Sallalia had a teacher but no schoolhouse, and that in Mostzatti there were two priests who had built a monastery with their own hands and would be formidable allies. By August, when he went to participate in a retreat for twenty-five priests of the Eastern rite, he knew every one of them by name, having visited each of their villages.

He wrote of his work to Ancilla:

> The Holy Father has given me one hundred thousand lire for the poor refugees who are returning to Bulgaria from Greece or Serbia. With this sum I have begun to provide one meal a day for 250 of the poorest children, not in Sofia but at Mesembria on the Black Sea. Just imagine that it takes two whole days to get there! . . . I shall soon be opening another refectory for the poor children—I have chosen to make them my special care—somewhere else where I am told that many die during the winter for lack of food. If you could see the destitution here! And this is still the result of the war. Imagine what it would be like for us if we had been expelled from our own land and obliged to go wandering

through the world, finding ourselves perhaps in Switzerland, in winter, without a roof over our heads and penniless, with old people and children in such weather.

Further along in the letter, he adds a typical little aside for Giovanni which indicates that, near or far, young or at middle age, his sense of what was seemly and proper remained unwavering: "Tell Giovanni . . . that with regard to that nun, the sister of that Gazzaniga whom I do not remember, it would not be correct for me to be the first to write to a nun whom I do not know. He will understand. For us priests all women, even nuns, must be like the holy souls in Paradise. We must do all we can for them, but with propriety."

There now began for Roncalli the most trying period of his life. In October 1925, having completed half a year in the new post, he returned to Rome to make a report to the pope. Pius was particularly interested in Roncalli's account of his visit to the metropolitan, Stefan Gheorgiev, patriarch of the Bulgarian Orthodox church. Like many of the visitor's early acts, this was without precedent—he simply decided it would be courteous and proper to pay a call on the Holy Synod—and it may have unsettled the metropolitan. In any case, he sent only a secretary to return the visit and in certain Vatican circles this was interpreted as an affront. Now the pope himself inquired about it.

"Was it not demeaning to the prestige of the Holy See, that they should send a secretary to return the visit of the apostolic visitor?"

"I do not think they intended it so, Holy Father," Roncalli replied. "It is just that the metropolitan is very busy."

Pius studied him over those little steel-rimmed glasses he wore. "One sows and the other reaps," he said at last, and Roncalli was glad to take that inscrutable judgment as closing the subject.

The balance of his report urged that administration of church affairs in Bulgaria be entrusted whenever possible to the Bulgarians. As matters then stood, ecclesiastical responsibility was divided among three foreign religious orders, the Assumptionists, Passionists, and Capuchins, and schools and hospitals were run by nuns of those orders from France, Italy, and Switzerland. The result, as Roncalli pointed out, was that Bulgarians tended to view their Catholic church as subordinate, a missionary institution directed from Paris and Rome. This was helpful neither to the Catholics of the country nor to hopes for an ultimate reunion with the Orthodox schismatics.

Roncalli's proposals were directed to that point. He suggested discontinuing the practice of sending an administrator from Rome to direct the religious affairs of Eastern-rite Catholics. Instead, he said, a bishop ought to be designated from among their own number, and recommended Stefan Kurteff. Then he asked that a new seminary be established in Sofia for the training of both Eastern- and Latin-rite priests. There, not abroad, and not by teachers of the established religious orders, a clergy could be educated in the Slavonic traditions that would be infinitely more meaningful to Bulgarians than would the ways of Western Europe.

His other proposals—the list was long and, to some in the Vatican, jarring—were similarly aimed at bringing the Catholic church in Bulgaria closer to those most concerned with it. He went back to Sofia to await results—and waited in vain. Except in the matter of Kurteff, his recommendations were ignored. When he wrote to Rome to ask what had happened, he received no reply. Nor did he receive any further instructions, so that when his pastoral duties ended with the elevation of Kurteff to exarch apostolic of the Bulgarian Catholics of the Byzantine rite, he was at loose ends.

It was frustrating and worrisome, but in the main Roncalli bore it stoically. Once, though, when he wrote to a friend in the Vatican about his problems, his letter came to the attention of certain curial officials. Hearing of their displeasure, Roncalli then sat down and wrote another letter. After a few lines in which he asked forgiveness in case he offended anyone, he proceeded to unburden himself of twenty typewritten pages on the subject of the difficulties caused him by his superiors in Rome. The letter soon found its way to the desk of the Holy Father himself, who read it with astonishment. "Behold the wrath of the lamb!" he said. But still nothing was done.

During a retreat at the end of 1926 in preparation for Kurteff's consecration as bishop, he made this entry in his journal: "I have been a bishop for twenty months. As I clearly foresaw, my ministry has brought me many trials. But, and this is strange, these are not caused by the Bulgarians for whom I work but by the central organs of ecclesiastical administration. This is a form of mortification and humiliation that I did not expect and which hurts me deeply."

That the Eastern Orthodox church had no interest in uniting again with the Roman Catholics did not greatly surprise Roncalli. His study of history had revealed to him the full bitterness with which the two houses of God had parted, the mutual persecutions and animosity of all the centuries since. But it pained him that the Eastern clergy seemed completely indifferent to the spiritual heritage of the Latin church, ignorant of its ancient glories and suspicious of its contemporary aims. He himself knew and venerated the Orthodox fathers. Now he hoped that this understanding, and a genuine feeling of brotherhood, would temper hereditary Eastern mistrust of every friendly overture.

Whenever there was an opportunity he attended services in the Slavonic liturgy. One day, without notice, he turned up at the Orthodox monastery of Rila, a Bulgarian shrine outside Sofia. The monks were astonished by the sudden appearance of the Roman archbishop, but nonetheless politely showed him through the beautiful old church, and were deeply moved when he knelt to pray at their altar. Someone had called him, "The monsignor whose approach is: 'Let us have good will for one another,'" and his own good will was so self-evident that men who met him with misgivings left him as friends.

Roncalli was to spend nearly ten years in Sofia, however, without narrowing the ideological gap between East and West by an iota. Nor did he substantially allay Orthodox suspicions that they were judged in the upper reaches of the Vatican, all one hundred million of them, to be vagrant souls, strayed from the one true church. But little by little he managed to thaw the official chill usually reserved for Catholic envoys in the Balkans. This was due not only to the warmth of Roncalli's personality, but to his demonstrated concern, especially in times of crisis, for all men, regardless of their religion.

In the spring of 1928, for example, a series of sharp earth tremors tore through the Maritza River valley in central Bulgaria. Roncalli rushed at once to the stricken towns and villages to see how he could help the homeless thousands. Day after day the terrible quakes continued, followed by savage rainstorms, and day after day the round, black-clad figure of the Catholic archbishop was seen moving among the refugees, directing the distribution of bread and blankets. He was in Philippopolis (now Plovdiv) when, at 9:00 P.M. on April 18, the whole city suddenly shuddered and sent the terrified population of one hundred thousand pouring into the streets. The next day, from Sofia Roncalli cabled the Vatican to ask for special relief funds, then took a moment to reassure his family that he was safe: "You will have heard about the earthquake in Bulgaria. Do not be alarmed on my account. It is far from here. In the last few days I have visited the scenes of the disaster—what a pitiful sight! Last night at Philippopolis I was present myself when there was an extremely violent shock which wrought havoc in the city. Like everyone else I spent the night in the open. Now I have returned to Sofia, the better to assist in rescue work. . . ."

But he would not stay away. With money sent to him from friends in Rome and Bergamo, he bought more relief supplies and returned again and again to the devastated valley. Drawn by the suffering, torn by it, he slept in emergency tents among the refugees, comforting them with his presence when he had nothing else to offer. Using the papal funds, he established what came to be known as "The Pope's Soup Kitchens," which dispensed food to all in need well into the month of June.

. "Unfortunately the continual rain has made life dreadfully hard for the numberless poor people who do not yet dare re-enter their tottering houses," he wrote. "Imagine so many old folk, and so many poor mothers who have given birth to children during these days and do not know how to shield them from the cold, the rain and the mire   . . if the rain does not cease there is danger of floods. . . ."

That crisis passed. But another, a long dark night of the soul, was gathering for Angelo Roncalli.

Around this time he began to hear the first of recurring rumors that he was to be assigned a new post. He had already been in Bulgaria far longer than he expected, more than three years, but he loyally stifled whatever hopes he might have had for a transfer. Thus when rumors reached the Sotto il Monte parish priest, Don Giovanni Birolini, Roncalli told him to pay no heed. "As Scipio was called 'Africanus,' the African, so I am ready to become '*il bulgaro*,' ['the Bulgarian'].", And when Cardinal Eugenio Tosi, archbishop of Milan, died, he wrote home, "There are some rumors about which associate my name with the nomination for Milan. Do not believe anything you hear. Beg the Lord to spare me greater dignities and responsibilities than those I have already assumed. It is no use letting one's imagination run riot."

But the stories persisted. Early in 1930, he heard that someone in Rome had proposed him for the post of apostolic delegate to Turkey, but it went to another. Later, it was reported in the press that he was to be promoted to nuncio and sent to Bucharest, and even in Rumania this was assumed to be so. But the honor went instead to Msgr. Valerio Valeri, whose diplomatic footsteps Roncalli would later cross in France.

He would have been less than human had he not felt passed over. It was not as though he was permitted to do what he believed needed to be done in Bulgaria. His plans for a new seminary were still bottled up in the Vatican bureaucracy, as were his other suggestions for emancipating the Bulgarian church from the rule of foreigners. So he busied himself as well as he could, remarking wryly, "I am like a beast of burden, always harnessed to this cart. I don't carry much weight, but I'm always at work."

He struggled against his frustrations, but his wounds were rubbed raw in the course of his periodic visits to Rome. "There are many people in Rome who ask me whether I do not consider my stay in Bulgaria has been unduly prolonged. I let them say what they like and remain calmly at my post." Once, returning to Sofia full of disappointment and distress, he uncharacteristically revealed the depth of his feelings in a letter to Ancilla and Maria, "I must tell you that I was very glad to get away from Rome where the sight of so much petty meanness got on my nerves. Everyone is busy talking and maneuvering for a career. Ah! How wretched a priestly life becomes when one is more anxious for one's own comforts than for the glory of the Lord and the coming of his Kingdom."

He commemorated his twenty-fifth year of priesthood before Christmas 1928. "Twenty-five years a priest!" he wrote in his journal.

> I think of all the ordinary and special graces I have received, of my preservation from grave sins. . . . I must always see myself as the poor wretch that I am, the least and most unworthy of the bishops of the church, barely tolerated among my brethren out of pity and compassion, deserving none but the lowest place: truly the servant of all, not merely in words but in a profound inner sense and outward appearance of humility and submission. . . .
>
> I will never take any step, direct or indirect, to bring about any change or alteration in my situation, but I will in all things and at all times live from day to day, letting others say and do, and suffering whoever so desires to pass ahead of me, without preoccupying myself about my future.

It was well that he had this selfless resolve to cling to, for now he was to be tested again. At the end of 1929, he was finally encouraged by Rome to begin negotiating for land on which to build the Bulgarian seminary. "The building will begin in the spring," he wrote exuberantly. "The total outlay will be 2.5 million Italian lire. The Holy Father will provide the money. I have only had the labor and strain of all the preparations necessary for the success of so important an enterprise, and now I shall have the joy of seeing that it was really worthwhile to make such great efforts."

His gratification was premature. The money never materialized and all his work and planning were for nothing.

He still lived in the small house at No. 2, Ulitza Massalà. It was inadequate as a mission and often overcrowded, for Roncalli shared it with the elderly Father Ustichkoff, who puffed the rooms full of cigar smoke despite his poor health and alternated between bouts of lonely weeping and holding court for throngs of unruly visitors.

Roncalli was lonely too. Thinking to have Ancilla and Maria with him, he sought permission from Rome to enlarge the house somewhat, writing home that, "Certainly some change is necessary: either I stay here with a well-established mission or I am sent elsewhere." Three weeks later he told his sisters, "Although I am not likely to stay here much longer I am nevertheless making my preparations as if you were coming here next year to keep me company. That is the only way we can live." But more than a year passed, and he wrote them, "I am awaiting a reply from Rome about the enlargement of my small house. As you know, they do things well in Rome, but one must learn to wait." He would wait in vain: The permission never came.

His pastoral duties having passed to Monsignor Kurteff, he was left in a sort of limbo. As he put it, "I have a dignity which I do not merit and the power of orders which I cannot even exercise as does a simple priest. I rarely have an opportunity to deliver a spiritual exhortation. I never hear confessions."

He traveled considerably, making several apostolic visits to Turkey and Greece and journeying to Czechoslovakia and Poland. Still he was left with time on his hands and had to force himself to keep occupied. "When there are no letters to be written and no visitors to be received, I study languages a little. I take an interest in the world at large by reading the papers. . . . I can give myself up calmly and regularly to worship and this brings me great comfort and helps me to endure the little pricks from the straw on which I lie like the Holy Child."

During this troubled time, Roncalli's letters made frequent reference to the state of his health, more so than at any other period of his life. He was approaching his fiftieth year, had grown corpulent enough to worry constantly about his diet, and was prone to colds and recurring gastric disturbance. In 1926 he had to have all his teeth extracted and a set of false ones fitted, a common enough occurrence at middle age in those days. "My dentist is clever," he wrote, "but all the same one has to suffer." The following year he had to return to Italy for treatment of a kidney ailment. Yet he came from hardy peasant stock and a long-lived family and one cannot help feeling that when, in December 1928, he remarked that "I myself do not expect to reach even my sixtieth year," he was expressing more a spiritual malaise than a physical one.

His ills of the spirit were made poignantly clear in his journal notes of April 1930: " 'Make me love my cross.' . . . The trials, with which in recent months the Lord has tested my patience, have late been many: anxieties concerning the arrangements for founding the Bulgarian seminary; the uncertainty which has now lasted for more than five years about the exact scope of my mission in this country; my frustrations and disappointments at not being able to do more, and my enforced restriction to the life of a complete hermit, in opposition to my longing for work directly ministering to souls; my interior discontent with what is left of my natural human inclinations, even if until now I have succeeded in holding this under control. . . ."

He did not yield. "*Obedientia et Pax*" was his episcopal motto, and seeking obedience and peace he found the forbearance to surmount this spiritual crisis. "I will be patient and good to a heroic degree, even if I am to be crushed," he wrote.

Six months later, an episode over which neither he nor the

Vatican had any control, a royal wedding, raised him from his patient obscurity and thrust him into the swirl of events.

A marriage between King Boris and Princess Giovanna, daughter of Victor Emmanuel of Italy, had been discussed from the beginning of 1930. The two were genuinely attracted to each other and it was felt that linking the royal houses of Bulgaria and Italy would be helpful to both countries. Mussolini was especially anxious for the wedding, seeing it as a funnel through which he could pour his influence over the Balkans. He made light of the single obstacle, Boris's Orthodox faith. Referring to the recently signed Lateran Treaty, he is reported to have said to Cardinal Pietro Gasparri, papal secretary of state, "Surely if we could resolve the great difficulties between us we can also settle this little Bulgarian business."

But it was not so simple. Before the Holy See could grant a dispensation for the Catholic princess to marry an Orthodox king it would require absolute guarantees that the ceremony would be carried out according to the canons of the Catholic church and that such children as might be born to the couple would be raised in the Catholic faith. Toward this end, Archbishop Roncalli spent long hours in the palace through the hot summer of 1930, entrusted with the delicate mission of winning the king's agreement.

He well understood Boris's great quandary. Eighty-five percent of his people were Orthodox and would wonder why their king had to submit to Catholic provisos, while the Bulgarian hierarchy would question the sincerity of his faith if he were not married in his own church. Moreover, the whole matter was out in the open, with daily newspaper speculation and heated street-corner arguments.

And yet the simple fact was that there could be no marriage with Giovanna unless Boris met the Vatican's conditions—a fact that Roncalli gently, but persistently, made clear. Finally, after weeks of talks, the king said he understood and was willing to sign the necessary documents to that effect. It seemed to be a diplomatic triumph for the apostolic visitor. Still, on the very eve of the marriage cermony he was cautioning that the closest attention be paid "if the slightest want of tact is not to arise which might compromise everything, even after the wedding is over. Here it is all going pretty well; but it is natural that the devil should use all his tricks to upset it."

Roncalli's fears were well founded. The royal wedding was duly celebrated in Assisi in accord with the Catholic rite on October 25. But six days later, as soon as Boris had returned with Giovanna to Sofia, he insisted that she submit to an Orthodox ceremony in the Eastern Cathedral of Saint Alexander Nevsky. This was announced as only a "nuptial blessing," although the marriage sacrament was repeated, and the ostentation of the entire affair made clear that it was intended to attract as much Orthodox attention as possible.

The repercussions were sharp. Roncalli himself was deeply hurt: He had come to like Boris, who had been astute and affable throughout their negotiations; but more, he was shaken to know that any man could so deliberately set out to deceive him. Even in Orthodox circles there were expressions of embarrassment and disapproval of the king's conduct.

Before making his report to the pope, Roncalli called on Signor Piacentini, the Italian ambassador to Bulgaria, to register his protest. The veteran Rome reporter, Corrado Pallenberg, has described what happened:

"Piacentini, with the skepticism and easy-going style typical of the Romans, replied, 'Don't take it too seriously, Your Excellency. Actually King Boris professes the Orthodox faith, and the matter is one for his conscience. As to Queen Giovanna, who is a Catholic, well, it means that she will go to confession.' On hearing these words Roncalli, as can well be imagined, flew into a rage. The conversation became very heated, and ended only when Piacentini rang a bell and told the footman to accompany the Vatican representative to his car."

Worse was to come. Summoned to Rome, Roncalli went at once to the papal apartments to make his accounting—and had an

opportunity to speak scarcely a word. Instead, he was kept kneeling while Pope Pius angrily rebuked him. He had compromised
the church in the eyes of the world, declared the pontiff. The
Holy See had counted on him and he had failed. He ought to
have seen through Boris's conspiracy, seen too that Giovanna
contrived in it, and he should have warned against granting the
dispensation.

Roncalli, though himself suffering from Boris's deceit and not
at all convinced that Giovanna was guilty of any more than the
same innocence, made no defense. Later he would say, "I had
done nothing to be blamed for, no, but the Holy Father had cause
to be angry and only my pride suffered." There was to be an
illuminating sequel to this incident, but for the moment the matter
was closed, and the archbishop returned to his post troubled and
heartsore. From Sofia he wrote, "Here my days are spent surrounded by storms. The business of the nuptial ceremony in the
Orthodox church has caused me much grief. I console myself
with the hope that a greater good may come out of the evil, and I
am content to keep calm."

The pot continued to boil. In the pope's Christmas speech on
December 24, he made public reference to the affair, speaking
with undisguised scorn of "these august personages" who did not
honor their promises. The result was a whole new spate of rumors
to the effect that the apostolic visitor would be forced to leave
Bulgaria. One diplomat told Roncalli confidentially that his expulsion was already arranged and set to take place immediately
after Christmas.

It did not, although echoes of the furor continued to reverber-
ate through Sofia. On January 23, Roncalli wrote Ancilla that the
pope's Christmas speech had put him in a difficult position,
"although I am on solid ground. It is possible that just because
some people would like to see me removed, the Holy Father will
keep me fixed in this post."

This was precisely Pius's tactic, and it brought an unforeseen
benefit. For a long time, the Vatican had sought to gain for the
papal envoy in Bulgaria higher diplomatic standing. In a country

where the relationship between the churches was at best wary, this was easier said than done and would require the assent of king and government. Now, when Boris was feeling conciliatory, if not contrite, the question was again put to him. And as the marriage ceremony in the Eastern cathedral had strengthened him with the Orthodox majority of his people, he decided that he could make this gesture to Rome. On September 26, 1931, the Holy See elevated its representative in Sofia to the rank of apostolic delegate, still not the diplomatic equivalent of a nuncio, but lofty enough in that it signified some degree of recognition by the Bulgarian state.

"From now on," Roncalli bantered in a letter home, "address me as apostolic delegate instead of as visitor. It is merely a question of title: I am still the same man. Nevertheless it is a good thing that this change has been made: It will please everybody here except perhaps the bearded worthies of the sacred Orthodox synod. But they too will learn to be patient."

One result of the change was that Roncalli was at last permitted to move to a larger residence, one commensurate with his new circumstances. It was appropriately furnished with the aid of his friends in Italy, who even managed to fulfill his request for a copy of one of the Trinity tapestries that once hung over the altar of the Sistine Chapel. This went into his own little chapel. In a land where the Holy Trinity was revered even more than in the West, nothing better proclaimed the delegate's sensibilities toward "the bearded worthies of the sacred Orthodox synod." On February 14, 1932, the tenth anniversary of Pius XI's accession to the papal throne, Roncalli welcomed the diplomatic corps to the delegation residence for the first time. Standing in the red reception room, he read to the assembled dignitaries a speech of welcome, speaking first in Bulgarian, then in French.

His sense of personal isolation was also ended. Rome sent him a young secretary, Giacomo Testa, who was to become a colleague and confidant, and like all Roncalli's aides of the future, a devoted apostle of his deepest conviction: that among all men there is more that unites than divides. Now, too, Ancilla and Maria came to stay with him for long periods. Delighted, as always, with their company, he took them on several trips, once to Constantinople, "so, when they are old and have nothing else to live on they will at least be able to live on the memories of things seen." Another time he wrote his mother, "Ah, how glad I should be if I could keep them with me always, not merely for three or four months."

But his trials in Bulgaria were far from over. On January 13, 1933, Queen Giovanna gave birth to a daughter. The following day, again in violation of his solemn promise, King Boris had the infant baptized with great pomp in the palace chapel by the Orthodox Exarchate Stefan Gheorgiev. Though Roncalli had suspected that this might be the king's intention, and had so warned Rome, the haste with which it was done, the callous swagger of the ceremony, stunned him. But when he went to the palace to register his protest, Boris would not receive him. He presented the official protest to the prime minister, and on January 15 addressed a stern letter to the king that somehow also conveyed his private sadness, "I think of the sorrow that will be felt by the Holy Father and by all good Catholics everywhere. I am all the more grieved because I know that no real advantage can come, either for the royal family, or for the Bulgarian people, from these continual violations of the human conscience in matters of religion which are repeated at every juncture of the history and life of this dear but unhappy land."

At this point Roncalli's primary concern was for Queen Giovanna. Was she involved in this latest breach of faith, or had Boris deceived her a second time? As soon as he was permitted to see her, the answer was evident. Giovanna was disconsolate. She told him that on the morning after the delivery, while she was still confined to her bed, Boris had come to her room and taken the child from her. Even as her mother, the Queen Mother of Italy, was on her way to Sofia thinking that she was to be godmother to her granddaughter at a Catholic baptism, Boris was going through with the elaborate but secretly organized Orthodox rite. And Giovanna, who had never consented to it, was powerless to prevent it.

Now she was gravely concerned lest the pope misunderstand this disturbing sequence of events and hold her to blame. On this score Roncalli was able to reassure her: He would himself affirm her innocence to the pontiff. Meanwhile, he cautioned her against attending mass at Saint Joseph's, her customary place of worship, where she might be subjected to the acrimony of staunch Catholics who did not know the truth of the matter. Instead, she should come to the chapel at the delegation, at least until tempers had cooled.

The pope, deeply wounded, addressed himself to the episode during a consistory on March 13. He had been painfully surprised, he told the cardinals vehemently, especially in light of explicit promises made "and signed by the royal hands." But he also made clear that he accepted Roncalli's view of Giovanna's blamelessness. He knew, he said, "how the responsibility was divided and that consequently we neither ought nor are able to inflict canonical penalties on, nor even to withhold our benediction from, a mother who is already distressed and who protested her innocence in all that has happened."

On January 19, Roncalli commemorated the anniversary of his consecration as a bishop by celebrating the mass at Saint Joseph's. Queen Giovanna, a great weight lifted from her spirit, insisted on being present. Afterward, in a characteristically kind and meaningful gesture, in the full view of the assembled worshipers, Roncalli gave her a beautifully bound missal. The matter of the baptism was closed.

It had closed for him on a mitigating note, as well. His faithful reports to the Vatican since the marriage finally brought Pius to realize that he had wrongly judged Roncalli three years before, that he had held him culpable and berated him without cause after the royal wedding. Now, according to the Vatican journalist Gabriele Carrara, he asked the delegate again to come to Rome. This time, as Roncalli knelt in obeisance, Pius, sitting before him, said that he understood more clearly what really had happened and who was responsible. "Now we should get up and excuse ourselves with you," the pope continued gently, "but if God should ever will you to sit in this chair, you will know that that is not possible." Then he rose. "As pope, no, but as Achille Ratti, yes. As Achille Ratti I stand and I ask you to pardon me. I give you my hand in friendship."

Roncalli was not received in court for a year, but in all other respects his life in Sofia went on as before. Encountering Exarchate Stefan at a banquet at the Hungarian embassy, he chatted pleasantly about everything but the baptism of the infant princess, Marie Louise. During Holy Week he went to observe the brilliantly staged service at Svate Nedelja, the Orthodox cathedral. By Christmastime, when he gave Communion to the queen, he had reestablished friendly ties with the Eastern clergy and, in March 1934, was again invited to the palace by Boris. Having made his point and held to his position, he could then say of the king, "Apart from the affair of the baptism, etc., he is a good man. But what a mystery the human heart is! We must pray for him."

Throughout this period, Roncalli's letters to Sotto il Monte reveal him more sharply than do biographers' portraits. And shining through them are the humor and gentle wisdom by which all the world would someday know him. Thus, writing one Christmas that he planned to celebrate the Solemn Pontifical Mass with the Capuchin Fathers, he said, "I hope to preach in Bulgarian," then, poking a little fun at himself, "The sermon will be short."

During a particularly severe winter, he counseled his mother and aunts on how best to treat a common cold, "We are poor, it is true, but resting in bed, keeping to a diet, taking a purge or an aspirin are simple little remedies which even the poor may adopt. . . . This advice I give to you all, old and young. To follow it costs nothing, and if you reject it you will have one expense after another, not excluding the cost of a funeral." Another time, though, he wrote, "Naturally . . . from time to time we must give the doctor and druggist something to do, or they would have to change their trade!"

Unlike some of his clerical brethren, he was not at all perturbed by the startling advances of twentieth-century science, never felt his faith threatened by material revelations and, indeed, gloried in their promise for mankind. In April 1930, he wrote his family: "You have heard of Marconi's latest discovery. [Guglielmo Marconi, the Italian Nobel Laureate and inventor of commercial radio, had recently demonstrated how microwaves "bend" around the earth's curvature.] He is a good Christian and a personal friend of the Holy Father. We shall soon be in such close communication that we shall be able not only to hear one another at a great distance but even to see one another. Just imagine: Every evening, by means of a little wireless which I have in my study, I can distinctly hear speeches, songs, news, etc., from very far away, without any effort on my part."

One can easily picture the wonderment with which the peasant family received this astonishing news. They did not have to rely on such "miracles," however, to communicate with their beloved Angelo. Each summer, usually toward the end of August, Roncalli returned to Sotto il Monte, remaining there until mid-October. These visits never failed to lift his spirits. He was nourished by his native soil and heartened in the presence of his family, now swelled by the children of his brothers and sisters.

Like any family, large or small, living in a single house, the Roncallis sometimes had their differences, and did not hesitate to seek the archbishop's support for one side or the other. In the beginning, he tended to soothe separate hurts and urge that ". . . we ought, like good Christians, to be able to find a way of living all together as separate families under the same roof."

Not that he could not be stern. One year, exasperated by the family wrangling during his previous visit, he wrote, "I do not want to find the same situation which I found before. Unless there is a change for the better I shall stay two or three days only, out of respect for my parents, and then go elsewhere for my vacation."

Finally, convinced that nothing would avail, he proposed that two separate kitchens be established in the house. He offered to pay, and instructed, "You, our father and mother, with Savero,

Alfredo, Giovanni and Giuseppe, and no one else—the women must obey orders, not give them—must hold a small family council and try to agree among yourselves about the minimum expenditure necessary." Then, as families so often do, the Roncallis patched up their quarrel and decided to go on living as before.

Meanwhile, the archbishop had found a little place of his own to retreat to during those family visits. The villa, which he rented from a young nobleman of Bergamo for a thousand lire a year, was still known as Camaitino—the Italian contraction for Casa Martino (the house of Martin)—after that long-ago Roncalli who first came to Sotto il Monte from the Imagna Valley. Now it is a museum, filled with souvenirs of John's papacy. But visitors who look out the window of his small bedroom will see, as he did, the tower of old San Giovanni at the top of the long green hill, and the world of his childhood below. When Camaitino was being put in repair for his occupancy, the workmen uncovered some fifteenth-century frescoes and an ancient coat of arms, a spire on a field of red and white bars. Reasoning that it must have been his ancestor's, Roncalli adopted it for his episcopal seal, incorporating the motto of Cesare Baronius, "*Obedientia et Pax.*"

Throughout the years, he maintained a lively correspondence about the refurbishing and maintenance of the house with various family members, mainly Ancilla and Maria, whom he had installed there permanently. His letters are filled with the most detailed instructions concerning the work to be done, at the same time cautioning frugality. Sometimes, though, principle or propriety took precedence, as when he asked his father, as a borough official, to see that the bathrooms were linked to the village water supply. "Naturally," he added, "we shall have to pay, the same as everyone else." Later, he wrote to express gratification that the repairs were proceeding well. Then, "But I am sorry that the lavatory has not yet been put in order. You must know that it is by the state of the lavatory that a family is judged, and if a distinguished stranger comes one feels ashamed to have to show him that ugly staircase with the ceiling of the attic, etc. Moreover, to arrange things as I have already indicated to you need not entail great expense. . . . Do what you can, but in any case I beg you not to leave it in its present unprepossessing state."

Often he brought guests to dine with the family at Colombera —members of the Bergamo clergy, Bishop Kurteff one Christmas, and some twenty-three of his seminary classmates who were commemorating their silver jubilee as priests the following summer—always sending some puckish note to his mother to "remind her of the chickens that must be fattened for the holidays." More often than not he enclosed a 100-lire note, more when he had it, toward the family household expenses or to meet the periodic mortgage payments. The scope of his financial assistance to others was in fact remarkable considering that, all told, the Vatican provided him with forty thousand lire a year, worth about $2,500 then, for his maintenance and expenses in Bulgaria. His personal needs must have been minimal, for out of this sum he managed to provide for his sisters Ancilla and Maria, to contribute to the support of an orphanage and the Sotto il Monte parish church, and to underwrite the tuitions of several worthy but poor local seminarians. Together, these expenditures—about which he continually admonished his family not to speak outside the household— came to more than twelve thousand lire annually, and he can scarcely be accused of exaggeration when he notes that ". . . although I lack for nothing which befits my state, I have nothing else, and most of the time I live in holy poverty, a dignified and in no sense wretched poverty but all the same very real."

In December 1927, he wrote his parents: "To remind you of me on Christmas Day I am sending you the last hundred-lire note I brought back with me from Italy. It is, so to speak, the last cartridge in my belt, and it is a pity there are no more. But this year I shot rather too many. . . . But there is nothing to be afraid of. I am a son of Providence, who will not allow either me or you to go without what we need."

This was a promise, not only to his aging mother and father but to all his family, that he never failed to keep. In the cruel winter of 1929, he wrote to Ancilla, "What our dear father tells me grieves me very much. I mean with the cold weather and other difficulties during these winter months, you are very badly off at home. In order to help you a little, at least to obtain the most necessary things, I am sending direct to you this money order for 2,897 Italian lire. . . . Now do as I say. Take out 1000 lire and give it to our parents, to satisfy the most urgent requirements of food during these bitter months. The rest, as last year, will be for your own needs."

In April 1930, he paid twelve thousand lire to the Bergamo bank, Piccolo Credito—all his painfully accumulated savings—to reduce the mortgage on Colombera Farm. "As soon as I can I shall send other small sums," he wrote, "because I can see that the income from the farm alone will never reduce that burden."

As there were so many relatives, he was at pains not to appear to be favoring one over another. Once, enclosing a small sum for his sister Assunta, "because she is the poorest of us all," he cautioned Ancilla, "Do not tell anyone else." But he turned his back on none of them. When Zaverio's daughter fell ill and required surgery, he wrote at once to his sister-in-law Maria to say that he would help with the expense: "I do for you and Savero what I would do for my other brothers and sisters-in-law in a similar situation. I had thought of putting a little money aside to send you with Savero to Lourdes this year, on the occasion of your silver wedding. But instead I will use the money to help you in this way. When the operation is over tell me what you need."

For a time he was helped in these benefactions by an American priest, Father Francis Spellman, who would one day become a power in the church as cardinal-archbishop of New York. Spellman had met Roncalli during his travels in eastern Europe and on his return began sending him regular sums to have special masses said for Americans of Bulgarian descent. Roncalli was scrupulous about not sending the money home until he had actually celebrated the masses. "There is a way to sanctify our poverty by spiritually uniting it to the sacrifice of Jesus who died in poverty for us." But by 1932, in the depths of the great worldwide depression, this welcome source of funds was drying up. On May 11 he wrote his parents: "I enclose a little check for twenty dollars which will serve for small household expenses. Every month I used to receive thirty dollars from America, corresponding to the intentions of holy masses which I celebrated. But now there is great poverty even in America. I was without requests for masses for two whole months, and now I have received a check for only twenty dollars. But we must have patience. Later on I shall try to help you in another way. . . ."

Then in 1934, eleven-year-old Angelo Roncalli, his brother Giovanni's eldest son, wrote to say that he felt called to the priesthood. It is doubtful if the prospect of aiding anyone had ever so gratified Roncalli, no matter the difficulties, and the proud uncle responded promptly:

> My dear Angelino, I was very pleased to receive the news you sent me in your letter of 17 April. If the Lord really calls you to the priesthood this is certainly the most precious grace he can grant you. But naturally only if you can become a good and worthy priest, useful to our Holy Church and to the souls of men. If you could not do this it would be better for you not to take a step along this road. But I hope the Lord, who has put this good purpose in your heart, will help you to consecrate your whole life to him. As you may well believe, I am willing, to the extent of my capacity, to be the instrument of Providence to help you along the road to the altar. . . . Meanwhile I bless you, I encourage you and your good resolve to our dear Mother Mary, the Queen of priests."

All that year the boy worked hard. By autumn, the arrangements had been made for him to enter the seminary in Bergamo. Then one wet November day he caught a chill, and within a week he was fighting for his life. The news reached Roncalli during an official visit to Rome and he immediately telegraphed Giovanni: "Follow doctor's advice/I will pay all expenses/Much distressed unable to come/Anxiously await news dear Angelo's illness praying, hoping, blessing/Telegraph news/Courage."

Days later the news came: Angelino, just turned twelve, was dead. Crushed, anguished for Giovanni and his wife Caterina, and for himself, Roncalli sent word to his brother that he was coming home, that he would pay the funeral costs. Then he wrote, "Be sure that Angelino, who is certainly now in heaven, and much happier and more content than any of us, will be a valid protector, first of all to you both who have brought him up so well and helped him on his way to the priesthood which he desired, and then to the whole family that now mourns for him. I am weeping. . . ."

A few months later, he had happier news: a promotion no longer even contemplated after ten years of waiting. On November 17, 1934, he wrote his parents, "It appeared as if nothing new was to happen with regard to my stay in Sofia but instead I hear this morning that the Holy Father has decided to send me to Constantinople as apostolic delegate. . . ." That was in August 1934. And on November 21, *L'Osservatore Romano* printed the following terse notice: "His Holiness Pius XII has appointed his Excellency Angelo Giuseppe Roncalli, Apostolic Delegate in Bulgaria, to Apostolic Delegate for Turkey and Greece."

It was not a spectacular advancement. Istanbul, still often referred to as Constantinople though the name had been officially changed in 1930, was not a nunciature. Indeed, there were fewer Catholics of the Latin rite in both Turkey and Greece than in Bulgaria. But of difficulties, there were plenty. Turkey's modern history had begun little more than a decade earlier, when Mustapha Kemal wrenched it from the ruins of the Ottoman Empire. Now he was called Kemal Atatürk, president of a proud and prickly republic, and among the first of his reforms was the absolute secularization of the national life and the consequent restriction of religious activity. It was generally understood, though never said, that it was the misguided fervor with which Roncalli's predecessor, Msgr. Carlo Margotti, contested these reforms that led to his replacement. Undoubtedly it was hoped in the Vatican that the new delegate, the genial, even-tempered Roncalli, might better adapt to Turkey's revolutionary heat.

Roncalli's reaction marked the man. He accepted the new assignment as the will of God, difficulties and all. Meanwhile, it was time for farewells. Bulgaria and its people had become dear to him, and in a Christmas sermon at the Church of Saint Joseph, delivered in Bulgarian and broadcast throughout the country, he expressed his feelings with heartfelt eloquence, to which many listeners responded with tears:

> Today I am with you for the last time. In saying this, I do violence to my heart. But you know that we are all pilgrims on this earth. . . . May God always protect you from any insecurity and keep the sky serene above you. I want to give witness before the altar of our Lord that the Bulgarian people, from their highest representatives to the most humble person, displayed love and respect for my office and that you deserve the respect of the world. I will never cease to say this. As for me, I have done very little for you. I failed in many respects and ask you to forgive me as good brothers forgive. I am a man like you. . . .
>
> And you, my beloved brothers, do not forget me, for I remain always, beyond wind and sea, the fervent friend of Bulgaria. There is a tradition in Catholic Ireland that on Christmas Eve each family puts a lighted candle in its window, so that if Saint Joseph and the Virgin Mary should pass they may know that within, beside a fire and a table blessed by the grace of God, a family awaits them. So it is that wherever I may be throughout this world, if a Bulgarian away from his homeland passes my house, he will find the candle of welcome burning in the window. He has only to knock on my door and it will be opened to him, whether he be Catholic or Orthodox. And inside, my Bulgarian brothers, you will find the warmest and most affectionate welcome. . . .

He left Sofia after the new year, taking the night train to Istanbul. He had come, nearly a decade before, alone and unnoticed, but his leave-taking was marked by a spontaneous outpouring of good wishes and by the official regard of the Orthodox church and the Bulgarian government. Newspapers extolled him. Catholics lamented his departure. And the king and queen invited him to an intimate little dinner at which Giovanna wept and Boris presented him with Bulgaria's highest decoration. Nor was any of this, the honors, the genuine regret over his going, merely formal recognition and thanks for the churches he had built and those he had rebuilt, or for the material aid he had brought to the poor and stricken people of the country. It was a testament to Angelo Roncalli, the good man, the great soul, to whom everyone was a brother.

On the day of his departure, January 4, it snowed and the evening was bitterly cold. But that did not deter the ordinary citizens who packed the railroad platform, nor the dignitaries who came to wish him Godspeed, among them bearded prelates representing the Exarchate Stefan, the king's personal emissaries, the prime minister, and the whole of the diplomatic corps. So moved was Roncalli, his eyes blurred with emotion, that he stumbled boarding the train and would have fallen had not someone rushed to support him. "Good-bye, good-bye," he called again and again until, as the train began to move, he was overcome and could say no more.

He is remembered in Bulgaria to this day, his spell mysteriously persistent. Cardinal Egidio Vagnozzi recalls that when he was in Sofia during the war, eight years after Roncalli's departure, he was constantly asked for news of "the Monsignor." Once, a shopkeeper who recognized Vagnozzi's clerical habit hailed him and ran out into the street to take his arm. "Tell me, Father," he said urgently, "how is our Monsignor—you know, the round one?"

And Robert Kaiser, then the *Time* correspondent in Rome, reported that during the 1960 Olympics in Rome, Pope John caught sight of a Bulgarian general he had known during the years in Sofia. He sent to ask if the general would call on him that evening, to the good soldier's considerable embarrassment, for Bulgaria by this time was under Communist rule. But the pope apparently only wanted to reminisce, and the conversation, about old times and old friends, lasted long into the night. At least, so the general reported to his skeptical colleagues, "He didn't ask me anything. He just said he loved Bulgaria very much."

Yet not long after the Olympic games, when the general returned to Sofia, it was learned that a Catholic bishop and a dozen priests, long imprisoned by the Communist regime, had been quietly released.

VIII

A BISHOP IN BYZANTIUM

Having left Sofia in triumph, Roncalli traveled 350 miles to arrive next morning in Istanbul as an unknown and unwanted alien. He had no diplomatic standing with the Turkish government and, in fact, had had to procure a visa to come and would require a permit to stay. A single secretary from the delegation met him at the railroad station and they went swiftly and discreetly to the apostolic residence in a taxi.

The old house, with which Roncalli was familiar from earlier visits, was full of dusty rooms and worn furniture. But he did not linger to contemplate his surroundings. Instead, in strict compliance with the law, he went at once to report to the governor of the city, then to register with the chief of police.

It was more a formality than a discriminatory measure. Catholics, although regarded as a tedious minority, were treated neither better nor worse than the country's seventeen million Muslims or its one hundred thousand Orthodox faithful. Turkey was in the throes of transforming itself from an Oriental sultanate to a modern Western republic and Atatürk had decreed that any kind of religious worship was an archaic stumbling block. Islam had been abolished as the state religion and privileges traditionally accorded the other faiths were summarily withdrawn. In their place, a series of annoying restrictions were imposed, one of which, to take effect in June, would forbid the wearing of religious habits. Roncalli noted that "the poor nuns in my entourage are most anxious about this," but for him it was a small matter.

He was familiar with the tangled story of Turkey's past, the excesses of sultan and caliph, and his grasp of history made clear to him the inevitability of an excessive reaction. From the time Emperor Constantine abandoned ancient Rome to the popes and built the splendid city of Constantinople on the shores of the Bosporus, that part of the Byzantine Empire, and later the Ottoman Empire, which we now call Turkey had served as a bridge between Europe and Asia, and also as a battleground for contending dynasties. Even as magnificent mosques and shining minarets rose on the Golden Horn, as emperors and sultans extended their sway over Eastern Europe and Persia and Arabia, Turkey remained a medieval state, corrupt, despotic, decaying. Known for a hundred years as "the sick man of Europe," still it refused to die.

The twentieth century issued in an era of deepening trouble. Under Sultan Mohammed V, Turkey fought and lost wars against Bulgaria and Italy and, allied with Germany in World War I, was again engulfed in defeat and forced to give up nearly all that was left of its European realm. In 1919, the Greeks attacked Asia Minor, sensing in the final disarray of the Ottoman Empire a chance to reestablish Greek power at the expense of a hereditary enemy. And they almost certainly would have succeeded—the new sultan, Mohammed VI, had in fact already agreed to humiliating concessions—had it not been for Mustapha Kemal and his Young Turks. Rallying an army in Ankara, where he had convened a provisional government, Kemal pressed the Greeks back and, in 1922, expelled them from Turkey altogether. The sultan fled with his wives, concubines, and slaves, thus ending seven

centuries of Ottoman rule, and Kemal Atatürk became president
of the new republic.

In the fifteen years of life that remained to him, Atatürk
changed the face of Turkey, hauling it up from the backward,
brutish morass in which its people had lived, with little hope for
change, since the Middle Ages. He ruled with dictatorial ferocity,
a brave, erratic, hard-drinking tyrant determined to sweep away
the rotten remnants of centuries by magisterial fiat. He abandoned the decadent capital of Constantinople with its ties to the
Moslem-messianic empire and built a new one inland at Ankara,
far from the pernicious influence of the European powers. No
vestige of the inglorious past escaped his notice. Polygamy was
abolished, the Gregorian calender was adopted, and new western-
modeled civil and penal codes were instituted. Arabic script was
abandoned in favor of the Roman alphabet, a measure which
simplified the monumental task of educating a population which
was 85 percent illiterate. Every Turk was obliged to take a sur-
name, as had the president himself: Atatürk (Father Turk).
Even the fez had to go, for it "sat on the heads of our nation as an
emblem of ignorance. . . . We accept in its place the hat, the
headgear used by the whole civilized world, and in this way
demonstrate that Turkey in no way diverges from civilized social
life." When an unwary Egyptian came to a diplomatic reception
wearing a fez, Atatürk knocked it off his head.

But none of the changes decreed by the Young Turks were
more revolutionary than those aimed at choking off the influence
of Islam, once an inseparable adjunct of the Ottoman rule. Religion was incompatible with the modern nation that Atatürk
envisioned. In 1924, he banished the caliph and four years later
abolished Islam altogether as the state religion. He was no less
hostile to the Christian minority, whose presence had historically
given the European powers a convenient pretext to intrude in
Turkey's affairs. Catholics and Orthodox, once free to pursue
their faiths without hindrance, suddenly found themselves regarded with official suspicion, warned against proselytizing, re-

stricted in those sacraments, such as marriage, which conflicted
with state law, and so circumscribed by the new bureaucracy as
to find it all but impossible to run their own schools.

Into this explosive atmosphere came the new apostolic delegate
—who promptly sought to defuse it with his innate good will and
bonhomie. Sunday, January 6, the day after Roncalli's arrival in
Istanbul, was the Feast of the Epiphany. Though the day dripped
with rain, it was an auspicious time to begin his new ministry, for
the Epiphany, commemorating Christ's manifestation to the Gen-
tiles, is more revered in the East than is Christmas. An archivist
recorded the archbishop's entry into the Cathedral of the Holy
Ghost: "If the sun did not shine, it was largely compensated for
by the face of the hero of this family feast day which was radiant
with kindness. Arriving incognito from Sofia on Saturday morning, Msgr. Roncalli was welcomed by the clergy and the faithful
in the basilica-cathedral on the morning of the Epiphany." The
papal bulls establishing him in his duties were read. Then the
assembled clergy approached to kiss his pastoral ring in token of
obedience.

In his sermon, Roncalli spoke freely of his love for the Bulgarian people he had just left. "But now my heart opens like arms
and leans toward you who are to form my new spiritual family.
. . . You know very well, and all the world knows, that I have
not been sent here to deal in politics or look after material interests; my functions are absolutely and exclusively religious. And it
is on these grounds that I wish to and must remain at all costs."

But he did not neglect to praise his predecessors, who had
sometimes fallen into disfavor for contending on temporal
grounds.

Of the eighteen million who then made up the Turkish nation,
there were perhaps twenty thousand Catholics, half of whom
lived in Istanbul. To them, Roncalli was not a diplomat but a
pastor, for as head of the apostolic vicariate of the city, he was

bishop of the flock with a full range of ministerial duties. The rest of the Catholic population was widely scattered: one thousand in Smyrna, two hundred in the 120,000 square miles of the Trebizond mission territory, forty-five in Tarsus, fifty families in Adana cared for by two Jesuits. As the pope's representative, Roncalli would visit them all. He had one further assignment, noted nowhere in his credentials: to initiate some sort of contact with the patriarch of Constantinople, Benjamin I, whose "primacy of honor" endowed him with the highest ecclesiastical ranking in the Orthodox world.

Meanwhile he was settling in. He wrote home to Sotto il Monte that he found in Istanbul a greater breadth of life than in Sofia, and although his residence was not so fine, "we are quite comfortably housed. If the Holy Father will send me the means to get rid of some of this old worn furniture we shall be even better pleased. But comfort matters very little when we know we are doing the Lord's will."

Soon there were painters and carpenters swarming over the house and, as he wrote to Ancilla and Maria, "Bit by bit I shall put nearly all the rooms in order, spending a little at a time, but wisely, so the Holy See will not complain and will be willing to pay." He added that he wanted them to come soon and said he was thinking of keeping some chickens in the garden so they could have fresh eggs. To his parents he sent 500 lire, "which I found at the bottom of my purse."

As the delegation was not provided with an automobile, he usually got about the city on foot or by bus. His position was, of course, not recognized by the government; like every other prelate in Turkey, he was barely tolerated in those years, but he was happier than he had been in a long time. Pastoral duties, for which he always longed, filled his hours and his heart. He felt himself truly a bishop for the first time, for at last he had a diocese. And though it was a small one, he devoted to it the most loving attention, and rare was the baptism, wedding, or funeral that did not command the archbishop's presence. In the journal he wrote,

"There is so much work waiting for me here! I bless God who fills me with the joys of his sacred ministry."

His household then consisted of Giacomo Testa, his personal secretary, Monsignor Della Tolla, a canon of Istanbul, and Luigi Bresciani, a young Bergamesque who had become Roncalli's devoted man Friday. In the beginning, the secretary to the delegation was Msgr. Angelo Dell' Acqua, the vicar-general, who had also held the position under Monsignor Margotti and who was to become one of Pope John's most trusted aides. When in due course Dell' Acqua was recalled to Rome, Roncalli had a chance to make amends for a hurtful decision of his predecessor.

There was an old curate of the cathedral named Collaro, who had once been vicar-general. A pious soul, Collaro's preoccupation with holy offices and the long hours he spent in the confessional had not, in Margotti's view, suited him to the administrative demands of the vicar-general's post, and in time he replaced him with the energetic young Dell' Acqua. Roncalli, whose patience was limitless, and who preferred suffering himself rather than give pain to another, saw the matter otherwise. Collaro, he reasoned, was a good and gentle servant of the church whose intimate knowledge of the diocese would make bearable his shortcomings as an administrator. In July, as soon as Dell' Acqua left, he returned the vicar-general's duties to the grateful curate.

On June 13, the edict banning religious dress in public went into effect, and Roncalli, noting that "after all, it is neither imprisonment nor death," saw to it that members of the delegation complied. His attitude seems to have been unique: It was reported that the Orthodox patriarch, Benjamin I, threatened to shut himself away for the rest of his life—a threat he never carried out—and at the behest of the Catholic religious orders, the French ambassador lodged a vigorous protest. The government replied that it was now master of the Turkish house: Gone were the days when a foreign power had only to dispatch a fleet through the Dardanelles to impose its will on Turkey. In point of fact, Roncalli, as head of a religious body, could have been exempted from the rule, but thought it more important to set an example. "If in Rome Christ is a Roman," he said, "let him be a Turk in Turkey."

Dell' Acqua, who was to be recalled in just a few weeks, saw no reason to order civilian clothes that he would never wear again. He would leave early, he said. But Roncalli wouldn't hear of it: The spirit of the law, as well as the letter, must be obeyed. A tailor was summoned, and Roncalli himself chose the fabric and colors for Dell' Acqua's clothing, as well as for other members of the delegation—and even taught them how to tie their neckties. "I learned it as a soldier," he explained.

Then they all marched ceremoniously to the Church of Saint Anthony to meet with the rest of the Catholic clergy and to make of the enforced surrender of their cassocks a sort of silent sacrifice to God. There was sadness in the bearing of the older priests and some embarrassment in the eyes of the watching congregation. But Roncalli seemed as genial as ever: no inviolable principle was involved, and as there was no choice but to obey the law, better to do it with a smile.

Later they had some photos made, Roncalli looking portly and a little self-conscious in a dark business suit and derby, rather like a Milanese bank clerk at the wedding of the managing director's daughter. He sent the photos to Sotto il Monte: "You will recognize your son the bishop dressed as the new law requires!" Afterward he would say, "I lived for ten years as a semicivilian, changing clothes every time I went in or out of church."

But it was just this attitude of conciliation that eventually persuaded the government that the Vatican and its delegate were prepared to abide by the changed circumstances. Unlike Margotti, who had pressed continually for diplomatic contacts, Roncalli hadn't even sent out the official letter announcing his arrival. "Quite unnecessary," he told his aides. "Let it be clearly understood, here and now, that in this country the apostolic delegate is a representative with no diplomatic standing." Such a gesture, one of many, enabled him to act more freely as pastor of his flock.

Roncalli well understood the precariousness of the Christian position in Turkey, and he was determined not to risk its complete obliteration by headstrong opposition to the government.

His strategy was to persuade his flock that a good Catholic could be a good Turk, despite the seeming contradiction, and his tactics were the same as those he had used in Bulgaria. He ordered that certain official documents be written in Turkish, and he himself set out to acquire a sound speaking knowledge of the language. Then he introduced it into the liturgy, having leaflets distributed to every pew so the congregation could recite the Divine Praises in Turkish instead of the French or Italian to which they were accustomed. Parts of the Gospel were read in Turkish, too, as were Roncalli's sermons.

There were difficulties: "Allah" would hardly do as a translation for "God," and the word "*Tanre*" was finally adopted; and he had to confront some antagonism, both from local Catholics, many of whom regarded the Turks as vengeful infidels, and from his superiors in Rome. But he saw the step as a simple token of respect for a country in which they were all visitors. He heard the criticism but ignored it, convinced that his way was right. It was Catholic. It was apostolic. On May 6, 1936, he wrote, "When the *Tanre mubarek olsun* (Blessed be God) was recited, many people left the church displeased. But I am happy. . . . The Catholic church respects everyone. The apostolic vicar is a bishop for everyone and intends honoring the Gospel, which does not admit national monopolies."

The good impression all this made on the Turkish people was to have lasting effects. It was soon after Roncalli was elected pope in 1958 that the Turkish government requested regular and permanent diplomatic contacts with the Holy See.

As soon as the apostolic residence had been brightened to his taste, Roncalli wrote to Ancilla and Maria, "I think the time has come for you to join me, as usual." The sisters had seen their parents through another biting winter, the household was tranquil, and they set out in mid-May, taking the steamer from Venice to Istanbul. But this visit was to be a short one. In July their father was taken seriously ill and they returned at once to Sotto il Monte. Roncalli, temporarily without a secretary and unable to leave his post, waited prayerfully for further news. When Luigi brought a cable to his study on the morning of July 29, he knew at once what it meant. Giovanni Battista Roncalli, aged eighty-one, was dead. He left his children no legacy but the example of his own life: seven decades of hard work without complaint, and an unfailing acceptance of God's will.

Roncalli was doubly grieved. He knew that his father had lived a long and fruitful life, but he knew too of the old man's deep peasant pride in his eldest son's station in the church. That Roncalli had not been there to share his father's last moments, to himself offer the solace of the final sacraments, was a deep personal wound. He cabled the family, "I mourn with you," and later in the day sought to assuage his mother's pain, and perhaps his own, with a long letter about the notice that would be taken in Rome and Istanbul of the death of a simple farmer in a remote Italian village:

> So the Lord has wished our sacrifice to be complete. . . . I would like to think that you, beloved mother, find consolation in my words. But what else can I say? The law of sorrow is the law of nature. Your children gather around you to comfort and support you. My house at Camaitino is entirely at your disposal. Go there with my sisters. You know that your son the bishop is not rich, but he would sell even his cross to satisfy your desires or your needs. . . .
>
> Meanwhile I must tell you that when the news of our father's death became known people began at once to call at the delegation. Tomorrow four newspapers of Constantinople and *L'Osservatore Romano* will print the announcement. Hundreds of requiem masses will be offered and thousands of Holy Communions. On Thursday there will be a solemn funeral service in this cathedral. I believe it will be a most impressive ceremony. In all this you will see some

compensation for the painful sacrifice I had to make in not
being able to come myself to Sotto il Monte. . . . I bless you
all together with great and tender affection.

He was able to come home at last in early September, to pray at
his father's grave, to see his mother settled in with Ancilla and
Maria at Camaitino. He gave some thought to the possibility of
having her visit at Istanbul, but the dangers of uprooting her from
familiar surroundings so late in life were only too apparent. Not
unnaturally, once he returned to Istanbul, she began to complain
more frequently about the ills of her advancing years, and even
remarked in a letter that she would probably never see him again.
Roncalli assured her that she would, then gently chided her with
one of those crisp aphorisms that would one day invigorate the
staid language of the Vatican: "One cannot get over old age, but
one can go on being old for a long time."

During these years, when he was further from Sotto il Monte
than he had ever been, or ever would be, he kept his ties close. He
was always asking for news, writing to the parish priest and, as he
once said, remembering "all that green hillside blessed with the
scent of spring in flower and rich with the gifts of summer."

When his youngest brother, Giuseppe, became the father of
twins, he wrote him joyously, "The Lord blesses the cooking pots
when they are large. You must have no doubts about the Lord's
blessing and his Providence. . . . Our dear father was right that
day when he came to the seminary to tell me that another little
Roncalli had been born at the Colombera (you were this new
baby!). He said: 'Oh, the Lord is great and good. Before us are
the fields, about us the splendid sun; within our hearts is the
Lord's own grace. What more can we want?' "

And of course, as always, he continued to take a personal
responsibility that the Lord's providence reached all Roncallis in
need. Thus he sent money to Giovanni in straitened circumstances, to Alfredo when he fell ill and, early in 1936, assumed a
staggering thirty thousand-lire obligation to relieve the family of

the pressure of its accumulated debts. Once, discouraged by this grinding burden, he wrote Giuseppe, "All this is crushing me and I shall never be free of it until my death, if I die soon, or some years from now when I shall be able to withdraw my insurance money and so free myself from any obligation at the bank." But by the time he had written a few more lines, his innate good spirits reasserted themselves: "Never lose heart, my dear Giuseppino. We are passing through hard times that we really did not expect. But you remember that when we were children it was very much the same story. Let us bless God in poverty as in prosperity . . . pray for me."

Meanwhile he worked on, fully engaged by the challenge of his new mission, content. In the autumn of 1936 he made a retreat at Ranica, the village outside Bergamo where twenty-seven years before he and Radini-Tedeschi had rallied to the cause of the striking ironworkers. Now, in the villa of the Daughters of the Sacred Heart, his world was full of peace and silence and he jotted down some reflections on his every-day routines and duties:

> I am pleased with my new ministry in Turkey, in spite of so many difficulties. I must better organize my days, and my nights too. Never going to bed before midnight is not a good thing. In particular these hours after supper need setting to rights. The wireless takes up too much time and puts everything else out of joint. . . .
>
> For my health's sake I must stick to a diet. I eat little in the evenings already but now I must eat less at midday too. It will do me good to go out for a walk every day. O Lord, I find this hard and it seems such a waste of time, but still it is necessary and everyone insists that I should do so. . . .
>
> I feel quite detached from everything, from all thought of advancement or anything else. . . . It is true, however, that the difference between my way of seeing situations on the spot and certain ways of judging the same things in Rome hurts me considerably: it is my only real cross. . . .
>
> I want to study Turkish with more care and perseverance.

> I am fond of the Turks, to whom the Lord has sent me: It is
> my duty to do what I can for them. . . .

The cross he bore, the sense that certain superiors regarded his work as insignificant because it produced no dramatic results, did not swerve him from the way of the Gospel to what he called "the wiles of human politics." He had come to Istanbul in circumstances that were not propitious and said, "Everyone knows, and the Vatican better than most, that these circumstances do not depend on me, and nobody expects me to bring about a change. It is best to get on with my work as unobtrusively as possible."

At the end of 1936, in his fifty-sixth year, he fell ill with a stomach disturbance that produced a small hernia. He promised his family that he would have the necessary surgery "as soon as I have the opportunity." He never did. Instead, he went on an even stricter diet, "no meat, a little light wine, plenty of vegetables and fruit. I shall be a bit thinner when I come home, but much better altogether. Such a strange thing: What they recommend most strongly is yoghurt! You see how it is—we must become like children again and eat the food of the poor."

Although Roncalli had also been named apostolic delegate to Greece, it was not at all certain that he would even be able to enter that benighted land. On Monsignor Margotti's appointment to that post three years before, too much had been made of the diplomatic import, with the predictable consequence that the Greek foreign ministry took offense and denied him a visa. Such visits as Margotti was subsequently to make to the Catholics of Greece were rare and roundabout.

Fully aware of this inauspicious record, Roncalli took care to avoid falling into his predecessor's trap. Calling on the Greek consul in Istanbul shortly after his arrival, he made formal application for a visa and said that its purpose was to enable him to see to the religious needs of the Catholic population. He made a point of not insisting on any diplomatic privileges. Then he went home to wait for a reply. It came within a week: He was granted a visa for eight days only, and with the understanding that he was traveling in no official capacity, but merely as a tourist.

He left for Athens at once and was plunged into another world. If Turkey was a land in turmoil, it was also full of energy and purpose, an old country transforming itself into vigorous young nationhood. But the Greece to which Roncalli came in May of 1935, menaced by revolution, torn from the Right and from the Left, seemed on the verge of violent death.

More than a century before, the whole of the civilized world had applauded the Greek struggle to break the Ottoman shackles. President James Monroe spoke in its behalf and Lord Byron died in its cause. But soon the world's attention was drawn elsewhere and for the next hundred years Greece, a poorly endowed nation, wracked from within, was left alone to fight a series of disastrous wars in the eastern Mediterranean. In 1924, the monarchy of King George II was deposed and succeeded by a strife-ridden republic that, at the time of Roncalli's visit, was already in its last days. By November 1935, the exiled George would be recalled to the throne and months later would dissolve the parliament and invest dictatorial powers in a general of the army, Joannes Metaxas.

Among governmental decrees affecting every phase of the national life, there were in preparation laws which would make it impossible for Catholics to undertake missionary work or to contract a mixed marriage in any but an Orthodox church; Catholic books were to be censored and their sales limited, and travel by the Catholic clergy was severely restricted. The Greek Orthodox leadership, historically the most anti-Roman in the East, was determined that the country's Catholic minority, whose liturgy was so close to their own, would win no converts for Rome. And Metaxas, anxious to avoid denominational divisions that might contribute to further disorder, would be happy to accept the advice of the Orthodox metropolitan, Papandreou Damaskinos.

All this was already in the wind at the time of Roncalli's first visit. But he quickly realized that he was to be paid special attention besides: Wherever he went, someone followed him. As he wanted it understood that the nature of his mission was entirely spiritual and within the law, he made no objection. However, one of the bishops who met him did take offense, and Roncalli had to restrain him. "When one goes about the business of the Lord," he said calmly, "one can afford to walk softly."

His discretion was rewarded. He was permitted to return in August and again in November, and the following year was finally granted a diplomatic visa that enabled him to come and go as he pleased. Eventually he managed to visit all Greece's fifty thousand Catholics, scattered in communities across the mainland and throughout the Aegean islands. He was also received by King George and by Metaxas, and was welcomed in the Ministry of Foreign Affairs. None of this wrought astonishing changes in the welfare of Greek Catholics, but as Roncalli was able to make their plight known, as he gained this small concession and that one, he could be convinced that "Here, too, the drop of water ends up by wearing away the stone."

If the Catholic faithful in their far-flung enclaves were often surprised by the unexpected appearance of the archbishop, usually puffing with exertion, for there were neither automobiles nor proper roads in much of that remote rocky land, the good friars of the thousand-year-old monasteries at Mount Athos were stunned. Catholic visitors to this citadel of Greek Orthodoxy, which barred the approach of any female, Catholic or Orthodox, human or animal, were rare enough; that the pope's own delegate should come plodding up the mountain on horseback was historic. Of course he came in a private capacity, because he was genuinely interested in the magnificent Orthodox libraries and art treasures, in their religious symbols and prayers. But he stayed three days and, by the time he left, had dispelled the monks' alarm at the sudden appearance of this representative of Rome.

Writing to his mother of the visit, he said, "There are up there more than twenty great monasteries and many other small communities; there is no other place in the world like it. . . . Unfortunately there are no roads at all. One has to go on horseback along most difficult paths, which many times made me pray hard to Saint Joseph and to our own dead, as I always do, to keep me from falling. And indeed I never fell, though my bones felt broken."

Inherent Greek suspicion of all Latins was intensified during these years by Mussolini's belligerent flourishes in the eastern Mediterranean. Yet Roncalli persisted with his work, and in time managed to ease the worst of the anti-Catholic strictures. He even won permission from hierarchy and government to have a cathedral for Catholics of the Byzantine rite built in Athens. This project involved him in long negotiations with his superiors, as well as with the Greeks, and entailed some compromise. In the end, it became possible only when the Vatican responded to Roncalli's urging and agreed to build the new edifice on the foundations of the ancient Byzantine cathedral and make it the seat of the Byzantine bishop, who was to have jurisdiction over all Greek Catholics, those in Turkey included. "The capital of Greece, Athens, is the capital of all Hellenes," said the Vatican announcement grandly. And this salute to the Greek national feeling won the day—as Roncalli knew it would.

His work in Turkey went on. He made regular visits to Ankara, the capital, and to the farther, smaller communities where separate handfuls of Catholics lived. Of continuing concern to him was the maintenance of the few Catholic schools still fighting to hold their doors open in the face of an adverse tide. Once they were among the best in Turkey; Atatürk himself had been educated in a French Catholic school. Now, the squeeze of the worldwide depression and the endless government pressure on the religious orders threatened to drive even the last of them out of existence. Only the archbishop's constant attention helped them to hang on.

His quietly pervasive influence was decisive in preserving the integrity of one of Turkey's own treasures, as well: the magnificent cathedral of Hagia Sophia (Holy Wisdom) in Istanbul. Built in the sixth century A.D. by the Emperor Justinian as a Catholic church of the Byzantine rite, its maintenance once required the full-time labor of six hundred men. With the Turkish conquest of Constantinople in 1453, it became a mosque, and its lofty central dome and slender minarets served as the models for innumerable other Islamic houses of worship. Now, with the antireligious Young Turks in power, plans were formulated to turn it into a secular museum.

The plans were never carried out. Somehow the Catholic archbishop convinced the atheist authorities that the historic and artistic importance of Hagia Sophia called for its restoration as a Byzantine shrine. Work was begun almost at once, and as five hundred years of paint and plaster were removed, revealing the glorious mosaics and paintings of the Christian era, the Turkish nation became the proud guardian of one of the world's great treasures in Byzantine art and architecture.

In January 1937, Roncalli had his first meeting with a minister of the government. In response to some inquiries, he was informed that Numan Rifat Menemengioglu, an under-secretary for foreign affairs, would receive him unofficially in Ankara. It was at least a chance to make his views known to the Turkish government, and Roncalli gladly made the journey to the capital. Leone Algisi, who observed the meeting, reported the guarded, painfully polite exchange between the two men—who liked each other on sight—one of whom dared not press his diplomatic presence, and the other who was not supposed even to acknowledge it. One would do well to read between the lines:

RONCALLI: As I am in Ankara on work connected with my ministry, I am very happy to have the opportunity of presenting my respects to a representative of Turkey.

MENEMENGIOGLU: And I am very happy to meet you personally and to tell you that the Turkish government has the deepest regard, both for you and the great and illustrious traditions which you represent.

RONCALLI: I thank you. I hope that the Turkish authorities
    have noted the way in which we Catholics have respected
    the laws of the country, even when these are sometimes
    trying to us. The suit which I am wearing is one example.
MENEMENGIOGLU: Of course, but we would like to point out,
    with great respect, that we are allowing you complete
    freedom to conduct your ministry, so long as it is not
    contradictory to our laws. Nor must it give the impression
    that we have relations with a religious power, a very
    respectable one, certainly, but alien to our way of life.
RONCALLI: I understand. That does not prevent that "religious
    power" from rejoicing in Turkey's progress, nor from
    detecting in your new constitution several of the
    fundamental principles of Christianity, although we
    naturally disagree with its antireligious spirit.
MENEMENGIOGLU: A secular state is our fundamental
    principle. It is, for us, the guarantee of freedom.
RONCALLI (smiling): The church will take care not to
    infringe it. But I am optimistic by nature. I always prefer
    to dwell on things that unite rather than those that tend to
    separate. Since we are in agreement on fundamental
    principles, we should be able to go at least part of the way
    together. As for the rest, we must have confidence. . . .

The two men became friends and, as it happened, in 1944, at
almost the same time Roncalli was named nuncio in France,
Menemengioglu became the Turkish ambassador there. He was to
remain a power in Turkish affairs for nearly two decades. Meanwhile, this first conversation led to others and, for Roncalli, a
widening circle of informal contacts among government officials.
There was no question of seeking diplomatic recognition, only
the hope of making his presence felt in the interest of Turkey's
little cluster of Catholics. It was a painstaking, plodding task,
without possibility of notable triumph, but with small, consistent
rewards.

On November 10, 1938, Kemal Atatürk, aged fifty-seven, died
in Ankara. To his people, who knew nothing of the relentless

pressures of his office, or of his loneliness and the whisky he drank to assuage it, the announcement of his death was a stunning shock. Roncalli immediately arranged for the delegation and the Catholics of Istanbul to join in the national mourning. He had never met Atatürk, but among their indirect communications was an expression of appreciation by the president when Roncalli encouraged the use of the Turkish language in Catholic churches. For his part, despite the government's official hostility to all religious practice, Roncalli never hesitated to voice his admiration for the president's remarkable efforts to raise his country from the wreckage of the Ottoman Empire. Now he made plain his deep sympathy for a people who had lost a beloved leader, and this was not forgotten.

Atatürk was succeeded by his premier, Ismet Inönü, a faithful follower of Islam who proved somewhat friendlier to this, the religion of most Turks. In the warmer political atmosphere, Roncalli was able to facilitate an important administrative change finally ordered by the Holy See at his longtime urging: In 1938, Catholics in the Eastern lands were removed from the jurisdiction of *Propaganda Fide*, with its missionary implications, and reorganized under the sacred congregation for the Eastern Church. Long before, Pope Benedict XV had said, "The Church of Christ is neither Latin nor Greek nor Slavonic. It is Catholic, and all her children are equal in her sight." Now Pius XI had moved to reinforce those words by elevating Eastern-rite Catholics from a state of vassalage to the West.

At the same time, Roncalli went on with his efforts to smooth the rough edges between the Catholic and Orthodox churches. This was less a Vatican assignment than an expression both of his abiding affection for the whole of the Christian brotherhood, and of his fascination with the history and culture of the Eastern churches. Nothing pleased him more than to appear at the door of some remote Orthodox monastery, to offer his respects to the bearded worthies who usually received him with consternation but invariably bade him Godspeed with esteem. He liked to pray

at their altars, to study their icons and talk about their manuscripts. Giacomo Testa, Roncalli's aide in Sofia and Istanbul, discussed this at length not long before his death in 1962 in a letter
to the church historian Zsolt Aradi:

> He took advantage of every good occasion to see again, at
> least materially, the places which were the centers and theaters
> of the ancient glories. And he always willingly approached
> those who are considered successors of the great ancient
> fathers, even though outside the Catholic family. It would
> take too long to enumerate his visits to the ruins of the great
> cities which were the seats of councils, and to the cultural
> centers of the ancient Greco-Byzantine world. . . .
>
> Above all he wanted people and authorities to feel that he,
> as a diplomat of the Holy See, was a bishop (pater and
> pastor); he wanted to be the living expression, almost the
> actual presence of the warm heart and helping hand of the
> pope in meeting his far-distant sons and those who did not
> belong to the Catholic family. Even under adverse conditions,
> he let his great heart be moved by everything that should
> fire the soul of a bishop.

Certainly during the twenty years that Roncalli spent in the
Near East, no other emissary of the Holy See was as understanding of all the subtleties of feeling and activity within the array of
Orthodox churches. Even when stony protocol foreclosed the
possibility of official meetings, he managed to convey to patriarchs and Eastern prelates the views of the pope, and his own
sincere regard. As Testa put it in 1959, "The announcement of
the preparation of an ecumenical council directed particularly to
the solution of the problem of the union of the churches is a clear
proof of the exceptional interest which Pope John XXIII has
always given to the oriental Byzantine question."

And Pope John himself, in his first address to the world, said
this of the Eastern schismatics, "With ardent desire we hope for
their return into the house of the common Father; they are not

going to enter into a house that is alien to them but into their own house."

He was endlessly fascinated by the teeming life of Istanbul. Here, at the intersection of three continents, empires had flourished and vanished and left behind a jumble of treasure and trash. Miles of bazaars snaked through the streets, open stalls heaped with prayer rugs, vegetables, shimmering silks, jewelry, and junk, thrumming with gossip and haggling. Here he would come to walk, sometimes with Monsignor Testa or Giovanni Dieci, who became his secretary at the end of 1935, but sometimes alone, to buy a book for his growing collection of Byzantine literature, or some *objet d'art*, but mostly to absorb the sights and sounds, to feel the ongoing excitement of sixteen centuries of living history. And above the chaos, thrusting to the sky, were the minarets and domes, the mosques and the great cross atop Hagia Sophia. "Here the stones speak," he once said. And he listened with his heart.

His work was difficult and sometimes tedious, but he was at peace in Istanbul. Late at night, when the house was still and he was alone in his room, there was time for reflection or a bit of quiet work. In the small hours of the morning, despite his repeated intention to be asleep by midnight, he would still be "tapping away at my little typewriter to get through all my business." But he felt now that his business had purpose, that no effort was too great. "I am tormented by the disproportion between what I do and what remains to be done."

At retreat once, near the edge of the city, he wrote:

> Every evening, from the window of my room, here in the residence of the Jesuit Fathers, I see an assemblage of boats on the Bosporus; they come round from the Golden Horn in tens and hundreds; they gather at a given rendezvous and then they light up, some more brilliantly than others, offering a most impressive spectacle of colors and lights. . . . It is the organized fleet fishing for bonito, large fish which are said to come from far away in the Black Sea. These lights glow all

night and one can hear the cheerful voices of the fishermen.

I find the sight very moving. The other night, toward one o'clock, it was pouring with rain but the fishermen were still there, undeterred from their heavy toil.

Oh how ashamed we should feel, we priests, "fishers of men," before such an example! What a vision of work, zeal and labor for the souls of men to set before our eyes! Very little is left in this land of the kingdom of Jesus Christ. Debris and seeds. But innumerable souls to be won for Christ, lost in this weltering mass of Moslems, Jews and Orthodox. We must do as the fishermen of the Bosporus do, work day and night with our torches lit, each in his own little boat. . . .

Once again there were rumors "of greater things in store," first that he was to be sent to Belgrade, a nunciature, and then that the cardinal's purple mantle was about to be bestowed on him. "I am not so foolish as to listen to this flattery," he wrote, "which is, yes, I admit it, for me too a temptation. I treat it as a joke. . . . I already have my purple mantle—my blushes of shame at finding myself in this position of honor and responsibility when I know I am worth so little."

He had begun to feel the weight of his years. The illness of 1936, the realization, repeatedly noted in his journal and letters of this period, that he was now as old as Radini-Tedeschi had been when he died, reminded him of his own mortality. In a letter of condolence to the widow of a cousin, he said, "Let us continue to hearten each other, my good Angelina, and to look to heaven. . . . What time still remains for us to live must be one long preparation for a good death. I too feel I am getting old. It is not only that when I look in the mirror I see white hair and wrinkles, but also because when I seek around me the dear faces so familiar to me in my childhood and youth, I find there is no one left."

But his energy was undiminished. Work, study, travel—all these went vigorously forward. In 1936, the first volume of his study of Saint Charles Borromeo, what Algisi calls "the distraction of a lifetime," came off the presses. It was dedicated to Pope Pius XI who twenty-seven years before, as Achille Ratti, prefect of Milan's Ambrosian Library, had encouraged the young priest to undertake the massive project.

His contacts with the English-speaking world and his innately ecumenical spirit were both broadened by friendship with the Reverend Austin Oakley, chaplain of the British embassy. Oakley was the first Anglican Roncalli had ever really come to know. The two dined together regularly and Roncalli had no hesitancy about praying in Oakley's chapel. Such comradeship between a papal representative and a Protestant clergyman was rare then, but as Pope John later told Oakley, with whom he never lost touch, "Whenever I see a wall between Christians, I try to pull out a brick."

Only once more, during the summer of 1936, were Ancilla and Maria able to bring to their brother in Istanbul the special companionship, that touch of family life, he cherished. Thereafter, it was understood that they would remain in Sotto il Monte to look after their aging mother. Discussing this with them in a letter, Roncalli wrote, "As you know, I enjoy your company immensely. . . . But I cannot deny that most of all I wish to give some satisfaction to our dear mother and to know that in these last years she has someone to care for her with filial love and tenderness. . . . Ah well, my sisters, you understand me even without words: You know how to read my heart."

His bond with home and family was transcendent. Most years he was still able to arrange a holiday in Sotto il Monte, although even then obligations in Rome or Bergamo invariably cut into the sunny days at Camaitino, and his correspondence with the widening circle of Roncallis was intense, as always. And as their needs continued to outpace their earnings, he continued to provide the difference—as always.

Once, wryly, he wrote, "Without having taken a vow of poverty as some religious do, I am in fact, practicing it." Because of exchange regulations that made it difficult to send money out of Turkey, he regularly deposited certain sums with Mario Tiraboschi, a Bergamo bookseller, and on Signor Tiraboschi's death, with the manager of the Piccolo Credito, on which Ancilla could draw at his instructions. Sometimes these drafts exceeded the funds available and he had to arrange to make up the difference when next he was in Italy. But to any request from home—for a bicycle for Giuseppe's little Anna, an additional field that Giovanni wanted to rent, Zaverio's baker's bill, Assunta's "family needs"—the answer was usually the same: "Ancilla is to go to Signor Tiraboschi. He will give her what you need."

Not until the very end of his life was he wholly out of debt. In May 1939, he could write to his sisters. "Just think that perhaps this year I shall be able to free myself entirely of that debt you know of, for the purchase of the Colombera. It has taken twenty years!" But a few months later he instructed her to get from the Piccolo Credito, for various family needs, twelve thousand lire, most of which he had had to borrow. Then, apparently feeling hard-pressed, he wrote, "But now for a little time I want to be left in peace and not appealed to for further needs of the Colombera."

Yet when the frugal Ancilla bewailed an increase in taxes on the Camaitino, he promptly replied, "You must not get depressed about the taxes, and still less must you complain. . . . Otherwise people will say I am mean and miserly, and this I could not bear. And after all a hundred lire will not be the death of me. . . . It is very easy for people without the responsibility of these matters to pass superficial judgments, but very hard to direct an administration. The public services must be well ordered. . . ."

To ease her concern, he revealed that "the Holy Father has now regulated our condition—but this is not to be bruited abroad." His monthly salary was to be slightly increased; he was to have a pension at the conclusion of his Vatican service; and were he to die before that time, a certain sum would be paid to his surviving dependents.

Soon after Mussolini boldly sent his army, with its bombers and modern weaponry, marching against Ethiopian spears and muskets, Roncalli noted, "The world is in a dreadful state." Mindful of his diplomatic status, he added nothing more specific than, "The big fish always want to eat the smallest fish, and the smallest fish say that the sea is wide and belongs to all." Even then, at the end of 1935, he seemed to sense the cruel and inevitable consequence of the Fascist adventure. In February he wrote to Zaverio, "Let us go on encouraging each other, and praying to God that he may save the world from further disasters. We must soon have either a clearer sky or a great storm."

But the skies continued to darken. The dictators were bent on domination and, in light of a reign of terror at home and repeated aggressions abroad, such lip service as they paid to the cause of peace deceived only the most wishful thinkers. In his last years, Pope Pius XI, who had doggedly sought an accommodation, first with Mussolini, then with Hitler, came to grasp their real purpose and the awful menace they posed. Without abandoning his desperate striving for peace, he denounced Fascist methods and the Nazi credo, particularly anti-Semitism. When in 1938 Hitler paid a state visit to Rome, the ailing old man pointedly departed for Castel Gandolfo. When the Führer expressed a desire to see the Sistine Chapel and Vatican museum, he was told that they were closed for repairs.

"We who are armed with nothing but the sword of truth speak to you in the name of God," said Pius in a public plea. "Justice is advanced with reason, not with arms. Nothing is lost by peace; everything is lost by war."

When Cardinal Pacelli begged him not to make such ruthless demands on his meager strength, he replied, "The church is better off with a dead pope than with one who cannot work."

Let that stand as his elegy. He died shortly before dawn on February 10, 1939, aged eighty-one, his great soul burdened by the almost certain knowedge of the calamity to come. The doors of the Vatican were sealed. The interregnum had begun.

Roncalli, who had last seen the pope in September, felt the loss deeply. He had known him for thirty years, from the time the

scholarly prelate and friend of Bishop Radini-Tedeschi had supported his ambitious plan for the Borromeo work. Now, Roncalli's steps toward amity with all faiths resulted in a significant
tribute to the dead pope. Present at the requiem mass in Istanbul
on February 19, were civic and diplomatic officials, as well as the
great rabbi of Turkey and representatives of the Greek and
Armenian patriarchs. Unity, said Roncalli in his sermon, was "the
most secret longing" of Pius XI, and the spirit of unity was served
when he arranged that the five funeral absolutions be given by
priests of differing sects, each in a different language.

The next morning there was a cable from Sotto il Monte: His
mother, who had been ill for some time, had died during the
night. That the news was not unexpected did not blunt its impact.
Again there was no possibility of his returning home; the worsen-
ing international situation and the pressing duties on the delegation between the death of Pius and the election of the new pope
made his presence in Istanbul mandatory. Helpless, anguished, he
cabled his brothers and sisters: "I mourn with you our beloved
and revered mother/Honor her memory/I thank and bless all
who in their prayers share our Christian mourning/I telegraph
Piccolo Credito asking provide funeral expenses."

A few days later a letter came to him from Ancilla, and he was
able to take a measure of comfort from what she wrote about
their mother's final hours: "She spoke often of her children, and
especially of you who are so far away. . . . How she brightened
when your letter came! She would not trust it to anyone else, but
insisted on holding it and reading it herself. Then, afraid she
might have missed something, she got Enrica to read it to her,
while she murmured: 'I see that he cannot possibly come; well, let
us hope: if the Lord leaves me here a little longer I shall be glad,
but if this is not to be I shall do his will and we shall meet again in
Paradise.' "

Although she died in the home of her son, the archbishop,
Marianna Roncalli made it clear that she was to be carried to
burial from the *casa paterna*, La Colombera. All the village came

to her funeral, and many from Carvico and Bergamo. In the midnight quiet of his study, Roncalli mourned alone and wrote this
poetic memorial for his mother:

> Dear and respected by all,
> Dearer to her children
> Who grew numerous and strong
> In the fear of God and the love of men,
> And to the sons of her sons
> Whom she saw multiplied in joy
> In her home
> Even to the third and fourth generations,
> Blessing her memory.

Then he conveyed to the family the last wish of this poor
peasant woman, the eternal mother: "I have found a paper which
she and our dear father left in my care, so that I might carry out
their instructions. The paper has written on it these words: 'As
my son Alfredo has remained a bachelor and so I could not do for
him what I did for my other sons, his brothers, Zaverio, Giovanni,
and Giuseppino, I ask that after my death Alfredo shall receive
my bed, complete with bedstead, springs, mattress and 8 (eight)
sheets and covers, etc., and the furniture that is in my room. I beg
my son Msgr. Angelo to see that this wish of mine is carried out.
Roncalli Mazzola Marianna.' "

To which the son, Monsignor Angelo, added a cautionary
word: "I am sure that these wishes expressed by our mother will
be held sacred by you all, and will cause no ripple on the peaceful
waters of your common accord."

Once again Roncalli felt laden by the passing years. A few days
before his fifty-eighth birthday, he wrote: "This year the Lord
has tested me by taking some very dear persons away from me:
my sweet, revered mother, and Msgr. Morlani, my first bene-
factor; Father Pietro Forno, my close collaborator in the *Records
of the Apostolic Visits of Saint Charles Borromeo* . . . and other

acquaintances and very dear friends. The face of this world is changing for me now. This, though, must encourage me to become familiar with the world beyond, thinking that soon I may be there myself."

On March 2, Eugenio Pacelli, papal secretary of state, was elected pope after the shortest conclave since 1623. Roncalli expressed his pleasure at the choice of this venerated man, long ago his lecturer in canon law at the Apollinare, and lately a staunch ally in the secretariat of state. "I am very pleased with this election, in which we can clearly see the Lord's hand," he said in a letter home. "Last Sunday I was able to listen in with my own ears to the great ceremony in Saint Peter's. What a miracle the invention of the wireless is!"

Nearly three months later, Roncalli made a visit to the patriarch of Constantinople, Benjamin I, first among Orthodox leaders. He expressed the appreciation of the Holy See that Benjamin had been represented at the requiem for Pius XI and at the thanksgiving service following the election of Pius XII. It was the first such meeting in nine centuries, and the patriarch received the pope's apostolic delegate with every courtesy. Although the Greek Orthodox newspaper made little of the event ("simply a courtesy visit between the two churches," was the detached comment), it had wider repercussions. Looking back from the perspective of our own times, it seems clear that that "courtesy visit" of three decades ago removed another brick in the wall between Christians, paving the way to the ecumenical council called Vatican II, a giant step in the repeal of mutual anathemas between the Catholic and Orthodox churches.

On September 1, 1939, Hitler sent his forces smashing across the frontiers of Poland. World War II had begun. The Poles fought bravely, but stunned by the Nazi *Blitzkrieg* and invaded from the east by the Soviet Union, they were soon overwhelmed. Then followed that peculiar twilight interlude, the months when Europe hung poised between peace and war. French and German armies crouched face to face at the Rhine but did not strike, and there were those in both camps who deluded themselves that Hitler's rapacity was appeased and that there was still time to turn back from the death struggle.

Mussolini, having crushed the Ethiopians and conquered Albania, declared Italy's "nonbelligerence" in this war begun by his Axis partner, to the immense relief of the Italian people. On Christmas Day, reflecting on the year ahead, Roncalli wrote home from Istanbul: "Who knows what mysteries it reserves for us? Think of those poor people who are at war, the Poles and those poor Finns, and the Germans themselves and the Russians. What do the soldiers know about it all? They suffer and die, causing grief to innumerable families. It is the leaders who are responsible. . . . We are fortunate in Italy. This time we must really admit that the *Duce* is divinely guided. . . ."

It was a difficult time for Roncalli, as well. Turkey clung to a precarious neutrality, although both sides pressured her to their cause. Bordering both Russia and the Balkans, one flank in the Mediterranean and the other in the Middle East, Turkey's strategic position was obvious. But as long as it remained uncommitted, it served the belligerents, all of whom were diplomatically represented, as a vast listening post, and Ankara and Istanbul became world capitals of intrigue and espionage. Roncalli, who maintained contact with the English, French, and German embassies, suddenly found his footsteps dogged by foreign intelligence agents, sometimes two or three at a time. Eventually he came to recognize them all and once said, only half-jesting, "After a while I didn't know whether they were spying on me or on each other."

His work was to grow more important, to involve him deeply in the welfare and survival of war-tossed thousands. But in these deceptive days of what came to be called the *Sitzkrieg*, there was still time for his normal duties. This was the time, too, when he learned that another of his nephews, twelve-year-old Battista, son of Giovanni, had declared a vocation for the priesthood.

To Roncalli this was of first importance. A few years after the death of Angelino, first among his brother's children to feel the call, he had written plaintively, "Is there no one among all my nephews and nieces who might feel drawn to follow me in serving the Lord with special dedication?" Now, especially gladdened that one who did was a brother to poor dead Angelino, he offered the most detailed counsel and every encouragement, even to the use of his own house at Camaitino.

"As for his studies," Roncalli wrote to Giovanni, "Battistino could make use of Camaitino and the help his aunts and his sister Enrica could give him. In so doing he would be removed from all the distractions of Colombera, and it would be easier for him to concentrate and to discipline himself in a way befitting a future seminarist."

Told that the boy's classmates teased him about the additional tutoring, Roncalli promptly responded, "One must take no notice. I remember they used to say to me that I wanted to be a priest in order to avoid working in the fields. This sort of thing always happens, and must really be ignored."

As the months passed, the boy remained in his thoughts. When winter came, he reminded Ancilla and Maria, "Look after Battistino. I think that when it is cold he might use the little bedroom at the end of the corridor between my study and the guest room. Treat him gently but firmly. . . . He must study."

But in spite of all, in the face of the family's hopes and his own longing to have a nephew take up the service of the Lord, he made it clear that if Battista's calling was not strong, he would do nothing to intervene on his behalf with church authorities. "I should like to have better news of Battistino," he wrote early in 1940. "I should like to hear that he studies diligently and with a good will. But you must try to encourage rather than frighten him. . . . Naturally, if he did not pass his examinations for admission to the seminary, one would have to think again. I should be sorry if this were to happen, but for my own part I would do nothing to recommend a boy, even my own nephew, if he were not serious in his studies."

As it happened, Battista's call to God was an honest one. In time he did become a priest, and now holds a post as a canon of Bergamo.

The uneasy stillness after the opening clamor of battle ended abruptly on the morning of May 10, 1940. German armor and airborne troops swept into neutral Holland and Belgium, then wheeled south to knife across France. The full fury of the storm had burst over Europe, a raging darkness that would cloak the continent for five terrible years. On June 10, with France dispirited and her forces in disarray, Mussolini took the fateful decision. Lusting for the spoils of war, falling on a people with whom he had no quarrel, the *Duce* sent thirty-two divisions through the Alpine passes to attack the French rear. Voicing the repugnance of most of the civilized world, including many Italians, Franklin D. Roosevelt said, "The hand that held the dagger has plunged it into the back of its neighbor." And Roncalli wrote: "We are about to go down into the valley of Purgatory."

France fell on June 22, but the war ground remorselessly on. The British continued fighting from their home islands, and in October, using Albania as a springboard, Italy invaded Greece. Outnumbered and outgunned, the Greeks not only held the Italians in check but by spring had driven them back into Albania. This was the moment King Boris chose to commit Bulgaria to the Axis cause, joining Hitler in simultaneous attacks on Yugoslavia and Greece. In little more than two weeks both countries had succumbed. King George II was compelled to surrender to the Germans, beginning the nightmare of occupation during which four hundred thousand Greeks were imprisoned, sixty thousand of them executed, and millions more were driven from their homes to wander starving through the ruined land.

Turkey's neutrality continued to be severely tested, especially after Hitler invaded Russia, its eternal foe. But calmer heads, mindful of Atatürk's deathbed warning against a Turkish war with England, prevailed over the firebrands. Not until the very end did Turkey join the battle, and then it was on the side of the Allies.

In the meantime, Roncalli's work became more pressing. The quickening pace of the war and its devastation greatly intensified the Vatican's relief effort and, as papal delegate in Turkey and Greece, he was at its urgent center. Emissary of the pope though he was, his position was not made easier by the fact that he was also a citizen of a belligerent power. The Greeks were particularly bitter that their country was now occupied by the very army they had earlier defeated. It was a time when only his tact and clear compassion for all of war's victims made it possible for Roncalli to function effectively.

He had prayed that Italy would remain at peace. Now that Mussolini had chosen otherwise, he was deeply troubled; but strove for a benign loyalty to his country. He cautioned his family to heed the episcopal letter of Msgr. Adriano Bernareggi, the bishop of Bergamo, issued on the day Italy declared war on France and England. "A grave decision has been taken by our country," the bishop wrote. "Our duty as Catholics is this: to obey. For the whole duration of the war we must try to live honestly, virtuously and in the fear of God, in order to deserve divine assistance."

It was the sort of advice that would stave off the wrath of the Fascists, yet fell well short of a flaming call to victory. It echoed Roncalli's own uneasy feelings. "These words are golden," he wrote to his family. "At home this is a time for us to speak little, to pray, work and accept some sacrifices. Pétain said very truly yesterday that one of the reasons for the French defeat was the extravagant enjoyment of worldly pleasures after the great war of 1914–1918. The Germans, instead, had voluntarily accepted all sorts of rationing and sacrifices, and so when the time came they were strong and prepared. It is like the parable of the wise and foolish virgins."

Here, his somewhat moralistic assessment of the French defeat includes no judgment of the morality of Germany's racist dictatorship. But he was not unmindful of it. With Germany at war with Russia, the German ambassador to Turkey, Franz von Papen, came to Roncalli and declared that now his country and the Vatican were really on the same side. Perhaps, then, the apostolic delegate could prevail on the Holy Father to lend his moral force to the Reich's battle against atheistic communism.

Roncalli did not take kindly to the suggestion. "And what shall I tell the Holy Father about the thousands of Jews who have died in Germany and Poland at the hands of your countrymen?" he asked sharply.

The journal entries for these years reflect his real feelings, anguish at the suffering of nations, and a scholar's grasp of the apostate and historical reasons for the war. At its outset he had written, "War is willed not by God but by men . . . deliberately, in defiance of the most sacred laws. That is what makes it so evil. He who instigates war and foments it is always the 'Prince of this World,' who has nothing to do with Christ, the 'Prince of Peace.' . . .

"Patriotism, which is right and may be holy, may also degenerate into nationalism. . . . The world is poisoned with morbid nationalism, built up on the basis of race and blood, in contradiction to the Gospel."

Two years later, with Italy at the crest of its wartime conquests, his analysis was unchanged, and he did not exempt himself from responsibility for the dangers of too great a love of nation: "The two great evils which are poisoning the world today are secularism and nationalism. The former is characteristic of men in power and of lay folk in general. The latter is found even among ecclesiastics. . . . We are all more or less tainted with nationalism. The apostolic delegate must be, and must be seen to be, free from this contagion. May God help me. We are living through great events, and chaos lies ahead. . . ."

At the outbreak of hostilities, Pope Pius XII, like Benedict XV twenty-five years before, organized the resources of the Vatican for the relief of Europe's afflicted millions. As one nation after another was bombed and beaten into submission, the efforts of the Pontifical Relief Commission to clothe the homeless and feed the starving were outpaced but never stilled. From Istanbul Roncalli wrote, "Together with Monsignor Testa I have organized several works of social assistance. The Holy Father has sent me half a million lire to begin with. But one needs miracle workers here."

The Vatican information office became a clearing house for relatives seeking some word of soldiers listed as captured or missing, and for refugee families torn apart and lost in the riptides of battle. Every plea for information, no matter where it came from, was accepted, some ten million by the time the war ended, and sent out for painstaking investigation by a network of priests, monks, and committed Catholic laymen.

The apostolic delegation in Istanbul was a mainstay of this vast operation, for Turkey, critically positioned with Russia to the north and the Allied Arab states to the south, now had the Germans on her Balkan borders as well. To the darkly nondescript house at Olcek Sokak 87 came the courier from Rome with urgent messages and cables destined for Syria, Palestine, Egypt, Iran, and India; to return with bulging mail bags from all those places. Apart from personal messages and official information, Roncalli was able to transmit a considerable body of intelligence gleaned from embassy contacts and the endless parade of diplomats, journalists, and military men who passed through Istanbul and Ankara, two of the world's most highly wrought cities, throbbing with clandestine dealings and open conspiracy. In a time and place where a German agent could masquerade as the British ambassador's valet and brazenly steal his most secret communications (as in the celebrated Operation Cicero), it is not surprising that a tenacious man of peace could gain information that, though less dramatic, was vitally important to the humanitarian strivings of the Vatican. What Roncalli learned was to spell the difference between life and death for hundreds of thousands.

He was able to locate prisoners of war and political refugees in concentration camps when even the International Red Cross had given up. Within his own troubled congregation, many of whom were members of the diplomatic corps, good Catholics whose countries were at war with one another, his watchword was peaceful coexistence. Blame and blind hatred served no one, he reminded worshipers—British, German and Italian alike. "Actually every one of us is at fault; there comes a time when every individual is involved in what happens to all the rest." When the French colony in Istanbul split apart in bitter discord after the surrender in 1940, partisans of both de Gaulle's Free French and Pétain's Vichy collaborators sought the archbishop's backing. Whatever his private feelings, his first duty was as minister to both groups, and he showed them an earnest impartiality: "I read in the Bible that the patriarch Jacob also had sons who disagreed among themselves. But he, the father, considered the matter in silence."

And Roncalli remained silent, but he kept their faith and friendship, for they came to understand that by disassociating himself from politics he was free to temper the suffering of political conflict. There were plenty of glib men on both sides to argue which was right and which wrong. In terms of suffering, it didn't matter. Once, at a reception at the British embassy, someone asked about the "little man in the dark suit" who seemed so out of place. The ambassador replied that the man was Roncalli, the papal delegate, "one of the few around here who's really doing something."

He was bishop to the Greek Catholics, and his efforts on behalf of that devastated land will not be forgotten, but he served the occupation forces of Germans and Italians, and celebrated mass for English prisoners in Greece as well. Sometimes he brought to the military camps a few bottles of wine, sometimes not. But his visits lifted men's spirits because he was his own ineffable self, homely, plain-spoken, warm. He shared their concerns and ate the same food from the same tin plates they did, and he never lectured them with the hollow phrases of nationalism and martial glory.

One day it was announced to an Italian regiment at the Albanian border that "the bishop" would visit them, that he was to be received with the honors due a lieutenant general, as prescribed by regulations. Wearily they lined up in parade ranks, expecting the usual grand entrance of an entourage, a few bombastic words, and the hasty departure of a motorcade that would leave them smothered with dust. Instead, a single small dark car came bouncing across the field and out stepped Angelo Roncalli, himself covered with dust, his guileless peasant face beaming as he walked among his countrymen shaking hands. When he came upon a soldier from Bergamo they broke into the Bergamesque dialect. Another soldier asked what they were saying and the archbishop replied, "It's not the meaning that matters. It's the sound of the old tongue that warms us."

He celebrated mass in the open field, then asked if there were any among them who had not been confirmed. A dozen men stepped forward. The bishop administered the sacrament. Then he sat and talked with them, and told them to pray for peace. It was growing dark when he rose to go and they followed him to his car, suddenly silent. When their officers ordered them back into ranks, a single soldier, young, awkward, stepped out toward the archbishop.

"What is it, *carissimo?*" Roncalli asked. "What can I do for you?"

"I want to embrace you, Excellency, for all of us."

In November 1940, Roncalli began his sixtieth year, "the year when we begin to be old." He was in excellent health but still battling girth and weight. He had limited his evening meal to soup and fruit, but it was a losing effort, perhaps because, as he wrote Ancilla and Maria, "Naturally at midday I eat like any other good Christian." At retreat that year, he reflected: "Advancing years, when one is in the sixties like me, wither the evil impulses to some extent, and it is a real pleasure to observe the silence and tranquility of the flesh, which has now become old and unresponsive to the temptations which disturbed it in the years of my youth and vigorous maturity. However, one must always be on the alert. The Bible speaks also of the foolish, doting old man. . . ."

As always, he had his family to think of. To help cover their daily needs, he withdrew fifteen thousand lire of his life insurance money (about $3,000) and turned it over to Ancilla, reminding her to be "kind and generous."

He now had an additional expense, Battista's seminary fees. He wrote to his brother Giovanni, "Apply to our sisters who know where to get the money. . . . If by chance the superiors are reluctant to accept fees because the boy's uncle is a bishop, you must reply that this does not enter into it, and insist on making the payment."

Battista had his troubles. He failed the first seminary examination and, as his uncle steadfastly refused to intervene, had to resign himself to another preparatory year, this one at the college in Romano. Even after his admission the way was difficult, for he was not a natural scholar. Roncalli urged him on and cautioned Giovanni, "I beg you not to be severe but to show your love for him even more than before. . . . He must be constantly encouraged, always with kindness and patience." But, set though his heart was on Battista's ordination, Roncalli never used his influence on the boy's behalf. "It is in his own hands, and God's," he said, and Battista's ultimate success is a tribute to his perseverance.

In September 1941, Battista's eldest sister, Enrica, entered the convent of the Sacred Heart. Roncalli was profoundly moved, for Enrica, named for his dead sister, had a particular place in his heart. When she declared her religious vocation to her uncle, he wrote, "I want to say that from now onwards you will have a special place in my prayers and blessings. As long as I live I shall take care of you.. . . I am now turned toward the sunset, while you are still in the dawn of life. But the light which enfolds us is the same."

Then, after little more than a year in the convent, Enrica fell ill and had to withdraw. This time there was a letter from Roncalli that, even for him, was remarkable for its sensitivity and understanding, and which, as Enrica later put it, "made it possible for me to accept myself."

"My dear niece Enrica, a word for you alone," he wrote. "You have already shed enough tears. Shed no more but be happy and content in the Lord. . . . If the Lord requires something else of you he will make his voice heard clearly and loudly. . . . Holiness consists not in penances and extraordinary practices but in seeking in all things the Lord's will, in obedience and humility. . . ."

Despite his advancing years and family concerns, however, Roncalli did not neglect his official duties. In 1941 alone he made four trips to Greece, most of them by air, a mode of travel with which he had become thoroughly disenchanted. "Flying is no fun in the winter," he wrote his family, then in spring confessed, "I am *always* nervous when I entrust myself to the air. . . . I commend myself to Saint Joseph, who traveled with only a donkey." But he knew that the world was changing, that events that once unfolded to a gradual, logical conclusion now went careening into history, and he accepted the airplane as part of this accelerated life. In any event, he was doing the Lord's work and "although I hold myself ready for anything that may befall, I set my mind at rest."

The work he had undertaken was the succor of the Greek people, faced with mass starvation as the second winter of the war loomed up. Farmers had been unable to plant crops; the Allied blockade of the occupation armies choked off foreign shipments of food; and the German and Italian forces were almost wholly concerned with their own pressing needs. In the face of disaster, the apostolic delegate sought to act.

In Turkey, he beseeched the German and Italian ambassadors to intercede with their governments for a promise of cooperation if some way could be found to bring food into Greece. In Bulgaria he won a pledge of assistance from King Boris and Metropolitan Stefan Gheorgiev. And on July 25, 1941, flying from Sofia in a German aircraft, he arrived in sweltering, starving Athens, not to leave again until October.

With funds provided by the Vatican, he established food depots and a commissary. Revamping the delegation quarters, he set up a clinic for civilian sick and wounded called the Good Samaritan, which continued to function long after the war ended. Through his good offices, flour began to trickle in from Hungary, and medicines from Monaco. Such hostility as the embittered Greeks may have harbored against Roncalli as an Italian national melted in the light of this selfless effort.

Yet it was only a drop of water on the fire of famine that swept the land. By September a thousand people were dying every day, and being buried in mass graves. Sensible men could see that an unspeakable calamity was in the making, and that a raising of the blockade was all that could head it off.

The king and Greek government had escaped to England, leaving the Orthodox church, with its metropolitan, Archbishop Damaskinos, as the only functioning national institution. Now Damaskinos, acting as regent, sought out the German military commander in Athens to plead that food in sufficient quantities to save his people from extermination be allowed into Greece. The *Gauleiter*, who had no interest in starving the conquered civilians, nonetheless posed some difficult questions. Where would the food come from? Would the Allies let it through the blockade? And most important, how was contact to be made with Germany's enemies? Who would be the intermediary?

Damaskinos could answer only the last. "I shall approach the representative of a Christian church," he said. The German knew that he referred to the Holy See. Aware of the bitter schism between Orthodox and Catholic and touched that the archbishop stood ready to humble himself for his people, he agreed at once.

No humbling was necessary. Roncalli, whose sources of information were not inconsiderable, learned about the meeting and moved at once. He sent a secret message to Damaskinos in which *he* requested an interview and asked the Orthodox archbishop to designate the time and place. This deference to the regent's painful position, Roncalli's effort to spare him public embarrassment —and possible underground charges of treason for dealing with an Italian—were not unimportant to the success of the mission. Its spirit marked their conferences.

They met first in a private apartment in the Paleophaleron Palace and thereafter in other unlikely places. Damaskinos revealed that the Greek government had sufficient funds deposited abroad to pay for the 370,000 tons of grain needed to prevent mass starvation that winter. The occupying powers had promised that the food would be distributed only to the civilian population. But how to contact the Western world, how to arrange swift shipment of the wheat? And even in consideration of the desperate circumstances, how to win from the British a guarantee of its safe conduct through the blockade?

"I am here to do whatever you ask," Roncalli told Damaskinos. He said that the Holy Father only waited for direct word before acting on Greece's behalf.

Then the regent handed Roncalli a letter for the pope—a plea for help, signed by the most eminent lay leaders of Greek Orthodoxy. At their final meeting, early in October, Roncalli offered also to take a letter to the exiled Greek government in London which would detail for the British authorities the terrible plight of the Greek people.

They parted with the kiss of peace, the gesture of forgiveness and brotherly love in both the Catholic and Orthodox liturgy, and on October 7 Roncalli flew back to Rome. His audience with Pius XII put the urgent plan into immediate action. Angelo Roncalli had done what needed to be done, and now the pope did the same. Before winter, the first wheat-laden ships passed through the blockade and safely reached Greek ports. The famine was averted. Hundreds of thousands lived who would otherwise have died. And when peace returned to Greece in 1945, Catholic and Orthodox churchmen stood side by side in gratitude and thanksgiving.

Roncalli returned to Greece four times within the next year. Then the military situation worsened and he was confined to Turkey.

But by this time Giacomo Testa, his one-time secretary, had been installed as his deputy in Athens, and he was confident that the church was well represented.

Nor did he have any lack of pressing concerns in Istanbul and Ankara. For in these final years of the war, as the Allies closed in on Hitler from east and west, the Nazis wreaked a terrible vengeance upon Europe's civil population, particularly upon the Jews. As the scope of the slaughter, the barbarity of concentration camps and crematoria, became known to an appalled world, men of good will sought by whatever means possible to save some last remnant of a whole people. They came, inevitably, to neutral Turkey, and to the apostolic delegate of the Catholic church, which still had contact with the warring nations, and which had committed all of its resources to the work of saving human lives, of whatever religion.

Two who regularly sought Roncalli's help were Dr. Isaac Herzog, chief rabbi of Jerusalem, and Chaim Barlas of the Jewish Agency's Rescue Committee. They never came away empty-handed. "Cardinal Roncalli is a man who really loves the People of the Book," Rabbi Herzog later said, "and through him thousands of Jews were rescued." And Chaim Barlas was to write, "Much blood and ink have been spilled in the Jewish tragedy of those years, but to the few heroic deeds which were performed to rescue Jews belong the activities of the apostolic delegate, Monsignor Roncalli, who worked indefatigably on their behalf."

To Roncalli, who referred to the virtual obliteration of European Jewry as six million crucifixions, this work was in no way singular but indeed mandatory on anyone who claimed to love God and humanity. And he acted with the consistent encouragement of the pope. Learning that the Catholic government of Slovakia, a Nazi puppet state, was about to comply with the "final solution" of Adolf Eichmann and deport the last of its ninety thousand Jews to Auschwitz, Roncalli sent an urgent protest to Slovakian president Joseph Tiso, himself a priest: "From various places the Holy See is requested to intervene on behalf of

people belonging to the Jewish race, against whom grave measures
are being carried out. The Holy See, animated by sentiments of
humanity and Christian charity which know no distinctions of
origin, nationality or race, cannot remain indifferent to these
appeals. The Holy See anxiously implores the Slovak government
. . . to assume an attitude consonant with the Catholic principles
and sentiments of its nation."

In this undertaking he failed; German troops rounded up
thirteen thousand Jews and sent them to the gas chambers, but
elsewhere, particularly in the Balkans, his direct intervention
contributed to the deliverance of thousands. In response to another appeal, he cabled the Vatican in February 1944: "Chief
Rabbi of Jerusalem Herzog came personally to apostolic delegation thanking officially Holy Father for many forms of charity
afforded to Jews these years. Implores papal interest for 55,000
Jews . . . gravely endangered during possible retreat German
troops." The sum of 1.35 million lei (more than $100,000) was
immediately provided to the Jewish Council of Rumania by Pius.
The result is reported by the historian Theodore Lavi: "This
interest manifested by the Vatican at this grave juncture . . .
was an important factor which greatly contributed to the rescue
of Rumanian Jews. Their moral power of resistance grew when
they saw that they were not abandoned to their fate."

In Bulgaria, where King Boris had early welcomed Eichmann's
"Jewish expert," clerical appeals finally stayed the planned depor-
tations. Msgr. Giuseppe Mazzoli, Roncalli's successor as apostolic
delegate, placed before Queen Giovanna the written plea of six
hundred women whose husbands were on the expulsion list. She
read it with tears in her eyes and promised to help. Meanwhile, in
Istanbul, Chaim Barlas showed Roncalli an *Aktion* report from
Bulgaria, detailing the final solution of the Jewish question. Barlas
later described Roncalli's reaction: "He rose in angry amazement
and said in a whisper, 'Good Lord! Is it possible? Lord in heaven,
help us!' And he rushed to his desk, opened a typewriter and
wrote a long message on a cable form to King Boris. Calling his

attendant to have it sent at once, he said, 'Let us pray that this will save us.' "

It did. Despite Nazi pressure, Boris repeatedly delayed the execution of their plan and in August 1944, with the Germans preparing to fall back, revoked Bulgaria's anti-Jewish laws altogether.

That same summer, Ira Hirschmann, a special emissary of the American War Refugee Board, requested an interview with the apostolic delegate in Turkey. Roncalli received him in the delegation's summer residence at Prinkipo, an island in the Marmara Sea. Hirschmann, who had come armed with statistics and eyewitness accounts of the Jews' desperate plight in Hungary, pleaded for help. Roncalli pulled his chair closer and asked whether Hirschmann had any direct contacts with the Hungarian Jews. Hirschmann said that he did. Whereupon Roncalli proposed a plan that was worthy of the years he had spent in intrigue-ridden Turkey.

He had heard that certain nuns in Budapest had given baptismal certificates to some Jews, mainly children, and that the Nazis had recognized these and left their holders unmolested. Now, said Roncalli, he was prepared to make available as many baptismal certificates as were necessary. He had no interest in whether any Jews actually received the sacrament or whether, when the war ended, any stayed in the church. He was concerned only with the saving of lives. So Operation Baptism was launched.

In his report to Washington, Hirschmann stated, "The Catholic hierarchy, which enjoys a large influence in Hungary, took unusual spontaneous measures to rescue Jewish citizens wherever possible. . . . [I refer] to the baptism of thousands of Hungarian Jews in air raid shelters." Discreetly, he did not mention Archbishop Roncalli.

In Budapest that autumn and winter of 1944, there was virtually no Catholic church institution where Jews did not find refuge. And when the Russians took the city in February 1945, some one hundred thousand Jews (two hundred thousand in the whole of Hungary) had been spared. It was the work of priests, nuns, and peasants. Armed with the simple conviction that Christianity meant more than Sunday piety, they knew what had to be done, and they did it.

Between the wartime vagaries of the mail (it sometimes took three months for his letters to reach Sotto il Monte) and a personal disdain for money, Roncalli was frequently overdrawn at the Piccolo Credito and rarely knew how his account stood. But he never hesitated to send Ancilla to the bank for whatever was needed. "Anyone who knows me need have no fear," he wrote. "The Providence of God never betrays those who trust in him."

Sometime early in 1943, he began thinking seriously about a plan to buy the villa at Camaitino and establish there an orphanage "as a charitable bequest to my dear parish and as my own memorial. As you know," he wrote his sisters, "I do not wish to live or die a rich man." This project never materialized, but about this same time he conceived another plan that remained close to his heart: to secure the future welfare of his family. He bought a second farm of about ten acres not far from Colombera so that his brothers and sisters and their children, who now numbered twenty-four, could properly support themselves. In January, he wrote to Giovanni, "It must be understood that I make this purchase under the name: *Fraterna Roncalli*, under which name our two sisters Ancilla and Maria would have exactly the same position and the same share as their five brothers. When the purchase has been made in good order we shall see what would be best to do, that is, either make a division of the land and houses or make the best arrangement we can. . . . I am still of the same mind: Peace and brotherly love are what matter most. And now give me all the advice you wish but obey me as your affectionate older brother, as you have done in the past, and remember that I shall be unjust to no one, but charitable with all."

Then, following a detailed itemization as to how the brothers were to proceed with the transaction, he added this postscript, "Lest you should be filled with wonder at the funds at my disposal, I can tell you that this money is in part a gift from the Holy Father, and in part my own salary."

He planned well. To this day the two farms, La Colombera and Le Gerole, are in the Roncalli family, cultivated by two of Pope John's nephews and providing for a score of children and elders.

Meanwhile the war was coming home to Italy. Long before the first Allied soldier set foot on Italian soil, Roncalli had sensed that his people would have to pay for their infatuation with Fascism. The devastation of Greece seared his mind, and he wrote his family, "Pray, and ask the children to pray, that we may be spared the horrors of a postwar period."

These prayers were in vain. In July of 1943, with all the force of their swelling strength, the Allied armies fell on Italy, battering their way across Sicily in thirty-eight days. Three weeks later, September 3, 1943, they landed on the mainland at Reggio, and on the 9th, the Italian government surrendered. But no one could now ward off the wreckage and ruin. The Germans swarmed down from the north and for twenty bloody months Italy was a battleground.

In October, Roncalli wrote to Sotto il Monte: "I have no special counsel to give you about the events which disturb the life of our country. It is useless to criticize: now there is war, the Lord's great scourge, which the Italians too have brought down upon their own heads. This is not the time to lay the blame here or there. We must all suffer in silence; everyone must do his duty in the painful circumstances . . . leaving soldiering to the soldiers and politics to whoever wants to play politics."

King Boris had died that summer, in somewhat mysterious circumstances, a week after his return from consultations with Hitler. The following Easter, Franz von Papen, the German ambassador in Turkey, asked Roncalli to convey to the Vatican a plea that the Allies recognize a difference between the Nazi regime and the German people. On June 4, the U.S. Eighty-eighth Infantry marched into the Piazza Venezia, where Mussolini used to harangue the Roman throngs, and two days later, D-day, the greatest armada in history landed an assault force in France.

The old order was changing. Even as the fighting went on and millions died contesting an outcome that was already inevitable, the postwar world with its new faces and new directions began taking shape. Among those scrabbling to avoid being swept into the dustbin of history was von Papen.

He was a faithful Catholic and former chancellor of the Reich, an aristocrat of the old school who, like so many of his peers, had been both hypnotized by the fanatical nationalism of Hitler and repelled by its moral bankruptcy. In the end, he and his class were seduced by the conviction that only the Nazis could stand against revolutionary communism, and von Papen himself helped Hitler to power.

Roncalli, who saw everyone's good side, considered him still another victim of the war. Von Papen had been consistently helpful in church efforts to spirit doomed Jews away to Palestine. Surely he was a gentleman, a distinguished diplomat and an exemplary Catholic, and now his world was coming down in ruins. What did Roncalli think when he learned that von Papen was also the mastermind behind Operation Cicero, that the obsequious valet Roncalli himself had seen time and again at the British embassy was in von Papen's pay, regularly delivering to him the most secret Allied documents? We don't know.

What we do know is that at the end he encouraged von Papen in whatever small ways he could. He told him that the German people would have to abide by the decision of the Western Allies, but expressed confidence in their judgment. He sent him a warm letter on his departure from Turkey in August: "You can well believe how sad my heart is that you are leaving. . . ." And later, when von Papen sat in the prisoner's dock at the Nuremberg war criminals' trial, Roncalli responded to a plea for a deposition that might strengthen his defense. And von Papen was acquitted. Still, a

German denazification court subsequently sentenced him to eight years' imprisonment, of which he served two.

Wednesday, December 6, was a dreary day in Istanbul, cold and gray with the threat of snow. In the early evening, Roncalli was at work in his study when Luigi brought him a cable from the Vatican. It was in code. His secretary, Thomas Ryan, who usually did the cumbersome work of deciphering coded messages, was out and Roncalli knew little about the procedure. Thinking that the message might be important, however, he got the code book out of the safe and set to work. The first words he cleared were "Nuncio" and "France" and, as he later said, "I thought they had made a mistake in Rome, sending me a message intended for Monsignor Valeri in Paris."

At that point Ryan returned and Roncalli turned the cable over to him. It was no mistake. After a few minutes Ryan looked up from the table, his full Irish face flushed, and he read it out very slowly, so as not to fumble the words: "His Holiness nominates you nuncio Paris. Letter follows. Montini."

Roncalli stood motionless, unbelieving. Nuncio in Paris! He, who had never been more than a semiofficial papal representative in obscure places, he who at the age of sixty-three had come to feel that only the grave lay ahead, he was now offered the Vatican's most eminent diplomatic post? He could not speak.

Ryan rose. "Congratulations, Excellency," he said, extending his hand. "God will go with you."

IX

ECCLESIASTIC ON THE QUAI D'ORSAY

France was a nation in crisis as the turbulent year of 1944 drew to a close. The Germans had been driven back, but the populace, four years under the enemy's heel, remained spiritually torn by the wounds of the occupation, divided by the hatreds and passions that sprang out of its profound humiliation before the world. De Gaulle was in power and Pétain was in prison, but the people were still gripped by an implacable rage for vindication and revenge against the collaborators. Caught in the crossfire was the hierarchy of the French Catholic church.

With the fall of France in 1940, Roncalli's predecessor as nuncio, Valerio Valeri, had accompanied the Nazi-certified government of Marshal Henri Pétain to Vichy. Similarly other bishops had carried on their duties under the Vichy regime. None were Nazi sympathizers. Many, in fact, were devout Gaullists, but most reflected the stand of the Vatican itself: The aged Pétain, *Pater Patriae*, headed the duly constituted government of France, and they supported him. In the course of their duties, some had had regular contacts with German officials. Valeri, it was said, had been friendly with Otto Abetz, the chief Nazi agent in Paris.

To the men and women of the French Resistance, this was treason and they were not inclined to forgive it, even of the clergy. *They* had not collaborated. They had hidden in the cities and forests and fought on. They had been hunted and gone hungry, seen their comrades massacred and innocent hostages shot dead by the invader. And they would not forget. Even the emergent Catholic political party, the *Mouvement Républicaine Populaire* (M.R.P.), whose loyalty to the church was unquestioned, pressed the government to expurgate the stain of Vichy.

Charles de Gaulle, provisional president, had led the Free French from abroad, and in his austere and dauntless person reposed the wartime hopes of the Resistance fighters. Now that they were triumphant and France liberated, they looked to him to spark the regeneration of French honor. One of his first steps in that direction was to have Valeri recalled. Writing in his memoirs, and referring to himself in the third person, as was his habit, de Gaulle said, "The Vatican, apparently, desired Msgr. Valerio Valeri to be accredited to General de Gaulle, after having been nuncio to Marshal Pétain. This was, from our point of view, impossible. After a number of fluctuations, the Holy See asked our approval of Msgr. Roncalli. We gave it at once." He also demanded that no fewer than thirty bishops be replaced.

But he did not want a break in diplomatic relations; he was a good Catholic and France a Catholic nation, and before Valeri's departure he invested him with the Grand Cross of the Legion of Honor. At the same time he pressed the Vatican to send a replacement without delay and offered to provide an airplane to speed the new nuncio to Paris. This last note of urgency was at least partly political. Since the Congress of Vienna in 1815, it had been accepted that the apostolic legate, regardless of the length of his tenure in France, was to be dean of the diplomatic corps. As such, he spoke for all the assembled envoys in presenting the traditional New Year's greeting to the president of the Republic. In the absence of a nuncio, the honor fell to the most senior diplomat present. And as 1944 moved into its final month, as de Gaulle was painfully aware, the ranking ambassador was Aleksandr Y. Bogomolov of the Soviet Union.

De Gaulle's first peremptory communications had touched off a flurry of deep concern in the Vatican. The pope was keenly aware of the dangerous winds that blew over France and, though saddened by Valeri's virtual expulsion, could not leave the church unrepresented there. But who to send? His two *sostituti*, substitutes in the long vacant post of secretary of state, Domenico Tardini and Giovanni Battista Montini, searched their minds for days. Of the experienced nuncios they considered, all were either better left where they were, or would be considered persona non grata by the inflexible de Gaulle for having served in countries politically inimical to France.

It was the pope who thought of the apostolic delegate to Istanbul. Roncalli was unspectacular but had steered a sound course through the diplomatic shoals of Turkey and Greece, avoiding collision with embittered factions and winning friends for the church with his unassuming warmth. He spoke French. He had a certain sympathy for the tenets of Christian democracy, then stirring to new life in France. And if he was a diplomatic unknown whose experience was limited to secondary assignments, he had a negative advantage that could not be overlooked. He was sixty-three years old: should he fail in France there would be no embarrassment in giving him some harmless job in Rome or returning him to—what was his home diocese?—Bergamo.

Nor did Roncalli himself have many illusions once he had absorbed the startling news. He was human and had naturally responded to the glamor evoked by the nunciature in Paris. For the first time he was being sent to a predominantly Catholic country and would have full diplomatic status. But he was a realist. As someone said, all that France really wanted was a black cassock with a white past. And Roncalli himself later told a friend, "When the horses break down they trot out an ass."

But the totality of the change and its abruptness unsettled him. "For the mission now entrusted to me I would need to be ten years younger," he wrote his family on the day after the cable arrived. "I shall do my best."

Once Montini's confirming letter had arrived on December 22, emphasizing the importance of his presence in Paris by January 1 and urging all haste, events moved at a breakneck pace. There was a farewell banquet in Istanbul, but he had to leave before the meal was finished to catch the train for Ankara. There, too, his good-byes were hurried, and on Wednesday, December 27, a dreary, overcast day, he boarded the war-battered American B-24 put at his disposal by the French government and took off for Rome. He sat hunched over in a bucket seat and almost at once the lights of Ankara vanished in the haze.

The exigencies of war had kept Roncalli from the Holy City for more than three years. Now he went directly to the Secretariat of State where Tardini, one of the two *sostituti*, awaited him. They talked for a while about the problems he would face in his new mission, and Roncalli expressed his astonishment that he should have been chosen. Tardini, a tough old Roman with decades of curial experience, promptly retorted, "You're not the only one who's astonished." And gestured toward the papal apartments. "It was all *his* idea."

On the morning of December 29, Roncalli saw Pius, who sought to encourage him by confirming that the appointment had been his own idea. "It was I, monsignor, who thought of you and took this decision, no one else."

He left Rome the following morning, this time in de Gaulle's personal aircraft, arriving over Paris in the early afternoon. But the city was obscured under a covering of winter fog; after a vain attempt to land at Le Bourget the pilot finally came down at Orly, then only a small military landing field. Of course there was no one to meet him. The welcoming contingents from the nunciature and the Quai d'Orsay were still awaiting the call from Le Bourget, but eventually someone rounded up a jeep and a driver and thus he made his entry into Paris. He reached the nunciature at No. 10, Avenue Président Wilson around 4:00 P.M. and knocked at the door. To the bemused priest who answered he announced pleasantly, "Good evening. I believe you have been expecting me. I am Monsignor Roncalli."

On the first day of the new year, a carefully prepared speech in his pocket and a devout prayer for guidance in his heart, Roncalli set out to present his credentials to General de Gaulle. The Élysée Palace, residence of French presidents, showed the ravages of war, but its inherent splendor could not be denied. De Gaulle received him in a small reception room whose threadbare drapes and magnificent eighteenth-century windows seemed an image of France itself: proud, fallen on hard times, but its essential worth intact. The general, towering over the stout Roncalli, stood rigid and unsmiling. He had not forgotten either Italy's heinous attack in 1940, or the Vatican's acquiescence in the German occupation. He confined his greeting to the bare amenities and Roncalli could do nothing but begin reading his speech, "I present to Your Excellency my letters of credence as apostolic nuncio. . . . You will understand, Monsieur le Président, with what sincere affection I accept the mission assigned to me by the Holy Father and come to this dear nation over which war has passed with all its devastations and destruction, without however impairing her vitality or the inspiration of her universal genius. . . ." It is said that some small expression of response softened the general's glare. No one could listen to Roncalli speak, not even in the high-flown phrases of diplomacy, without knowing it came from his heart. And his French was excellent.

Barely an hour later, the various ambassadors and ministers plenipotentiary assembled in order of rank in the Élysée's grand salon. Roncalli, standing next to Bogomolov, the Russian ambassador, murmured his apologies for reaching Paris just in time to deprive him of the honor of the New Year's greeting, yet not soon enough to allay his concern for its preparation. The ambassador smiled knowingly; he was not a novice in these matters.

But Roncalli was genuinely concerned. It was simply not in his nature to offend anyone. "I should like my first official call to be at the Soviet embassy," he said. "Will tomorrow be convenient?" Papal representatives rarely visited Communist embassies, and never with such deference. But Roncalli did. Upon another occasion, when it began raining at a Bastille Day ceremony, journalists and everyone else present noted how the nuncio sought shelter under the Soviet ambassador's umbrella, and how the two chatted animatedly afterward.

At half past ten, General de Gaulle appeared and Roncalli stepped forward:

> Monsieur le Président, it is a great honor for me . . . to express to you, in the name of our sovereigns and heads of state, our best wishes for the New Year.
>
> In spite of inevitable trials and sufferings, the year just ended has been marked by events of the greatest significance for France. Thanks to your labors and farsighted statesmanship this beloved country has in fact recovered at the same time her liberty and her faith in her own destiny.
>
> We do not doubt that the new year will see new progress and new triumphs. So France once more assumes her traditional role and her rightful place among the nations. With her clearsightedness, her zest for work, her love of freedom and her spiritual ardor . . . she will be able to point out the way which will, at last, lead our human society toward periods of tranquility and lasting peace. . . .

The president was listening intently. Roncalli had touched a responsive chord in the fiercely patriotic de Gaulle, and his parting handshake was warm. Again Roncalli had begun well.

But all through that winter of cutting cold and a record snow-fall, he was acutely mindful of the magnitude of his task, and of his advancing years. "I must not disguise from myself the truth," he confided to his journal, "I am definitely approaching old age. My mind resents this and almost rebels, for I still feel so young, eager, agile and alert. But one look in my mirror disillusions me.

This is the season of maturity; I must do more and better, reflecting that perhaps the time still granted to me for living is brief."

One of the most explosive situations that faced him in his new post was de Gaulle's call for the resignation of the thirty bishops accused of Nazi collaboration, among them Cardinal Emmanuel Suhard, archbishop of Paris. Roncalli did not formally protest the government's demand. He understood the feverish wellsprings out of which it spilled. But the spirit of revenge was repellent to him; he would not be a party to a witch hunt. He proposed to M. Georges Bidault, the French foreign minister, that an investigation be conducted into the specific charges against the accused, and within a few days he had plump dossiers on each one. He read them with disbelief. "What I have thus far seen consists of newspaper clippings and gossip," he wrote Bidault. "There is no documentation, nothing that would be regarded as evidence under any system of law. If this is all, I am afraid that any action against these men would be discreditable to me and to the justice of France."

There were further inquiries, more negotiations, but meanwhile the months passed; passions cooled. And in the end, only three bishops were removed. Cardinal Suhard was not among them. It was a signal achievement. Roncalli had faced a crisis that might well have shattered the French church, with repercussions throughout the Catholic world, and with calm and reason he had won out.

Soon after, he had occasion to assist a French priest who had actively resisted the Nazis, thereby striking a blow for all who had refused to collaborate, and, not incidentally, winning the deep gratitude of the de Gaulle government.

The archbishop of Toulouse, Msgr. Jules Saliège, was a frail old man, almost completely paralyzed, but neither his courage nor his compassion was impaired. In the summer of 1942, when the full horror of the Nazi roundup and deportation of French Jews had become clear, he had drawn up a thundering declaration of conscience and ordered it read from the pulpit by every priest in his diocese. When the police told him the order must be withdrawn, Saliège replied, "It is my duty to teach morals to the members of my diocese, and when it is necessary, to teach them also to government officials." And on the following Sunday he himself was carried into the cathedral on a stretcher and spoke these unforgettable words—which were echoed in four hundred churches, smuggled to Resistance hideouts and the BBC in London, reprinted in *L'Osservatore Romano* and twice broadcast by Radio Vatican:

> There exists a human morality which imposes duties and recognizes certain rights. Both come from God. They can be violated, but they must never be suppressed. . . . Children, women and fathers have been treated like animals. That the members of one family can be severed and shipped like cattle to unknown destinations is a sad spectacle reserved for our days. Why does the right of asylum no longer exist in churches? Why have we surrendered? Lord, take pity on us! Our Lady of God, pray for France! In our diocese horrible scenes are taking place in the camps of Noé and Récébedou.
>
> Jews are men, Jews are women. They are part of mankind. They are our brothers. France, my beloved France, France which cherishes in the conscience of all its children the tradition of respect for the individual; France the generous and chivalrous—France is not responsible for these horrors.

Though repeatedly threatened with arrest, Saliège survived the war and was not forgotten. When Giuseppe Saragat, the Italian ambassador, conveyed to the nuncio the French government's special regard for Saliège, Roncalli saw at once that not only the government, but every Frenchman who had fought Hitler and resisted Vichy, would stand honored by church recognition of the brave archbishop of Toulouse. He immediately sent to Rome a vigorous recommendation that Saliège be made a cardinal, and this was done at the next papal consistory. Roncalli himself went to Toulouse and presented Saliège with the red biretta.

There is a maxim that the nuncio to France carries a red biretta in his knapsack, meaning that unless he dies or disgraces himself he is almost certain to be elevated to the college of cardinals. Always careful not to seek—or to appear to be seeking—personal advancement, Roncalli forewarned his family, "I do not want to hear any talk of my being made a cardinal, because if this were to happen it would mean nothing to me but only make me very melancholy. I do not care about it at all, and for this reason I am vexed when people, thinking to give me pleasure, pay me compliments on this score. You must do as I do. Do not speak of it, or let others speak of it. . . . I might run into some serious trouble which would make nonsense of all this gossip."

Mostly, though, he was far too occupied with present duties to concern himself with future glory. As nuncio, he was not directly responsible for the spiritual direction of French Catholics, as he had been for the Catholics of Turkey and Greece, but he nonetheless made himself available for feast days and special ceremonies at parishes all over the country. As Msgr. Loris Capovilla, his loyal aide, put it, "As nuncio, Monsignor Roncalli did not shut himself up in an imposing palace at the end of a street in Paris, but went every day in search of a community, or a soul, that for him was France: the *clochards* of the Seine embankments and the young seminarists of Cannes, the fishermen of Sables-d'Olonne and the wine-growers of Beaune, the parish functions of Saint-Séverin and the patriotic celebrations of 14 July." Roncalli used to say that the pope was parish priest of the world; as nuncio, he liked to think of himself as Pius's delegate in his parish of France.

He was also having the long-neglected nunciature on Avenue Président Wilson put into proper repair and suitably decorated. Often he would stand in the debris chatting with the workmen, then invite them to join him in a glass of wine. Once an Italian welder came to move some radiators and Roncalli was so delighted with the man's company that it was 6:00 P.M. before the work was finished. Whereupon Roncalli sent the welder home to fetch his wife and children back to the nunciature for dinner.

Another time, as the story is reported, he overheard a carpenter whose work was not going well loose a stream of blasphemies, some highly original and all in thorough keeping with the volatility of the French temperament. Roncalli, hoping that the tirade would simply pass, tried closing his study door against it, all to no avail. Finally he marched in to confront the erupting carpenter. "What is all this, my good man?" he said earnestly. "Why can't you just say *merde* like everyone else and get on with your work?"

Before long the refurbished nunciature became a favorite gathering place for the leaders of European politics, the diplomatic corps, members of the French cabinet, visiting dignitaries. They came not for the excellent food and wine, although Roncalli had hired a chef who did incredibly well with sometimes meager postwar supplies, but for the company of the nuncio himself. Robert Schuman, who became the French premier in 1947, said of Roncalli, "He is the only man in Paris in whose company one feels the physical sensation of peace."

That Roncalli's innate warmth and cordiality could kindle friendship among disparate leaders of men is understandable. It was this very warmth, his longing to abet amity between people and nations, that led him in a perfectly natural way to a high order of diplomatic competence. His approach was always honest and straightforward. Complimented once for his adroitness at representing the Vatican's interest, he said of himself, "I deserve no credit. It is just that my friends in the government are accustomed to diplomatic indirection. When they discover that I am telling only the simple truth, they say, 'How clever that man is!'"

He saw it as part of his mission to draw all nations closer to one another. At a banquet commemorating the sixth anniversary of Pope Pius's coronation, the first gathering of the French diplomatic corps since the end of the war, he left it to others to extol the Holy Father. The nuncio's toast was to France and England. Addressing Monsieur Bidault, the French foreign minister, he said: "We have heard you inaugurate the new radiophonic transmission service between Paris and London. You spoke of the sad night through which the entire world had had to pass, and of the joyful dawn which gleams before our eyes and brings consolation to our hearts. . . . Permit me . . . to invite you to raise your glasses to this dear and welcome dawn, and to these reconciliations of people."

It is the consensus of the dignitaries who regularly came together at his table that Roncalli himself usually led the conversation, some say dominated it. That this son of the soil, whose formal learning had been heavily religious, could guide these worldly men in wide-ranging discussions is an eloquent tribute to his remarkable gift for self-education, to the developing forcefulness of his personality, and to his agile wit.

Once, confessing his fondness for the fables of La Fontaine, despite their sometimes dubious morality, he said, "La Fontaine teaches us to walk with our two feet on the ground. Everyone finds himself in these tales, from the great statesmen and industrialists to the lowly laborer, from the famous artist to the poorest *clochard*. We all discover that we are part of these fables, and it is good to lose ourselves there for a while." When someone mischievously asked in which one he found himself, Roncalli replied, smiling, "But surely you know that a good diplomat never gives up the key to the safe in which he keeps his secret documents."

Jacques Dumaine, chief of protocol at the Quai d'Orsay, wrote in his memoirs, "Monsieur Roncalli is a man of experience and picturesque good spirits. . . . He was extremely popular, and deservedly so. I recall seeing him at a reception, spinning like a top, all purple and russet colored, between the minister of foreign affairs and his secretary-general, in the midst of five ambassadors, several cassocks and a few academicians. He was equal to all occasions."

Indeed he was. Cardinal Vagnozzi, who was at that time Roncalli's chargé d'affaires, told of a time one of the newer ambassadors arrived for a state dinner with his wife, "We never invited ladies to the nunciature, it was not done. But apparently this gentleman had misunderstood and so there we were, with this—this lady! I was terrified." Not Roncalli. He called Vagnozzi to one side and instructed him to slip into the dining room and rearrange the place cards, seating the ambassador's wife at his right. Vagnozzi was in the midst of this agonizing chore when, as it happened, the lady recognized the situation and made a graceful exit. "But that changes nothing," said Vagnozzi, recalling that day. "He would never have asked her to leave, and was even prepared to give her the seat of honor to put her at ease."

He is remembered in France as "a powerful fork," but although the luncheons and dinners he gave gained a well-founded reputation for their full measures of delicious food and wine, Roncalli himself ate less and less. His chef, Roger, a zesty soul who later became proprietor of an intriguing Left Bank restaurant, Roger à la Grenouille, learned to make his favorite dishes—polenta, deviled chicken, tripe Bergamesque—but lamented, "For a man who is fat as a curate, he eats like a bird. It must be those books and papers he devours that filled him out."

It was about this time that he began to take an occasional cigarette after a meal. Later, when newspaper photos showed him with a cigarette in hand, there were those who clucked that he had fallen on bad habits. But the fact is that he was not a real smoker. He would accept a cigarette if a guest offered one, to make him feel at home, but he never learned how to inhale and simply puffed away in the inept manner of the nonsmoker.

Roncalli's sense of humor never deserted him, even in the face of his excessive girth. On the occasion of his first visit to the august French Academy, an aide asked for his impressions. Still sitting in his seat, he looked about and murmured, "Beautiful, beautiful." Then, struggling to get up, added, "Unhappily the chairs are only wide enough for a demi-nuncio."

The French, sincere admirers of the bon mot, came to delight in Roncalli's quips, and they were often repeated, office to office, through an entire ministry. Later he would regret being quoted so much, confessing that his quick tongue sometimes got the better of him. But the fact is that his stories usually sprang from his urge to break down barriers of awkwardness and never had any malicious intent. It was the protocol chief, Dumaine, who told of the time Roncalli found himself at a dinner party seated next to a lovely lady in a dazzlingly low-cut dress. There was a long moment of horrified silence at the table, until Roncalli broke the ice. "I do not find it very courteous," he said briskly, "that no one is admiring the gown that this good woman has gone to such pains to choose for this affair. Instead, everyone is looking at the nuncio—to see how *he* is taking it."

Another time, at a diplomatic reception, Roncalli was engaged in conversation with the chief rabbi of Paris. As they started into the dining room, the rabbi said, "After you, Excellency."

"No, no," replied Roncalli, gently steering the rabbi forward. "The Old Testament before the New."

Because Roncalli was the doyen of the diplomatic corps and the Russian ambassador, Bogomolov, was the next senior member, they were often side by side at official functions. Once, noting that Roncalli was on his left, the ambassador puckishly asked, "Does that mean that the Vatican is now taking a leftist position?"

"Only to move you further to the right," Roncalli shot back, then tempered any hint of a rebuke. "I mean, of course, the right path."

No one who was there is likely to forget Roncalli's New Year's greeting to President Léon Blum on December 31, 1946 (de Gaulle had resigned the previous January). Roncalli had contracted a bad case of laryngitis and it was necessary for his auditor, Monsignor Oddi, to read the address. "But Monsignor Roncalli could not stand being voiceless on such an occasion," recalls Dumaine. "It was contrary to his expressive Italian nature. And so he mimed the talk, emphasizing every sentence with appropriate facial expressions and gestures, which made clear, if that were necessary, that the words came from his heart."

And they did. Blum, a socialist, had been deported to Germany in 1941 and imprisoned there for four years. Roncalli alluded to this painful experience when he said, "You, Monsieur le Président, and innumerable noble sons of France with you, have given a shining example of endurance. . . . Your brave acceptance of the reins of government was, with good reason, applauded by all."

But he also said, and his meaning was plainly understood, "Two years after the end of a war, the most dreadful ever known, millions of human beings are still living in anguish and suspense as they wait and hope to rejoin and reform their families and homes."

He was referring, of course, to the German prisoners of war, 250,000 of whom were still locked away in French internment camps. Before Christmas that year, he had visited some in a hospital near Fontainebleau and written, "Poor lads, many of them married and far from their dear ones, many of them without news of home for seven years—and they are sick and captive, and who knows when they will be set free? . . . So many people, now well out of danger, still cherish hatred for their late enemies, as if we were not all proud sinners." When he learned that a camp near Chartres held some two hundred young German seminarians, he arranged to send them books so they could continue their ecclesiastical studies behind barbed wire, and he himself ordained the first priests from this "underground seminary."

He did not conceal his feelings from the French authorities, and repeatedly urged a spirit of charity. The Vatican, too, appealed for repatriation of the prisoners, but one government after another, fearful of public opinion, hesitated to act. Not until March 1948, nearly three years after the war, when the French bishops, in a pastoral letter, declared the issue to be a matter of conscience, were the Germans finally sent home.

Roncalli was almost continually involved in the question—for him, it had been a matter of conscience from the start—but tried not to thrust himself too forcefully into French affairs. Here, too, Jacques Dumaine's reminiscences provide some candid insights. This is his entry for November 20, 1946: "I paid a call on the nuncio. . . . He is at great pains not to become involved in internal politics nor to exceed his functions as diplomatic representative of the sovereign pontiff. Indeed, he is well aware of the reproach habitually cast at the nuncio in France, which is that of interfering with the domestic affairs of the French clergy and of meddling with the bishop's prerogatives." Dumaine then conceded that the indiscretion was not always one-sided: "One of our worst faults is that of inveigling foreigners to take part in our domestic problems."

Roncalli likened his mission in France to that of Saint Joseph, "I must watch over and protect the interests of our Lord, but always discreetly. I show myself to the government as infrequently as possible." It has been said that he bent as much energy to the task of noninterference as some of his predecessors had devoted to intrigue.

Once Bidault reproached him because they met so rarely, reminding him that one nineteenth-century nuncio had come to see the foreign minister every week. "Yes," Roncalli replied, "but in those days your ministers were, almost to a man, enemies of the church and the poor nuncio had to remind them of his existence. But now I am among friends, whom I have no desire to embarrass." Nonetheless, he agreed to meet with the foreign minister more regularly.

Guarding his political impartiality, steering a severely objective course, Roncalli satisfied neither the extremists of the Right nor the Left, and both found occasion to attack him with relish. They were a small minority, to be sure, but highly vocal, and persisted in attempts to lure the pope's emissary into a political ambush. Maurice Thorez, leader of the French Communists, tried once to draw from him an opinion on a volatile issue of the moment. Roncalli parried with a discourse on Italian wines and grape-growing, talking on unflaggingly until Thorez, outflanked and with new respect for his adversary, smiling, raised his hand, "Peace, Your Excellency! My next question, I assure you, is only about your impressions of our Paris weather."

Another who tried embroiling him in partisan politics was Pierre de Gaulle, brother of the general, and then mayor of Paris. But he pressed too hard and not only came off second best but also felt the subtle sting of a rare Roncalli riposte. At a reception commemorating the two-thousandth anniversary of the city of Paris, the mayor alluded to the political undercurrents of the moment, then tastelessly tried to twist Roncalli's presence into a church endorsement of the newly formed Gaullist party. In the hushed embarrassment that followed, the nuncio calmly rose to reply. After greeting the distinguished assemblage, he said, "I have had pleasure in visiting the international book fair in connection with these celebrations, and particularly to discover that among the earliest books published in France was one written by a fellow Bergamesque, the sixteenth-century humanist Gasparino de Barsizzi." Glancing briefly at the mayor, then returning his serene gaze to the audience, he added, "It is all about good manners."

Following General de Gaulle's resignation and through the troubled days of the Fourth Republic, when governments sometimes came and went in a month's time, some leaders of the Catholic party, *Mouvement Républicaine Populaire*, were not beyond soliciting Roncalli's support for this or that candidate. To one such entreaty, he replied, "*Cher monsieur*, you know that at the conclusion of the Lenten period, all the holy images in our churches are covered with a violet veil. Please permit the nuncio this privilege during the election campaigns, to cover himself with a veil of silence."

His graceful style, the ability to soften even a disappointment with gentle humor, enabled him to maintain political detachment while building firm friendships in all camps. Once, when Vincent Auriol, who was to become one of Roncalli's warmest companions in France, came to ask him to intervene with the M.R.P. on a school matter that Catholics could wholeheartedly endorse, Roncalli declined. "It is true that I am close enough to the M.R.P. to have some small influence," he said. "But that is because I never exercise it."

Having passed his sixty-fifth year, he was trying to look after his health. He dutifully went to bed at 10:00 PM., but usually was up and working by four. His portly figure had become familiar among the bookstalls that line the Seine and visitors to the nunciature were hustled into the library to see his fine collection of ecclesiastical works. He recognized a touch of vanity in this, but did not unduly tax himself over it. It was a small transgression.

He continued to give his money away to anyone who came to him in need. Vagnozzi tells of the time they were confronted by a beggar, a man who had once done some work at the nunciature. Roncalli gave him twenty francs. "Excellency," Vagnozzi scolded as they walked on, "that man is fit to work. He deceives you. Why do you give him charity?"

"He has to live," Roncalli said. "He has a wife."

"That woman is not his wife! They have never been married—at least not to each other."

"That may be, but they still have to live," he said firmly. "I prefer to be deceived by nine people rather than deny help to one who needs it."

There were two on his episcopal staff at this time, in addition to Vagnozzi, a young Swiss, Don Bruno Heim, and Monsignor Oddi, the auditor. They got on well, but it seems apparent from certain references that Roncalli sometimes felt himself not sufficiently stern with them. In the journal he wrote that his temperament inclined him toward pliancy. Accepting only the good side of people, he shied away from criticism and harsh judgments. "This and the considerable difference in age . . . often make me feel painfully out of sympathy with my entourage. Any kind of distrust or discourtesy shown to anyone, even to the humble, poor or socially inferior . . . makes me writhe with pain. I say nothing, but my heart bleeds. These colleagues of mine are good ecclesiastics: I appreciate their excellent qualities, I am very fond of them and they deserve all my affection. And yet they cause me a lot of suffering."

He recalled the household of Bishop Radini-Tedeschi where there had never been a disrespectful or irreverent reference to any Vatican official. "As for women, and everything to do with them, never a word, never; it was as if there were no women in the world. This absolute silence, even between close friends, about everything to do with women was one of the most profound and lasting lessons of my early years in the priesthood."

Even fifteen years later, when he remarked about some long-ago sins against chastity—"nothing serious, *ever*"—his attitudes toward sex were those of his seminary years. In that simpler Victorian time, before Sigmund Freud and the explosive influence of the new forms of entertainment, it was unquestioned that the sexual impulse in priests was evil, devil-sent. Roncalli still thought so. But it is likely that his younger colleagues, while conscious of the dangers of temptation, felt freer, in the franker atmosphere of those later years, to discuss such things among themselves.

But even that troubled Roncalli less than their occasional disparagement of superiors. He considered this shocking and immoral. Still, it was not in his nature to rebuke them, not even when, as once happened, the criticism was aimed at himself. What he did say, however, may have been even more effective. He had come a bit late to the luncheon table and, when the conversation stopped abruptly, shrewdly guessed, "I take the sudden silence to mean that you have been talking about me, perhaps not too kindly." By their stricken expressions, he saw that he was right. "Well, priests have to give up so much," he calmly continued, "marriage, children—so many pleasures forbidden. They must be allowed the greatest clerical sport: criticism of superiors."

He had again taken up the practice of vacationing at Sotto il Monte, where young Enrica, striving to make a new life after her disappointment at the convent, had moved to the Camaitino to look after her aging aunts, Ancilla and Maria. Gradually she assumed their function as her uncle's chief correspondent, courier, and spokesman when he was away. "You seem to be the most popular scribe in the Roncalli republic," he wrote her fondly, then again urged that she seek within herself for spiritual peace: "To have the grace and charity of Jesus in your heart, and to be able constantly to spread this grace among those who make up your close family circle, your aunts' and your uncles' families, so as to become a real peacemaker with them all, with your prudence, gentleness and patience—does this not seem to you a fine apostolate, or do you think you must look elsewhere?"

To each member of the family he managed to convey this essence of a unique relationship, his special concern, a particular feeling that applied to no one else. To Alfredo, who had never married and was now slowly losing his sight, he sent "a special word" just after the new year in 1948. "You too are my brother and, with your sisters Ancilla and Maria, particularly dear to me because . . . we are in the same position: We have sought no other life companion but the Lord himself, who must regard us with special affection. I say this without implying any disparagement of the others. For if they had followed our example the Colombera would really have been like a monastery!"

To Ancilla and Maria, he wrote at Christmas that year, "My good wishes come first of all to you two, who are nearest to me. . . . You have given up all thought of what most daughters of Eve enjoy, in order to remain in the company of your brother who is a priest."

Giuseppe was especially dear to him because he was the youngest brother and father of ten children. Following the purchase of the new farm, however, Giuseppe had suddenly disrupted the family harmony by objecting to the division of the property, and this brought forth a gentle admonition. "What was done," Roncalli wrote, "was prompted by my special consideration for you, and our brothers and sisters have faithfully carried out my instructions not to restrict themselves merely to giving you your legitimate share but to exceed this, bearing in mind your numerous children whom I have always loved and will always love."

It pained him deeply, he went on, after his financial sacrifice in the purchase of the land and house at Le Gerole, to learn that Giuseppe was against leaving Colombera. "It was almost as if you wanted the other three brothers and the two sisters to move out instead of you. . . . I have said these things to you, dear Giuseppino, not to grieve you but because truth and charity must go hand in hand."

In the end, the eldest brother's gentle persuasion restored peace to the family—and peace of mind to himself. His family and his village, his roots in the stony soil of Sotto il Monte, were more precious to him than the golden glitter of Paris, and his lofty station and high honors. He wrote home that the company of kings and princes, statesmen and ecclesiastics, only put him in mind of "the simplicity of our fields." Amid the splendor of the Élysée Palace, he wrote his brother Zaverio, he thought of their mother. "It was just as though I could see her, popping out of some corner and saying with her usual simplicity, 'Madonna! where on earth has my Don Angelo got to? Well, we must just pray for him, and think no more of it.'"

And as the years closed in, as another harvest approached, he wrote them poignantly, "I am content to know that you are all well and attached to your land. Believe me, I often think of you all and I like to imagine you all together, enjoying the new wine, chatting harmlessly about this and that. . . . Enrica is right when she says that the best life is the life of the fields."

He was gladdened to learn that two more of his brothers' children, Giuseppe's Anna and Giovanni's Giuseppina, had chosen the religious life. He promptly informed them that he would pay all the necessary expenses although, as he wrote to them both, "I hope the nuns will be content to let me provide this little by little." In time, Anna chose to serve as a missionary nun with the Congregation of the Sacred Mother of the Blacks in Africa. And when Giuseppina pronounced her perpetual vows, to become Sister Maria Angela, Roncalli made the trip to Rome so that she could receive the sacred veil from his own hands.

Over the years to come, he never lost close touch with these two nieces who had joined hands with God. And throughout the early, difficult years of the cloistered religious life when, as so often happens, they faltered and felt lost in worldly fantasies, his letters, full of tenderness and compassion, turned them gently back toward their sacred calling. Once, in response to a plea for guidance from Sister Angela, he wrote, "What you tell me in your letter about the temptations to which your fervor is subject does not alarm me because it is very usual in the spiritual life, especially during youth. . . . Often it is our bodies which cause the trouble. We are not to blame for this, except that sometimes we are too indulgent toward its natural inclinations."

Around this time, he had some correspondence with a second cousin who, because of an involvement with two women, was about to be made to answer in a court of law. Roncalli wrote that he could not intervene: "And I beg you not to be offended by my refusal. I am a priest, and therefore trained to understand, pity and pardon human weaknesses. . . . But the prudence I must observe with you and concerning your affairs is closely linked with the responsibilities of my ministry, and I must respect it at all costs." He did, however, send him twenty thousand francs (about $40.00).

There were other family expenses, most of them unexpected, but all of which he continued to meet. A cousin who lived in France, near Metz, had a sick wife; Giuseppe wanted to buy a cow; the tax on La Colombera came to a painful eighty thousand lire. "The uncle the archbishop may look rich but is really poor," he once said, "But there is not much satisfaction in doing good when there is no difficulty about it."

When he heard that Giuseppe was not well, he expressed his anxiety, offered to pay the expenses of treatment and ventured an astute diagnosis, "I have noticed that all we Roncalli brothers suffer with our teeth. . . . But with poor teeth a man eats his food badly and digests it even worse. If your cure ought to begin here begin it at once."

And the cure worked. But more than a year later, Roncalli was writing to Enrica, "Send me information about your father's new teeth. Tell him not to get impatient with them, and to wash his mouth and those two contraptions every morning."

He provided a radio for the families of La Colombera and Le

Gerole, but advised them "not to let the excuse of the wireless rob your fine homes of that atmosphere of tranquility."

In the autumn of 1948, the Sisters of the Poor in Bergamo, whom he had helped to buy a house for a new foundation in Paris, sent Servalli, a distinguished artist of Bergamo, to paint his portrait. When it was completed the following spring, he wrote, "Everyone says it is very handsome—more handsome than the original."

The real surprise is that he found time to sit for it. In addition to official functions and his duties on religious occasions, he made time for a whole range of activities that had nothing to do with either. No one in Paris was surprised to see him at the theater, the Louvre, the Sorbonne, a Boy Scout jamboree, or at the top of the Eiffel Tower.

He visited all but two of the eighty-seven dioceses of France, some of them several times. For though his primary mission was to serve as the Vatican's ambassador, apostolic duties gave him the greatest pleasure. Once he said, "We all tend to judge events from the vantage point of this handful of earth beneath our feet. This is a great illusion. We must take our view from the heights and courageously embrace the whole."

And so he set out to know, and embrace, all France, at a pace that belied his age and exhausted his aides. He turned up in remote parishes, at far-off monasteries and obscure shrines, curious to see everything, glad to talk with bishops and monseigneurs, but with time, too, for the people. Once, on a visit near Amiens, surrounded by officials, he broke away to join some farmers. "You are country people, aren't you?" he said to them. "I, too, was brought up in the country."

Early in 1950, he set out on a six thousand-mile automobile trip through Spain and North Africa to visit Algeria, which the French had made an integral part of the Fourth Republic in an effort to blunt a restive movement for independence. In Algiers, which was torn by dissension and terrorist violence, he went to the cathedral and spoke of peace to the largely French congregation: "Algeria is living in a period that is full of sadness. Never until now had two ideologies clashed in such a tragic way: love and hate, war and peace, kindness and violence. . . . My dear brethren, resist the voice of hate. Remain faithful to love, peace, kindness. My thoughts and my heart turn not only to our Catholic brethren but . . . to the great masses of many different races and tongues who constitute the majority of Africa, a territory full of mystery and attraction."

His willingness to travel to the farthest reaches of his episcopate did much to regain for the church the esteem it had lost in France. Yet eventually it was brought to Roncalli's attention that his frequent trips displeased the pope. Nor did Pius XII take kindly to the nuncio's taste for strolling about Paris and poking into shops and bookstalls. It was not seemly for an emissary of the Holy See. Roncalli replied calmly to Rome, "Holy Father, a mere remark becomes a rule of life for me. As far as my goings and comings in France are concerned, I go only where the bishops insist that I be present. And with my presence, as I did in the East, I attempt to be the eye, the heart, and the helping hand of the pope."

In addition to his other duties, Roncalli, in 1951, became the first permanent Vatican observer to the United Nations Educational, Scientific and Cultural Organization (UNESCO), headquartered in Paris. The delegates, many of whom feared that the views of the Holy See would be at sharp variance with those of UNESCO, responded to Roncalli, first with a collective sigh of relief, then with considerable enthusiasm. He did not pontificate about what the church thought in this or that instance; he did not pretend that the Vatican was the last bastion of morality in a modern materialistic world. Nonetheless, observed an American delegate, people seemed to remember what he said, "Even the Russians praised him for not handing down pious lectures. They did not rush to the nearest church to be baptized . . . but the seeds of his activity bore fruit."

Addressing the general conference shortly after his appointment, Roncalli sounded the keynote of unity. He was, he said, the representative of the oldest cultural organization in the world. When, two thousand years ago, Jesus sent his disciples forth with words that rang out from the hills of Galilee—"Go, teach!"—he set in motion a force still vibrantly alive "wherever liberty is more than an empty word."

"UNESCO," he went on, "[is] a great burning furnace, the sparks from which will everywhere kindle enthusiastic and active energies, and widespread cooperation in the interests of justice, liberty and peace for all the peoples of the earth, without distinction of race, language or religion. . . ."

The following year, at a mass celebrating the new session of UNESCO, he repeated this theme of unity and mutual progress. But he added a cautionary note in response to what he called

> . . . the feverish cry that "We must swim in the current of history!" . . . as if the world were still taking its first tottering steps! . . .
>
> We who are assembled here feel indeed that we are moving in the current of history: not to be dragged along with it, or overthrown, but to control and direct it toward the salvation, not the shipwreck, of the world. Modern inventions and techniques, their unexpected applications to all forms of life and human society—all this is interesting and worthy of respect, but it is not enough, not even for man's happiness in this life, let alone for the eternal bliss of his immortal soul. . . .

If all roads lead to Rome, most of them seemed to pass through Paris in the eight years Roncalli was nuncio there. Thus he was host to church worthies from around the world, gaining an insight into their homelands and special problems. And the roster of prominent laymen whom he met and entertained in this period is glittering indeed: Churchill, Nehru, Eisenhower, Paul Henri Spaak, Thomas Mann, François Mauriac, as well as every political notable in France.

He struck up some remarkable friendships. Ambassador

Menemengioglu of Turkey, who had been so coolly aloof in Ankara, was free to express his real feelings in Paris. "What we could not do for you, Excellency, in Turkey, we do now here in France," he told Roncalli at the very outset. "My government authorizes me to convey to you my deepest respect and most sincere gratitude." They were particularly close thereafter, Roncalli once referring to Menemengioglu as "my favorite infidel."

Still another nonbeliever who freely admitted to seeking the nuncio's counsel and friendship was Vincent Auriol, who became president of France in 1947. "An honest socialist," Roncalli called him in his first New Year's greeting, and his remarks grew warmer in tone with each succeeding year. There was a roguish interplay of banter between the two, such as is possible only among friends. In his final New Year's address, Roncalli turned, as he so often did, to a fable of La Fontaine to illustrate a point. Afterward, Auriol approached the nuncio and said, "La Fontaine is really a strong writer, Excellency. I could recognize him in spite of your accent." Roncalli beamed, and playing on Auriol's country background in the Haute-Garonne, replied, "I can understand your difficulty, Monsieur le Président. It took me a long time to get used to yours."

This easy bonhomie was not as simple as it appeared nor, obviously, was it the whole substance of Roncalli's success in France. He practiced a sort of intuitive diplomacy. He had a sure sense of when it was safe to ignore protocol and when silence was his strongest ally. His wit was based on intelligence, restraint, and sensitivity—as genuine wit always is. But in the end he was popular and hence, successful, because beneath the light touch lay the deepest of feelings about men and issues. Roncalli wrote in his journal:

> The longer I stay in France, the more I admire this great
> country. . . . I am aware, however, of a contrast, which
> sometimes gives me a twinge of conscience. I am delighted
> to praise these dear brave Catholics of France, but I feel it is
> my duty, one inherent in my mission, not to conceal, through

a desire to be complimentary and not to give displeasure, a certain disquiet concerning the real state of this elder daughter of the Church and certain obvious failings of hers. I am concerned about the practice of religion, the unsolved question of the schools, the insufficient number of the clergy and the spread of secularism and communism. My plain duty in this matter may be reduced to a question of form and measure. But the nuncio is unworthy to be considered the ear and eye of the Holy Church if he simply praises and extols all he sees, including even what is painful and wrong.

Decades and even centuries may pass before his secret reports to the Vatican are made available to scholars. Publicly he maintained "a gentle silence." Yet, in some circles he was gratuitously labeled a conservative, which is one reason the innovations of his papacy struck the world so forcibly. He did vigorously defend the forms of his faith. He did fill his addresses with the religious allusions of his youth. But he failed one important test for Catholic conservatives: He did not believe that God penalized anyone for not being Catholic. He even went so far as to include nonbelievers in his prayers.

All this may have had something to do with his relatively low standing in the Roman Curia, where he was lightly held and sometimes dismissed as "our good Roncalli." He was well aware of this, and of the sort of diplomat preferred in some secretariat cliques —someone who would summon press conferences, mount protests, call meetings. Roncalli had once said, "I usually find it more rewarding to pay a visit than call a meeting." Now he went serenely on his way. As it happened, his way endeared him to the French; the curial way, in that explosive time, would almost certainly have gotten him thrown out of the country.

In 1943, two young chaplains of a Catholic workers' movement, the Abbés Daniel and Godin, wrote one of those landmark books that illuminate and alter our times. It was called *France: A Missionary Country?* and bluntly detailed the striking de-Christianization of this "eldest daughter of the church." It is said that when Cardinal Suhard read it he crossed out the question mark, then grieved all night. In many regions, said Daniel and Godin, and particularly in the cities, large masses of the population no longer considered themselves Catholics. Among the workers, there was increasingly intense feeling that the church was allied with the established social order, responsive to rich and middle-class employers. It was insensitive to the laboring man's needs, and so had become irrelevant in his life. The figures produced by Daniel and Godin were stunning: In a country that was 80 percent Catholic, at least nominally, only one in four went regularly to mass; in some areas fewer than 20 percent of the newborn were being baptized; throughout France there were more than fifteen thousand parishes without a priest, and without serious complaint.

How to reclaim these millions? So long as the priests remained comfortably locked away in their rectories and the working classes in their shops, factories, and mines, there was no way. The answer was suggested by the example of those brave wartime priests who had chosen to accompany thousands of Frenchmen to the slave-labor camps of Germany. Forbidden to go as chaplains, they went as workers, accepting their countrymen's bitter lot to bring them the comfort of faith. Now the war was over, but the experience of those years, a new understanding of labor and laborers, led directly to the worker-priest movement.

Cardinal Suhard and the French bishops supported this bold, indeed, revolutionary, experiment to take the church to the people. There were, of course, dangers. The plan involved nothing less than consigning priests to the secular world, sending them out into the industrial areas and waterfronts, to bring the word of God to men who had scorned it, to work alongside the disaffected, to share their meager lives and so, finally, to persuade them that the church did care. But the need was pressing. "A wall of separation divides the church and the masses," said Suhard. "One must tear down this wall at any cost."

In Rome, the plan was regarded with suspicion from the first. But the earliest results were marked by such a surge of optimism that no action was taken. Idealistic young clerics, trained in special mission seminaries, went to live in the laboring quarters of the cities and their shabby outskirts. Wearing laborers' clothes, they celebrated mass at factory benches or kitchen tables, using a simplified liturgy that could be understood by their new parishioners. Suddenly there appeared a breach in that great barricade of working-class alienation. Religion became meaningful.

But as so often happens in revolutions, the greatest danger was success. Their close association with the workers made the priests natural candidates for posts of leadership within local unions, including those affiliated with the Communist-led *Confédération Générale du Travail* (C.G.T.). Inevitably, many became involved, not only in labor negotiations and strikes, but in political protests and street demonstrations. Some of them were even arrested.

None of this was overlooked by the press. The idea of priests living in slums and working alongside their neighbors had strong appeal, and before long there was a steady stream of stories and speculation, much of it, not surprisingly, sensational and distracting. What about the celibacy of priests who lived in temporal surroundings? When, if they worked all day, did they find time for holy offices? And wasn't there a grave danger that, instead of winning men away from skepticism they were falling victim to it?

These reports were read with alarm in the Vatican. Curial anxieties were transmitted through the office of the nuncio. In turn, Cardinal Suhard—and later his successor as archbishop of Paris, Msgr. Maurice Feltin—went to Roncalli for advice. Typically, Roncalli decided to see for himself what the situation was. Traveling to regions where the worker-priests were active, he quickly perceived that, whatever the problems, the movement had won the sympathy and confidence of the people. Precisely what he reported to the Vatican remains undisclosed, but the obvious essence of his recommendations was patience, for no action was taken as long as he remained in France. Indeed, when the decision was made to terminate the experiment, he was replaced as nuncio by someone who was willing to carry the ax to Paris.

"In France ideas are born with wings," he used to say, but he did not shrink from high-flying ideas. "Without a touch of holy madness, the church cannot grow."

He was not blind to the hazards of the worker-priest movement. But he came to agree with Archbishop Feltin that all who troubled to penetrate the screen of second-hand information and really came to know these earnest young missionaries had to applaud their apostolic zeal and be heartened by their achievement in reaching souls. He had not forgotten his own years with Radini-Tedeschi and the workers of Bergamo. And he simply was not the man to counsel suppression of such an effort, especially when it had the support of the French hierarchy.

But suppression was in the wind, and gathered strength after the death of Suhard in 1949. A month later the Holy Office decreed the punishment of excommunication for all who collaborated with Communists. The following year, in an easily transparent apostolic exhortation, Pope Pius declared, "We are sure that you are well aware that among certain priests, not distinguished for learning or austerity of life, there has been an alarming spread of revolutionary ideas." And in 1953, the year Roncalli left Paris, his successor came with clear instructions to prepare for the curial intervention which effectively ended the worker-priest movement.

After Roncalli became pope, the French, who have never forgotten his sympathy with the experiment and still believe its final chapter remains to be written, reopened the question. Their request for reconsideration of the entire matter arrived during the first months of his papacy, when he was still learning how to manage the amorphous and determined curia. It was channeled to the Holy Office and decided there, and the answer was no.

The sense of the approaching end was nearly always with him now. In 1950, his seventieth year, he wrote in the journal, from

Psalm 89, "The years of our life are threescore and ten, and even if we are strong enough to reach the age of eighty, yet these years are but toil and vanity; they are soon passed and we also pass away." Some of his loved ones had been claimed by the passing years, his sister Assunta's husband Giovanni and Giuseppe's Ida, and he wrote:

> So it is no use nursing any illusions: I must make myself familiar with the thought of the end, not with dismay but with confidence. . . . Some time ago I resolved to bear constantly in mind this reverent expectation of death, this joy which ought to be my soul's last happiness when it departs from this life. I need not be wearisome to others by speaking frequently of this; but I must always think of it, because the consideration of death, the *judicum mortis*, when it has become a familiar thought, is good and useful for the mortification of vanity, and for infusing into everything a sense of moderation and calm. As regards temporal matters, I will revise my will once more. I am poor, thank God, and I mean to die poor.
>
> As for my soul, I shall try to make the flame burn more brightly, making the most of the time that remains as it passes more swiftly away. Therefore, total detachment from the things of this world, dignities, honors, things that are precious in themselves or greatly prized. I want to redouble my efforts to complete the publication of the *Apostolic Visits of Saint Charles Borromeo to Bergamo*, but I am also ready to accept the mortification of having to give this up.

He planned to spend all his leave at Camaitino that September, working on the last of the Borromeo volumes. But arriving home on September 24 after an exhausting trip from Paris, he heard on the radio that a busload of French seminarians, in Italy on a pilgrimage, had been injured in a highway accident and taken to a hospital in Ravenna, on the Adriatic coast. This was a hard day's drive from Sotto il Monte, but Roncalli felt compelled to go. He set out on the twenty-sixth and was at the seminarians' bedsides by nightfall.

He took up the Borromeo work on his return, and continued into the spring, devoting three hours a night to it. That summer of 1951, he wrote to his niece Enrica, ". . . I have almost finished it [seven more years would pass before he actually did]. This volume, the last, is very precious to me. After my death the humble name of Msgr. Roncalli will be remembered for this alone."

In April 1952, he launched a campaign to persuade his four brothers to visit him in Paris. Ancilla and Enrica were his agents, and all that spring and summer he peppered them with letters anticipating the brothers' objections and countering them. Was it too far? He would send his own car to fetch them—they could even make a pilgrimage to Lourdes en route. Did they lack money, proper clothing? They would have no expenses, not even for clothes. Enrica was to choose the material and have the suits made in Italy. "*I will pay for everything*," he wrote, and the emphasis is his.

"This is a gesture of affection I want to make to them while there is still time. . . . Nor must they think of sending their wives, sons, or daughters in their place. We shall think of something else for the women. . . . And they need have no fear of feeling embarrassed. Here they will be treated by everyone with great courtesy and will have no cause to feel ill at ease."

Finally he wrote directly to the four themselves, "My dear brothers, do not say 'no,' and do not try to make excuses; come as if you were under orders." So they went, in August, and had a splendid time.

For the evening of their arrival in Paris, the nuncio had invited some friends to a small dinner in their honor. But long after the guests had appeared the four brothers were still secluded in their rooms on the top floor of the nunciature. Finally Roncalli himself went to fetch them, and found the four milling around a single mirror vainly trying to properly knot their neckties.

"So that's what's keeping you," he said, laughing. "I suppose one of the women should have come along after all."

Swiftly he performed the miracle of tying the ties for them, and they went down. Roncalli introduced his brothers to the guests, then explained the delay: "They were waiting for the nuncio to play his other role—substitute wife."

Many years later, when Zaverio was eighty-five years old but still crustily self-contained, he was asked why the brothers had been so reluctant to go to Paris.

"Because it's far," he replied, clearly baffled as to why anyone would ask a question whose answer was so obvious. "To go to Paris—ha!—it's not like going out to the orchard for some salad or vegetables."

What had he seen there?

"Everything. My brother the archbishop took us everywhere, and in a week we saw it all. Then we came back to Sotto il Monte which I like better than Paris."

What had he liked best of the visit?

"That everyone treated us with great respect, though we are poor peasants. Now I will tell you what I liked least: that people traveled underground—under the soil!—like rats. They took me on that Métro one time, then I said, 'Excuse me, signore, I prefer to walk, even if it is twenty kilometers!'"

Was the story about the neckties true?

"Naturally," he said, vigorously pumping his gray and grizzled head. "What do we know of neckties?"

It is safe to assume that there were some carefully guarded questions during this visit about the nuncio's future. It was equally sure that Roncalli's reply was a repetition of what he had already written to the family: They were neither to speculate nor heed any gossip about "further honors, etc., in the church." Anyway, he said, he was a little late in life to have need of the red biretta. "As my little boat seems able to navigate the waters of the Seine satisfactorily, I neither desire nor covet any other position." But of course he was not insensitive to the diplomatic guessing games, or the currents of conjecture that flowed through his own household. Once he said to his secretary, "I am now the oldest nuncio who has ever served in France. At my age, the others were cardinals or long dead and buried."

Then, on November 10, 1952, there was another of those secret messages from the Vatican: Msgr. Carlo Agostini, patriarch of Venice, was incurably ill; Pope Pius had chosen Roncalli to replace him when the See became vacant. On November 29, the Vatican announced that his name was on the list of cardinals to be nominated at a consistory on January 12. Immediately thereafter thousands of congratulatory messages descended on the nunciature. On December 29, Monsignor Agostini died, whereupon it was announced at the consistory that Roncalli would succeed to the patriarchate of Venice.

And in the midst of it all, that very winter, came the jolting news from Sotto il Monte that Ancilla was suffering from cancer of the stomach and could not be expected to live long. "Ancilla, my dear Ancilla," he wrote, "you who are nearest to my soul, be of good heart; do your best to get better, with rest and good food (without thought of expense), with confidence in the Lord. . . ."

All through this period of imminent change, Roncalli's letters were understandably ambivalent. On the one hand, there were all those elated expressions of congratulations and good will to respond to; but in few did he fail to note that the laurels now accorded him came accompanied by "a thorn that pierced the most sensitive part of my heart."

To his "dear sisters, brothers, nephews, nieces, and relations," who had already heard the first rumors in mid-November, he wrote at the end of that month, "As you see, some news spreads so quickly that the people it most concerns have no time to impart it themselves. So it is true: My humble name is included among the twenty-four churchmen whom the Holy Father, on 12 January, will nominate cardinals of the Holy Church."

He wrote to Battista, cautioning him against daydreams animated by his uncle's new circumstances. "Even in our prayers we ask for *our daily bread*, not for tomorrow's trimmings." A few days before Battista was to receive the sacred tonsure introducing him to the ranks of the clergy, he wrote again. "The Lord blesses dawns and sunsets. You are going forward, . . . toward the dawn of your priesthood; I instead am turned toward the sunset, but we are still in the same light and we must bless the Lord together as we both draw strength from the same light."

Then, two weeks before Christmas, he tore himself free from the activity at the nunciature and hurried to Sotto il Monte. He stayed barely twenty-four hours, but spent them, except for a snatch of sleep, entirely at Ancilla's bedside. She knew that she had not long to live but did not grieve. It was the will of God. As always, her first concern was for her brother: He was not to worry about her; he was to sleep well at night—she might yet surprise them all. In fact, she did, living nearly another year, relatively free of pain.

Meanwhile, Roncalli prepared for his investiture.

It had long been a privilege of the heads of state of Catholic countries to confer the biretta on cardinal-nuncios. And so, on January 15, 1953, Roncalli accepted the honor from his good friend Vincent Auriol, then President of France. Roncalli knelt and Auriol stood gazing down on the bent white head, then gently put the biretta on it. "It was a great honor for me," he said later. "I was deeply moved. The new cardinal went down to his knees to receive the biretta, but he did not prostrate himself before me, an agnostic, but before a person who for that moment represented the sovereign pontiff. . . . I saw his friends weep for joy and pride and I was not ashamed to join them."

And what were Angelo Roncalli's feelings? Now that he was a prince of the church and, at the age of seventy-one, possessed of all the honors any priest could reasonably expect, was he at peace? Or as he knelt there in the company of distinguished statesmen and boyhood friends, did he feel an intimation of some greater work yet ahead?

There is no answer. He rose, smiling that warm, good-hearted smile that reflected his warmth and goodness, and was now His Eminence, Cardinal Angelo Giuseppe Roncalli. Addressing

Auriol, he said, ". . . Monsieur le Président, your presentation of the cardinal's biretta in the Holy Father's name is for me an honor but at the same time, I admit, inspires some sadness, for it signifies that my mission is at an end and that I must leave France. . . .

"For my own consolation, as long as I live and wherever it may please the Holy Father to assign to me a task and a charge in the service of the Holy Church, I shall be satisfied if every good Frenchman, remembering my humble name and my sojourn among you, can say, 'He was a loyal and peaceable priest, always and in all circumstances a sure and sincere friend of France.' "

He had come at a dark and trying time and worked to heal the old wounds. He had helped to restore peace within the church and exercised a benign influence on the moods and clashing convictions that beset France and French Catholics. On February 25, he left with the genuine regard of the people, returning to take up a mission in his native Italy for the first time in nearly thirty years.

X

PATRIARCH OF VENICE

His entry into Venice was fixed for Sunday, March 15, and in the interim, he went to Sotto il Monte and Bergamo. Delegations and distinguished visitors from all over came to call on him, and he received them with unassuming courtesy, although their regard was often directed less to him than to his new office. "It is true that princes are esteemed more than people," he remarked ruefully. A petty nobleman, seeking a favor, slyly asked whether the family of a certain Count Roncalli was not related to him. "Not to this date," he replied, "but I have the impression that from now on the family circle will widen considerably."

One visitor in whom he delighted, however, was Bruno Vianello, concierge of the patriarchal palace where Roncalli was to take up residence. With his wife, and at his own expense, this unpretentious Venetian came unannounced to Sotto il Monte to pay his respects to the new patriarch, and to bring the considerable stack of mail that had already accumulated for him. Roncalli was enchanted. He entertained the humble couple, introduced them to his family, and sent them on their way with a special blessing.

On Tuesday, March 10, he set out from Bergamo, stopping in Verona and Vicenza, and on the afternoon of the fifteenth, a brilliant day of full sunshine and the promise of spring, he entered the city of Venice.

He was welcomed with tumultuous warmth. The people turned out in every available launch and gondola to meet him, then fell into procession behind the vessel carrying Roncalli along the Grand Canal to the Piazza San Marco. Palaces and bridges were emblazoned with bunting and the banners of the ancient Venetian republic, its emblem, the winged lion of Saint Mark, snapping in the wind. The banks were crowded with cheering faithful, and Roncalli waved, his beaming smile embracing them all. Overhead, the open windows were filled with exuberant faces and cries of greeting. Only the windows of the town hall were shuttered, for the city council had a strong Communist representation. But when an official apologized, Roncalli, invigorated, replied, "Very well, we shall try to open those, too."

At the piazza, the carabinieri made a file for him through the happy crush of the citizenry. Wearing the scarlet robes of the cardinalate and a short ermine cape to keep his shoulders warm, he walked slowly toward the basilica, a thousand-year-old glory of Byzantine architecture. Inside, a solemn *Te Deum* was sung. Then the forty-third patriarch and 139th bishop of Venice peered through his steel-rimmed glasses at some pages of notes headed, "*Ecce homo, ecce sacerdos, ecce pastor*" ("Here is the man, here is the priest, here is the shepherd"), and spoke to the people:

> I want to talk to you with the greatest frankness. You have waited for me impatiently. Things have been said and written about me that greatly exaggerate my merits. Now I humbly introduce myself.
>
> As does every other man who lives on earth, I come from a family and from a particular place. I have been blessed with good physical health, with a little good sense to see things quickly and clearly, and with an inclination to love men. . . .
>
> Here I am, at the end of much experience, turning again

toward Venice, the land and sea familiar to my ancestors. . . .
No doubt the great position entrusted to me here exceeds all
my capacities. But above all I commend to your benevolence
the man who simply wants to be your brother. . . . I have
never aspired to any role other than to be a simple pastor in
my native diocese of Bergamo, but until this day Providence
has deemed otherwise. Now that I am a shepherd at last, your
shepherd, my first desire is to count the sheep, one by one.

The Venetians were plainly delighted with him. The festivities
continued into the evening as they came by the thousands to wish
him well. It was nearly midnight when the crowds began to leave,
and Roncalli turned to Pio Pietragnoli, editor of the diocesan
newspaper, and said, "Well, the bride has been married off and
the guests of the party have all gone home. Now I am alone in
this great beautiful palace and I do not even know how to find
my way around in it. Would you be good enough to lead the way
for me?"

Thereafter, he found his own way in the new surroundings. In
many ways, the next five years were the happiest of Roncalli's
life, for as Pallenberg points out, "A great, spontaneous sympathy
was established between the Patriarch and the Venetians, a kind,
tolerant, soft-spoken, somewhat skeptical people, who immediately appreciated the geniality and good humor of their new
pastor."

The local clergy was soon referring to him as "the calm after
the storm," for his predecessor had been a nervous, furious whirlwind of a man. Roncalli, in his mild, unhurried way, sought the
friendship of everyone. He was available to all in his residence
next to the cathedral, and walked about the city without fuss. A
journalist who called on him tried to cut the interview short in
deference to the patriarch's busy schedule, but Roncalli chatted
serenely on. When the man finally did rise to go and bent to kiss
his bishop's ring, Roncalli took the other's hand instead and shook
it, and still chatting, walked with him out to the stairway.

Not a week had passed before he went to the town hall to pay a call on the mayor, Armando Gavagnin, in thanks for the warmth of his welcome. Present, as Roncalli anticipated, was the entire city council, Socialists, Communists, and all. He told them that he was glad to be in the house of the people, the place where men worked for good government. "Only he who works for good is a Christian," he went on gently, "even if it happens that there may be several here who do not call themselves Christians. Yet they may be truly considered such for the good that they do, and so to all of you, without distinction, I give my paternal blessing."

In May, during a retreat at the villa of the Venetian seminary, he wrote: "In April last year I sought shelter under the roof of the Sacred Heart of Montmartre in Paris, and spring this year finds me here at the foot of the Grappa, Cardinal and Patriarch of Venice. What a transformation in all that surrounds me! . . . Now I am ministering directly to souls. To tell the truth, I have always believed that, for an ecclesiastic, diplomacy (so-called!) must be imbued with the pastoral spirit; otherwise it is of no use and makes a sacred mission look ridiculous. Now I am confronted with the church's real interests, which is to save souls and guide them to heaven."

Venice has always been a magical city. It was settled soon after the fall of the Roman Empire, by refugees fleeing barbarian invasions from the north. They built houses and palaces of great beauty on the marshy islands of their lagoon and counted on the sea to protect them. Facing the Adriatic, seemingly afloat in that cerulean light between water and sky, they created a thriving city-state that came to dominate the Mediterranean world.

Then Venice fell on evil days. Even as great schools of painting and music flourished in its magical light, the discovery of new trade routes to the East cut deeply into its economic strength and influence. It submitted to Napoleon without a battle, came under the rule of Austria and, in 1866, was united with Italy. And as the twentieth century entered its second half, it lived still on past glory. For except for a naval installation and a seasonal tourist industry, there was nothing to keep young people from seeking livelihoods on the mainland. Atop its noble column, the winged lion of Saint Mark gazed out to sea, but saw only transients arriving while Venetians left for good.

Within a few weeks of taking up residence, Roncalli wrote, "I have already two painful problems here, amidst all the splendor of ecclesiastical state, and the veneration shown to me as cardinal and patriarch: the scantiness of my revenue and the throng of poor folk with their requests for employment and financial help." By the end of that first year, as he told his family, he felt like the mother of a poor and very large household. And in his Christmas message of 1955, he made it clear that he considered the social and economic well-being of the poor to be a responsibility of the rich, and a legitimate concern of the church. Detailing the hardships of widespread unemployment in Venice, he said, "I turn to the industrial leaders and business firms, to their technical consultants and economists, and I implore them in the name of God to consider that the active intelligence and the goods of fortune given to them were placed at their disposition, not merely to adjust budgets, but to be the ministers of providence for all the human family. Thus they should consider themselves engaged in the most difficult but essential of the social services—a title of merit and honor for him who works in the spirit of the Old and New Testament."

Fascinated by the history of his ancient diocese, he was incessantly made aware of its modern problems. His personal charities cut sharply into the funds allotted to him, and he had to humbly solicit for badly needed new churches and church schools. Eventually he even sold the patriarchal summer villa at Fietta to pay for a new seminary. When someone protested that he was giving up a haven where he could count on a bit of respite from the pressures of his office, he replied that the needs of the diocese were more important, adding, "And I sleep quite well here in Venice."

Soon he was the first citizen of the city. The people grew accustomed to seeing his rotund figure striding along the streets and squares looking, except for the red and gold band on his broad-brimmed hat and a flash of red socks beneath the cassock, like an ordinary parish priest. He owned neither a gondola nor a private motor launch, hiring them as needed or, more often, riding the *vaporetto*, the community boat bus. Recognizing their cardinal-patriarch, other passengers bustled to make room. But he wanted them close: "Come and sit by me," he encouraged them. "You pay the same fare as I do. Come, we'll talk."

Often, when spring tides flooded the great square in front of Saint Mark's, Roncalli cut through a café called the Birreria Leoncini (the Beer Hall of the Little Lions). At first his appearance signaled only an uneasy silence among patrons and proprietor. Then a predictable colloquy developed:

"Want to wet your throat, Eminence?" someone would call out.

"No, nor my feet either," was the patriarch's reply as he scurried through.

He rose regularly at 4:00 A.M., although if insomnia wakened him earlier he would get out of bed and work until he felt able to sleep again. By seven, he had prayed, recited the breviary, and celebrated mass. In summer he sometimes climbed to a terrace at the top of the palace and looked out over the city's maze of roofs as the rising sun turned them fiery red. After breakfasting on coffee, warm milk, and some fruit, he turned to the business of the day, always varied in detail, but always the same in intensity. In his office, a medium-sized, vaguely unkempt room with pink brocade walls and a massive desk under which rested a footwarmer, he went through half a dozen newspapers. Beginning at ten, he was available to anyone who wanted to see him, receiving visitors in the audience hall of the doges of the Venetian Republic. His aides tried, but eventually gave up any attempt to cut these hearings short. "Let them come!" Roncalli protested. "Let them all come—some among them may want to confess."

Luncheon was at one, the main meal of the day, followed by a short rest. The afternoon was devoted to the endless details of administering the nine dioceses of which he was metropolitan.

There were meetings, consultations, correspondence. Or, as frequently happened, he was off to visit the sick, greet a distinguished visitor, bless a rugby team, or show a group of vacationers through the palace.

At 7:45 P.M. he joined the members of his household in the chapel for the recitation of the rosary. Dinner was at eight, perhaps some vegetable soup, fruit and cheese, then Roncalli retired to the small study next to his bedroom. Often he had a pastoral letter or an address to write, and this might keep him awake until 2:00 A.M. Otherwise he read or worked on the final Borromeo volume and was in bed by ten.

Roncalli did not consider this an especially rigorous regimen. "In my humble life I've never been a race horse," he wrote a Bergamo colleague. "I go to bed early, at ten, and rise at four because this gives me time to pray in peace and go to work with a quiet mind."

At this time two people came into his life who would serve him for the rest of his days, Loris Capovilla and Guido Gusso. Capovilla, a thin and earnest young priest of Venice, became his secretary during that first summer, and between the two there came to be the same warm filial relationship that Roncalli had shared with *his* bishop, Radini-Tedeschi. To this day, Capovilla, now Pope John's literary executor, considers himself to be in the late pontiff's service.

Guido Gusso joined him just a few days after his arrival in Venice, when he had no staff except a few reluctant holdovers from Agostini's patriarchate. "I had to do everything," Gusso, a tall and engaging young man, said years later. "I was the butler, the driver, the sexton, the major-domo, because for months there was no one else." Then, smiling, "And all for that miserable salary."

Not long ago Gusso, who is now assistant head usher at Saint Peter's, sat in his neat little apartment in the Vatican and recalled those days. Asked why, if the pay was so poor, he hadn't left for another job, he looked through the window, far away, and replied, "Who could leave that man? He had such a soul. It

wasn't his fault that they didn't give him enough money. Sometimes he gave me his own.

"And I wasn't afraid of the work, that every day I had to wake
up at six so I could serve his mass, that I had to drive him from
parish to parish for festivals and confirmations. And I wasn't
ashamed to clean the bedroom and study, and serve the food—
because no matter how hard I worked or anyone worked, he
worked harder, that old man.

"Once I got into a big fight with a bunch of Communists about
him. We had driven to a little village in the Veneto—he was
giving the sacrament of confirmation in that region—and it was
one of those very hot days of May. I waited in the car while he
went into the church. I could see from the way he walked that he
was already tired out, and there were still other places to go.

"This was a working-class village, with many Communists, and
soon enough they gathered around the car and began to talk:
'Oh, these priests, they live in luxury. They drive around in new
automobiles and never work.'

"He had this small Fiat—it was a present, that's what made me
angry—and I said to them, 'Do you know how old that man is?
He is seventy-five. If he were anybody else he would be retired
now, living on a pension, happy to do nothing. But he is still
working, and has worked all his life, far away from his home, and
he will work until he dies. Is that what you call luxury? Do you
know what time he left the patriarchate this morning? At 5:00
A.M.—to be here in time to confirm the children of this place. He
has already been in Mestre and this afternoon he must be in other
places and it is the same all through the month of May. Should he
walk? Should he send for the children to come to him?'

"But you know how it is, there are people who will not listen.
'Yes, yes,' they said, 'but when we are in power we will take care
of the priests.'

" 'Go ahead,' I said, 'but when you take care of this one you are
going to make a lot of enemies.' "

A few years after he joined Roncalli, Gusso became engaged to
a girl from his home town, Caorle. Finally he decided that if he

were ever to afford marriage he would have to leave Roncalli's service. In the early fall of 1958, gathering his courage, he went to tell him so. He was not pleased with the patriarch's reply: "He said he didn't want me to leave. No matter what I said, he answered me from the Gospel, from Matthew's Sermon on the Mount, about how our heavenly Father feeds the birds of the air, and how we mustn't be anxious about tomorrow because tomorrow will look after itself. It was as though he didn't even understand—I wanted to get married!"

But a few days later Capovilla came to Gusso with astonishing news: At Roncalli's request, he had telephoned the manager of a bank in Venice and gotten him a new job. The pay would be nearly double what he was getting and he could start the following week. Gusso was elated and set the wedding date.

"That was the first week in October," recalled Gusso, smiling wryly. "On the ninth, Pope Pius died and I postponed the wedding once. Capovilla telephoned the bank manager again and said I had to go with them to the conclave—the patriarch needed me. We would all return in a fortnight and I would be free to start at the bank at once. Well, everyone knows what happened at the conclave, why I had to postpone the wedding again, this time for six months: The patriarch was elected to be the pope and none of us ever came back to Venice again."

The evidence of Roncalli's five-year patriarchate is visible to anyone who knew the city before he came. He established thirty new parishes and a center for patriarchal archives, built a minor seminary, and launched a program of restoration at the palace and basilica that went forward even after his departure.

One of his first renovation projects was the burial crypt beneath the main altar of the cathedral. The tomb of Saint Mark, which had been hidden from sight, was raised so that it could be seen as well as venerated. The remains of other former patriarchs were then entombed there, and the magnificent Byzantine mosaics were rehabilitated. It was here that Roncalli himself planned to be buried, but of course this was not to be.

Behind the palace stands a row of church buildings, which were then in serious disrepair, where the aged canons of the city resided. Roncalli ordered a complete reconstruction, only to be informed by his emissary, Count Vittorio Cini, chairman of the lay committee of Saint Mark's, that the old monsignori refused to vacate while the work was done. Roncalli went to see for himself, and returned to say that all was arranged. Cini, who later recounted this episode himself, asked, "But what did you say to them, Eminence?"

"The same thing you did, my dear Count," was the reply. Then, putting his hand on Cini's arm, added, "But I kept it in mind that these good fathers are all past seventy years of age and a little frightened of having to leave their home, even for a little while. And so I said it in a softer way."

Another problem gently resolved by Roncalli, but not until he became the pope, was the placement of the iconostasis of Saint Mark's, a rood screen of splendidly adorned marble that, unfortunately, obscured the main altar from the view of worshipers. In the ancient days of the Venetian Republic, the doge and his little entourage could get close enough to watch the mass, and it was of no importance that no one else could. But now that Saint Mark's had been the patriarchal basilica of the city for a century and a half, Roncalli decided the time had come to let all the faithful see the altar and participate fully in the liturgy. He talked with various committees, the mayor, the fine arts commission, but nothing was done.

Finally he proposed that rather than remove the masterpiece, it be mounted on pivots and wheeled to one side during the services. Still there was criticism: He was trying to mutilate the historic cathedral; camera-carrying tourists of every faith and no faith would profane the sanctuary.

Was Saint Peter's profaned, then, Roncalli asked mildly? For millions came every year to gaze at its high altar. But he said no more. Then, a few months after he succeeded to the throne of Saint Peter, he remarked to a visiting Venetian, "About the iconostasis at St. Mark's . . ." Within weeks it was mounted on pivots, exactly as he had originally suggested, and there was nothing but praise for the transformation.

It is said that he celebrated mass in every parish of the Venetian diocese. The record of his engagements shows repeated trips to the new parishes, and to those on the mainland where mostly working people lived. And he invariably put the stamp of his own style on these visits. A group of officials awaiting his arrival in a town square, saw his little Fiat turn off on a side street. When he did not reappear, the dignitaries, concerned, went to find him: Was he ill?

"Not at all," he told them. "I thought you would not object if I spent a moment in your church. First God, then the reception committee."

Busy as he was in his patriarchate, Roncalli found time to go abroad, sometimes at the pope's behest, sometimes to speak in countries where he had once served. In the summer of 1954, he led the bishops of the three Venetian provinces on a pilgrimage to Lourdes. Then, putting aside his scarlet robes for a simple black cassock, he spent two weeks touring Spain. Later that year he went as papal legate to a Marian congress in Lebanon where he met again with many of the prelates of the Eastern rite.

In Paris, his duties had brought him regularly into the company of world leaders. In Venice, he moved among the ordinary people of his flock with no change of manner. A delegation of gondoliers went to see him and reported that he had risen when they entered, asked their views on a multitude of local questions—"Go on, go on," he kept saying, inviting the freest discussion—and saw them personally to the door. "The president of the Republic could not have received better treatment," said one, a Roncalli partisan for life.

How was it that he got on so well with everyone? someone once asked him. "Why not?" he replied with a smile. "There is nothing wrong with my nerves or my liver."

Nor with his heart. During the Christmas season his first year in Venice, he read in the newspaper that Eugenio Bacchion, a leader of the diocesan Catholic Action, had just lost his wife. He telephoned to offer his condolences, then said, "This will be your first Christmas with an empty place at the table. Will you come, then, with your children, and have Christmas dinner with me?"

When Vincent Auriol came to see him, Roncalli asked the municipal band in Saint Mark's Square to play "*La Marseillaise*," to the undisguised delight of the patriotic old Frenchman. The Venetians were fascinated by the warm bond between Roncalli and this socialist nonbeliever who had been president of France. But having learned to expect the unexpected from their patriarch, they were not really surprised. Auriol has left an account of how Roncalli showed him through the patriarchal palace, and of the prescient moment when they came to the apartment occupied by a predecessor, Giuseppe Sarto, who became Pope Pius X and later was sainted.

"Showing me a modest, poorly furnished little room, Cardinal Roncalli limited himself to saying, 'Here lived Pius X.' I believe he used this brief phrase only because emotion had prevented him from saying more. It was Pius X who had blessed him the day after his ordination as a priest, more than fifty years before. I realized at that moment that at my side there had faded away the man who for eight years had served as a most astute dean of the diplomatic corps in France, the cultured, articulate and pleasing humanist. He was now no more than the humble priest, overcome with piety."

Auriol was profoundly moved. "Perhaps," he said as they turned from the simple room, "the successor to the present pontiff will have lived in this palace, too."

Roncalli did not reply. The memory of Pius X lived in Venice, like a benediction renewed day after day. And he heard the comparisons. "That one," the people said, meaning him, "is a saint, too." Around this time he wrote to his sister Maria that some irrational people were already predicting "greater things" for him. "In France . . . some crazy Frenchmen, who rejoice in revelations and second sight, have even announced the name I shall assume when they make me pope. Crazy, crazy, the whole lot of them. I am preparing for my death."

But it all made him uneasy.

Roncalli had been in Venice only a few months when his nephew Battista, whose path to the priesthood seemed beset with obstacles, encountered still another. He had come to the age of twenty-six without having been ordained a subdeacon, not in itself a serious matter, except that Italian law excuses from military service only those seminarians who have attained that state by the time they are twenty-six. When in April 1953, Battista received his notice to report for duty, he was heartsick at the prospect of another two-year delay. He took the notice to his superior, Monsignor Battaglia, Bishop of Faenza, who sent him straightaway to Venice to see his uncle, the cardinal-patriarch: He could surely do something.

Battista himself later told what happened, "I went at once with the vicar-general of the diocese—the bishop sent him with me, for he attached that much importance to the matter—and we arrived just as my uncle was leaving the patriarchal palace. We met him in a hallway and he said at once, 'What is it? Why aren't you at school?'

" 'It is this,' I told him, showing him the notice.

"He looked at it. Then he looked at the vicar, and again at me. He said, 'I don't understand why you have come here. If this is what you must do, do it. I did it, too. There is nothing in life we cannot learn from.' Then he excused himself, for he had a group of children waiting to be confirmed, and saying good-bye, he rushed out.

"I was ready to leave, but the vicar said we must wait for him to return. The cardinal had not understood, he assured me. I must explain it to him—two wasted years!

"I knew that my uncle had understood very well, but we

waited. When he returned, I held the notice out again—I was nervous for I thought, now he will be angry—and I said, 'The bishop sent me here, he said you would help me.'

"He was not angry at all. His face had that look of patience and loving. He took my arm and said, 'My dear boy, I cannot help you. I cannot do for you what is not done for others. That you are my nephew means that I can give you what is mine to give—my love, my money—but nothing else, not what rightfully belongs to this office I am privileged to hold for a little while. Surely you see that, do you not, dear Battista?'

"I said that I did. I thanked him and we left. The vicar was so amazed he could not speak. When we returned, the bishop was amazed too, but he spoke. 'How can it be?' he said many times. 'How can it be, when you are his own flesh and blood?'

" 'It is because he is a saint, Excellency,' I said, 'nothing less.' "

In the end it was arranged by Monsignor Battaglia to have Battista made a subdeacon in advance of the normal time, and he managed to avoid military service after all. Then he received a letter from his uncle. "By the time you get this I hope you will have got over your difficulties in a way that satisfies your own desires and the secret purposes of Providence, who directs human events for our own true good.

". . . This initial consecration pledges you to an angelic purity, a sincere and serene humility, a confident and unfailing trust in God and a fervent desire, but without emotional exaggerations to become a priest. . . . And think of nothing else."

On August 10, 1953, Roncalli began the fiftieth year of his priesthood. It was to be a time of trial. Ancilla was approaching the last days of her life, and before long it was learned that Maria, too, was suffering with cancer. "All my relations are *dear* to me," Roncalli once wrote, "but no one will be offended when I say that my two sisters Ancilla and Maria are *dearest*. I might even say that we three are like three candles burning on the same altar." Now two of the three candles were flickering out.

Ancilla died early in November, just before Roncalli arrived for what was to have been a final visit. Instead, he stayed for the funeral, returning to Venice emotionally spent. It was some time before he could write to Enrica that he was more serene.

". . . I think of her, now in Paradise, watching over us and blessing us. When I left Camaitino I went back to the cemetery once more, and found the young sexton Mapelli filling up the grave. I cannot tell you how I suffered when I saw her there at the feet of our dead. May she pray for us. Let us pray for her."

Over the next three years, he was besieged by a grim sequence of bereavements. They were not entirely unforeseen in a family whose members had reached the sixth and seventh decades of life, but of course this did not make the loss of loved ones easier to suffer. Another sister, Teresa, died suddenly, only two months after Ancilla, and then Maria began the long, painful trial that could have only one outcome. Roncalli wrote to her frequently, never attempting to deceive her about the true nature of her illness, nor of his grief at the imminence of their separation, yet bolstering her belief that the best was yet to come:

> This is very sad for me. To have two sisters who have given up the thought of marriage in order to remain with me . . . then one sister leaves us for heaven and the other also seems on the verge of departing. I do not say this is bound to happen in the near future—I might go before you, for I am now in my seventy-fourth year. . . . I have become so used to the thought of my departure that I no longer have any fear of it, because I know that Paradise is even more beautiful than Venice or Camaitino and that there we shall really know eternal joy, for we shall meet our Blessed Jesus and our Lady, and be reunited with our dear ones who have gone before us and await us there.

Maria died on April 18, 1955. Less than a week later, his nephew, Assunta's Giuseppe, was killed in a motor accident on his way to work. Roncalli wrote immediately to console his sister and offer financial help. "Poor Beppino! I saw him on Tuesday at Maria's funeral: he was so good and kind. His death is like a tree falling to the ground. . . . I believe the Lord has already received him. . . . I continue to pray for him, for his widow, for you and for his little fatherless daughters."

In the autumn, still another blow fell: Giovanni, the next to youngest of his brothers, who was the father of Enrica, Battista, and Sister Angela, fell ill with an intestinal malignancy. Masking his sorrow, Roncalli once more sent words of comfort and encouragement, reminding Giovanni of the great dangers he had escaped as a soldier during World War I, evoking the time, "far back in 1898, when our parish priest Rebuzzini died and you were only a little boy, you barely escaped from death. If God would but grant our prayers this time, too, as I beg him most earnestly, always, day and night." But like the others, Giovanni lingered only another year, then passed on, and again the mourning brother returned to Sotto il Monte to bury a loved one.

But it was not a time of unrelieved sadness. In 1954, Roncalli commemorated his priestly jubilee, fifty years in the service of God, quietly at Sotto il Monte. He had to take stern measures to prevent the occasion from being turned into a diocesan celebration, writing sharply to Battista, who seemed to be the motive force behind these preparations. "I have had enough festivities in my life to exceed any merit won in this half century. . . . Under the trees in the cemetery the earth which covers our dear sisters Ancilla and Teresa is still newly turned. How could we think of celebrations? You understand me, dear Battista; see that the others understand too. . . . Arrange everything very simply and receive my blessing."

Poor Battista, who wanted only to do what would please his uncle, arranged everything simply as instructed. For Roncalli, the peace of Sotto il Monte was blessing enough, and it was seen that this was provided him. On the momentous anniversary, he wrote in his journal, "My golden jubilee as a priest at Sotto il Monte, 10 August 1954. A wonderfully bright sky after beneficial night showers. . . . What is my poor life of fifty years of priesthood? A faint reflection of this poem: 'My merit—God's mercy.' "

And the following summer, another great blessing occurred. In the patriarch's chapel in Venice, in the warm circle of the family, he ordained Battista a priest. Thereafter the earnest young man was a particular comfort to his uncle, especially through those final years when he was pope, when life in the uppermost reaches of authority was sometimes very lonely indeed.

Meanwhile, the life of the fields went on at Sotto il Monte. The elders were reduced to four, Zaverio, Alfredo, Giuseppe, and Caterina, the widow of Giovanni—Assunta now lived with her children near Milan—but in their midst, what Roncalli called "a wealth of children" grew and began families of their own. To ensure that the Colombera would long remain the *casa paterna* of the Roncalli clan, extensive repairs were undertaken in 1956, to which the patriarch contributed a million lire (about $570) as his initial share.

When his namesake, Giuseppe's son Angelo, was called up for his military service, the uncle wrote him a long and affectionate letter, recalling his own years in the army during World War I. The world and its ways had changed greatly since those days, he knew, and was particularly concerned that his nephew not be caught up in the swirl of pleasure-seeking that seemed to mark this new era. "Above all beware of women," he warned. "Have nothing to do with any of them for any reason at all, and do not let them accost you. One such experience is enough to ruin a fine young man. And do not be influenced by the crazy ideas current today. Think your own thoughts, not those of others."

His sense of rectitude was of an earlier, simpler time. But it was uniquely and immovably his, and stood like a rock against currents of hedonism and a tide of self-indulgence. A niece came to stay with him in Venice, a lovely ingratiating girl who remained for two and a half weeks and transgressed in only the most minor way, as any attractive teen-ager might. Soon her father had a tactful letter from his brother, the patriarch. It praised the girl without reservation—yet made it perfectly clear that it would be better if she did not visit him again: "Here in December we were cheered by the company of your little daughter . . . who behaved *very well indeed, to everyone's satisfaction.* . . . But you will understand . . . what sort of house this is. [Your daughter] is almost twenty and this is a house made of glass. As you know, tongues wag about everything. I was glad for her to stay here eighteen days, but I could not grant her this favor again. This house is good for putting up my relations for two or three days. . . . Everything must be done *with prudence and moderation.* Enough: You have already understood me."

There were many family visits to Venice—in time, everyone came—but none that moved the patriarch more than that by Enrica escorting her Uncle Zaverio and Aunt Maria on the occasion of their fiftieth wedding anniversary. Even before they came, Roncalli wrote his brother that although this golden anniversary, materially, had brought neither gold nor silver, "its spiritual significance is worth more than these." And at his behest, Pope Pius sent the couple a "long and beautiful" telegram of congratulations.

The bond between Roncalli and his secretary, Loris Capovilla, grew very close. The patriarch could count on his brilliant aide to relieve him of innumerable small burdens and to speak plainly on large issues. There quickly developed a deep mutual devotion that transcended their ecclesiastic relationship and was apparent to all who saw them together. In one letter home, Roncalli said that Capovilla had become "like a member of the family." In another, in the spring of 1956, when Capovilla fell seriously ill, he wrote anxiously, "For more than a month my dear and precious secretary Msgr. Loris has been suffering with a glandular inflammation of the neck which gives him a lot of pain, although he bears it very patiently."

The Venetian photographer Borlui, who came to be a favorite

around the patriarchal palace, tells of visiting early one morning around this time and finding Roncalli at Capovilla's bedside. He had been there all night.

"Eminence," said Borlui, aghast, "why have you done this? Surely the sisters could have looked after him, someone else . . ."

"No, no," Roncalli replied briskly, "the sisters are busy with other duties. They need their rest. Besides, I know exactly when to give him his medicine."

Capovilla, who came from a poor family of the Veneto, presented a striking contrast to the calm, portly patriarch. He was highly-strung and hyperactive and Roncalli once said, "We get along well because we are opposites." *Time-Life* correspondent Robert Neville called Capovilla "Roncalli's window to the world's youth." He liked speed, airplanes, television, to all of which the patriarch quickly grew indifferent.

The contrast extended to their attitude toward money. Roncalli was certain that Providence would somehow see to his needs; Capovilla did not doubt this, but saw no harm in trying to check Roncalli's inclination to cheerfully give away everything he had to anyone who petitioned for help. And Roncalli, who did not like anything to do with business, not even his personal business, and was far from adept at it, was most happy to pass the burden on to his secretary.

But when it came to the patriarch's little charities, Capovilla fought a losing battle. Once Roncalli saw him tipping a motor boatman a hundred lire and lectured him on the high cost of living: "What is a hundred lire these days, my dear Don Loris? A thousand is little enough. Come, where is my wallet? This good man deserves something more." But when he finally found his wallet in the swirls of his cassock, it was empty, a not uncommon occurrence, and Capovilla had to produce the additional nine hundred lire himself.

The concierge Vianello tells of the Christmas when Roncalli secretly tried to supplement the little gift envelopes which Capovilla had distributed to the staff. "My salary was low and my family big," he recalled, "and this was his way to help a little." As the patriarch shook his hand and wished him well for the holiday season, he tried to press a packet of money into Vianello's palm. The concierge, not realizing what was happening, let it fall to the floor, all fifteen thousand lire of it. Then he stared at it dumfounded—as did Capovilla. Only Roncalli was unflustered. He smiled and said, "Well, Bruno, now that you've given my secret away, pick it up and be off."

When the work of restoring the angel atop Saint Mark's was completed, Roncalli climbed the narrow ladder to the bell tower to bless it, Capovilla doggedly following. Borlui, who went along to photograph the event, tells how Roncalli teetered on the narrow landing three hundred feet high, leaned out and conferred his blessing. Then—"as long as we are here"—he got up on a workman's bench, Capovilla clinging to his robes, to bless the entire city. "When we got down," said Borlui later, "I could see who was the nervous one—Don Loris's face was white as milk!"

Venice is a lively city, host to an important international film festival and biennial art show. Unlike some of his predecessors, Roncalli did not try to ignore the cultural life, though some of its aspects dared the bounds of propriety. He personally celebrated the traditional "Movie Mass" at film-festival time in September, and each year held a reception at the palace for the film-makers of all nations, not excluding those from the Communist world, or those among the celebrities whose real-life amatory adventures were sometimes more colorful than their screen roles. But he never failed to use the occasion to remind producers, directors, and actors of their enormous influence and responsibilities. "The spirit governs even entertainment," he told them one year. Speaking in French, he said, "Messieurs, my brothers, the world of today is shrouded in a suffocating atmosphere. Purify it! Let the fresh air into it! And you will make a contribution both to the cinema and to society as a whole. I pray for you; come, pray with me."

In 1954 he became the first patriarch to attend the celebrated

Venice Biennale, the show of modern art held there every second year. It had been Cardinal Sarto (later Pope Pius X) who forbade priests to visit the exhibit because of the shocking—for those days—nature of some of the paintings. But like his Renaissance predecessors, Roncalli felt art to be "a noble human activity," and indeed knew a great deal about painting, although he always tended to minimize his intellectual attainments. He also thought it important to keep in touch with worthy new trends of artistic expression. At a reception for artists and guests in the Sala Maggiore (grand salon) of the palace in 1956, he announced a lifting of the old ban against clerical attendance at the exhibition.

He inaugurated an annual mass for journalists, held on the Feast of Saint Francis de Sales, patron of Catholic writers. He remained an avid newspaper reader, though he had come to understand during his service in some of the world's great cities that what happened and what was reported to have happened could be quite different, the variable factor being the newsman's imagination. But his reaction was usually mild and occasionally antic. In Venice he said to the writer of a story about him, "You put too much salt in it." In Rome, years later, he waved a magazine article at Capovilla and, on the verge of laughter, exclaimed, "You must read this if you want to know what the pope is up to. In these pages I have just found out not only what I am doing, but what I'm thinking!"

Another of his innovations, perhaps the one best remembered in Venice, is the way he brought modern music into Saint Mark's during the music festivals. It was Roncalli who invited the Russian composer, Igor Stravinsky, to conduct the premiere of his oratorio, *Sacred Canticle in Honor of Saint Mark the Evangelist*, in the basilica. Two years later, in September 1958, Stravinsky returned to conduct his *Laments of the Prophet Jeremiah* at Saint Mark's. It was noted that the patriarch was present at the rehearsal.

This is not to say that he accepted everything about Venetian life and every proposal to enliven it for the beguilement of the tourists. When the city council proposed to move the gambling casino from the Lido to the center of Venice, indeed, to Saint Mark's Square, he registered a protest. It was characteristically tactful, but so firmly framed that no more was heard about the matter as long as Roncalli was patriarch. And when finally the move was made, the casino was relocated in an inconspicuous part of the city, near the railroad station.

A shaft of the Roncalli wit was directed at tourists who engulfed Venice in summer and, showing more bare flesh than they would have dreamed of doing at home, made straight for Saint Mark's: "We do not live in the tropics or in the arctic, so it is quite easy for women to decide what is proper to wear. People need not come to Italy in furs or woolens. They can come dressed in that modern American silk, which is a veritable refrigerator at low cost. Italy, after all, is not on the equator—and even there, by the way, lions wear their coats and crocodiles are covered by their valuable hides."

On February 11, 1954, the twenty-fifth anniversary of the Lateran Treaty which ended the long conflict between the church and the Italian government, Cardinal Roncalli demonstrated again his uncircumscribed spirit of charity and rare courage. In a commemorative address at Saint Mark's, at a time when the name of Mussolini could still rouse terrible passions in Italy, he praised the dishonored *Duce* for his "decisive part in concluding the agreements."

"This was the man whom Providence brought face to face with Pius XI. . . . He later became a cause of great sadness to the Italian people. Yet it is human and it is Christian not to deny him at least this claim to honor after his immense misfortune . . . and after his humiliation to commend his soul to the divine mercy of our Lord who . . . is in the habit of choosing the most appropriate vessel and who, once the work has been accomplished, breaks it as if it had not been prepared for a special purpose. My brothers and sons, I know you can understand how I feel. Let us also respect the fragments of the broken vessel and let us turn to good effect the lessons they teach."

All his life he remained an ardent supporter of Catholic Action and the Christian Democratic party. And in the initial fervor of the postwar renewal, the Christian Democrats were strong enough to command an overall majority in Italy's Chamber of Deputies. But as the tensions of the cold war began to fade and politicians could again indulge their ingrained genius for petty disagreement, the Christian Democrats were forced into coalitions with other parties in order to keep the government from falling to extremists of the Left or Right. When they turned to the Socialists, they incurred the sharp displeasure of the Holy See. The seventy-eight-year-old Pope Pius XII had been afflicted by serious illness in 1954, and although he recovered to live another four years, he was never the same man. His single-handed control over the machinery of the Vatican slipped and, as it did, the curial conservatives strengthened their position—and their fixed focus of the world beyond Saint Peter's allowed for no differentiation between atheistic Communists and moderate Socialists.

In August, 1956, when a Christian Democratic "opening to the Left" was being hotly debated, Roncalli spoke against it, as did Montini in Milan, where he had become archbishop. Both were loyally following directives from Rome. Their separate papacies are perhaps better evidence of their true beliefs, as is Roncalli's hospitable welcome to a Socialist congress in Venice only six months after he had called the coalition with the Left "a very grave doctrinal error." He had posters put up all over the city heralding his personal greeting and the hope that the Socialists would devote themselves "to doing everything possible to improve living conditions and social well-being." In a pastoral letter which conceded that it was painful for him to recognize that honest, intelligent men could believe in an ideology not inspired by the Gospels, he expressed the wish "that the people of Venice, welcoming and amiable as is their custom, will help to make this meeting of so many of our brothers from all regions of Italy a contribution toward the ideals of truth, goodness, justice, and peace."

The shocked reaction among conservative Venetians stirred a

brief newspaper tempest. To one journalist who came to the patriarchate seeking a statement, Roncalli said, "No one should be disturbed by my initiative. One day all those people [the Socialists] will come to church again." And to another, he explained, "Alongside purity of doctrine there open up fields for the exercise of charity, which begins with respect and courtesy."

But the controversy in Venice was as nothing compared with the silent disapproval that surged from the Vatican. "Our good Roncalli" had done it again.

As he would, once again, when he assumed the throne of Peter. His essential faith was open, not closed. He was the same man who befriended Vincent Auriol, "an honest Socialist," and Numan Menemengioglu, "my favorite infidel." His deepest beliefs as pastor and patriarch were explicitly put in his address to a diocesan synod in November 1957. In the liturgy, he explained, the bishop is called father and pastor. He must provide for the spiritual welfare of his children and protect them against threats to their faith. But in so doing, the bishop himself must guard against two threats: authoritarian arrogance and paternalism. "Authoritarianism suffocates truth, reducing everything to a rigid and empty formalism that is dependent on outside discipline. It curbs wholesome initiative, mistakes hardness for firmness, inflexibility for dignity. Paternalism is a caricature of true fatherliness. It is often accompanied by an unjustifiable proprietary attitude to one's victim, a habit of intruding, a lack of proper respect for the rights of subordinates."

He was not insensitive to the suggestion by some that his forbearance was really weakness, his quest for simplicity really a gullible simple-mindedness. But he was determined to pursue "the perfection of mildness, patience and charity," he wrote, "and this at all costs, even at the risk of seeming to be, and being considered a person of little worth."

Once he was urged to take action against a priest who had gotten into some difficulty in his diocese. He refused. "If you break a glass it is broken," he said. Again he suffered the charge of weakness, felt though unspoken. But the priest eventually redeemed himself.

Sometimes he was forced to take disciplinary measures, then almost always found some way to temper them. In 1957 his auxiliary bishop, Augusto Gianfranceschi, an officious and difficult sort, was transferred to Cesena. The reaction among the clergy there was glum: The bishop's reputation had preceded him. Then, with diabolic Italian humor, there mysteriously appeared throughout the diocese cards bound in black mourning bands announcing the new appointment. Roncalli sent off a letter of reprimand to the priests suspected. But not long after, he was heard to remark, "Ah, that Gianfranceschi—if he had been present at the Creation, our dear God would have had to do it *his* way."

Although he was immersed in his duties as patriarch, he did not then, or ever, forget the lands or the people he once served. In 1954, speaking of the Eastern churches, he said, "The road to unity between the different Christian creeds is love, so little practiced on both sides." He reminded his listeners of Joseph's cry of forgiveness to the brothers who had betrayed him, stepping down from the throne to declare, "I am Joseph, your brother!"

As pope, he himself would have occasion to speak those momentous words, and soon. Without his knowing it, his days in Venice were drawing to an end. In August 1958, he took his annual holiday in Sotto il Monte, a pleasant, restful time during which he visited a summer camp maintained by the Pontifical Relief Organization. The children performed a little entertainment that poked fun at the oddities of old age. Roncalli, laughing, called out to them, "Yes, yes, I did the same as a child. But don't forget that some day young ones will say all this about you!" He left in the car with Gusso on a calm summer day, unaware that he had seen the village of his birth for the last time.

He had completed the final volume of the Borromeo study, which was then being printed, Roncalli having raised the money in Bergamo. In a foreword, thanking all who had helped him, he wrote, "In normal conditions five years of hard work would have sufficed for this; it took me fifty years." It seems clear that he felt his worldly commitments to be nearly fulfilled. At retreat in September he wrote, "My advanced age means that I should now be much more chary of accepting engagements to preach outside my own diocese. I have to write everything down first, and this is a great effort, besides the constant humiliation of feeling my own insufficiency. May the Lord help me and forgive me."

That same month he celebrated the centenary of the sainted Pius X, who had also come from a peasant family, also risen in the ranks of the church to become patriarch of Venice, leaving there in 1903 for Rome and immortality.

But in Venice that early autumn of 1958, there was no visible sign of the events that would change Roncalli's life. Bruno Vianello, the faithful concierge, recalls that the patriarchal palace was still in process of renovation: "He had ordered a lot of work, because it was all very old-fashioned. There was to be running water everywhere, even in my apartment, and central heating and a new elevator." The work never seemed to end and all that fall, Roncalli, full of apologies, had to pass through Vianello's flat to reach the motor-boat landing. Once he said of the disorder, "You will see, Bruno, when the cage is finally ready, the bird will escape."

Not long after, in Rome, when Vianello reminded him of this prophecy, Pope John XXIII said, "Yes, I remember, but I did not mean it *this* way: I thought I would escape to Paradise."

But as September ran its course that fateful year of 1958, as October came with disturbing hints of Pius XII's incapacity, a certain feeling, an apprehension such as he had never felt about the future, took hold of him. This may account for the peremptory tone of his letter to Enrica on October 6, "As you have heard, we must all pray for the Holy Father's recovery: I would not like to have to leave in a hurry for Rome. I add no more: It is our duty to pray and to fear nothing because the Lord rules his church. *Nor must we indulge in daydreams* . . ."

In Venice during that climactic week, a medical convention was in progress and events were foreshadowed by an urgent call from Rome: The Vatican was trying to locate Dr. Antonio Gasbarrini, a specialist in internal disorders who was in attendance on the pope. Next came a warning from the Secretariat of State, the official notice sent to members of the college of cardinals throughout the world: Each was to hold himself in readiness; the condition of the pontiff was grave.

At Castel Gandolfo, the pope's summer retreat, the eighty-two-year-old Pius, weakened by the same racking bout of hiccups that had almost killed him four years earlier, now slipped perceptibly toward the end. Within hours of the first public announcement of his illness, newsmen were camped in the small piazza outside the papal residence, watching the bedroom window on the third floor, and hundreds more were on the way. The Vatican Radio began issuing periodic bulletins.

On the morning of Monday, October 6, Pius suffered a stroke, collapsing at his desk. Incredibly, the enfeebled old man rallied and Tuesday's medical reports were guardedly optimistic. But on Wednesday he was felled by a second stroke, and muttering, "Thy will be done," he lapsed into coma. An hour before dawn on Thursday, the light in the third-floor window went out. After a pontificate that had lasted nearly twenty years, Pope Pius XII was dead.

In the patriarchal palace in Venice, at the same time, Angelo Roncalli was listening to the radio in the hush of his bedroom. An important announcement was promised. His thoughts were fixed on the man with the gaunt face and good heart who had sent him to France with the words, "It was I, monsignor, who thought of you and took this decision, no one else." He prayed for him, as he had repeatedly through those anxious days, and he waited.

Then there came the familiar ringing theme of the Vatican Radio, and the flat, tired voice of Father Francesco Pellegrino reading the last bulletin: "The supreme pontiff is dead. Pope Pius XII, the most esteemed and venerated man in the world, one of

the greatest pontiffs of the century, with sanctity passed away at
3:52 A.M. today, October 9, 1958."

Roncalli rose heavily and went alone to his chapel.

On October 11 he celebrated a High Requiem Mass for the Holy
Father at Saint Mark's. Then he had Gusso pack the bags for the
trip to Rome where he was to bury the dead pope and, in solemn
conclave with the other cardinal princes of the church, to elect
his successor. He took his *cappa magna*, the ceremonial red cape
which he had never worn, which cardinals wear only in paying
first homage to a new pope. But he took little else, none of the
personal papers or books that usually went with him, even on a
short trip. He *wanted* to come back. But as he left his quarters on
the morning of Sunday, October 12, Capovilla noted that he took
a last lingering look around.

Once more he had to pass through Vianello's little flat to reach
the boat landing. The children scurried to make a path so he and
Capovilla could get by; Gusso had already left the mainland by
car with the baggage. He stopped to apologize, saying to Vianello, "Perhaps this is the last time I shall have to disturb you."
Then, suddenly aware of the unintended significance of his
words, he said quickly, "No, no—it is that the repairs will be
finished when I return."

The boat chugged through the waters of the Grand Canal and
all aboard were silent. It was raining and, unlike his entry to the
city, few people watched as he left. There was a small crowd at
the railroad station, some officials, and it was in everyone's mind
how that earlier Venetian patriarch, Giuseppe Sarto, had gone to
a conclave with a return ticket in his pocket but remained in
Rome as Pope Pius X. But when someone wished this for Roncalli, he replied that his own wish was to be back in Venice within
fifteen days. To another he said, "There is a matter I want to
discuss with you when I return."

A last photograph of him in Venice shows him standing in the open window of the train, smiling down at his friends on the platform. There is a certain sadness in the smile, a reflection of the moment, surely, but also perhaps of his most private thoughts as the train began to move. The past, the long preparation, was behind him now, and ahead lay his ultimate destiny.

XI

SOLEMN CONCLAVE

He arrived on Monday morning, October 13, and went at once to the Domus Mariae, headquarters of Women's Catholic Action in Rome, where he was to be quartered until the conclave was actually convened. It stands near the top of the Aventine Hill, a new building overlooking the ancient city and the great dome of Saint Peter's. It seems safe to say that Cardinal Roncalli became familiar with this prospect during the next twelve days, for apart from prescribed obligations at the Vatican he did not often leave his sanctuary.

On that first Monday, the third day of the *novendialia*, he stood in prayer with the other cardinals as the body of the Holy Father, encased in coffins of cypress, lead, and elm, was lowered to the burial crypt beneath the Clementine Chapel. Thereafter, still in the purple cassocks of mourning, the cardinals met each day in the Hall of the Consistory to conduct the business of the Holy See and to prepare for the conclave. Among their more unpleasant duties was the dismissal from Vatican service of Dr.

Riccardo Galeazzi-Lisi, who had been personal physician to Pius XII for the past twenty years. At the end, it appeared, he had also been an uninhibited entrepreneur, having sold to the more sensational picture magazines in Italy and abroad photos and a lurid account of the pontiff's desperate last hours. Soon after, the medical society of Rome struck Galeazzi's name from its membership list.

Sometimes, in the afternoon, Roncalli visited the churches in Rome that had marked the turnings of his life: Santa Maria in Monte Santo where he had been ordained fifty-four years earlier, San Carlo al Corso, the church of Saint Charles Borromeo, where he had been consecrated a bishop. But mostly he remained closeted in the Domus Mariae, thinking and praying. Like the other cardinals, together charged with the awesome obligation of choosing the next vicar of Christ on earth, he was determined to remain apart from the cries and the conjecture that now ran rampant in the world outside. For as no favorite became apparent, as no single name emerged to dominate this *sede vacante*, as had Pacelli's in 1939 and as Montini's would in 1963, the uncertainty mounted to a fever of speculation. Even the staid *L'Osservatore Romano*, which had cautioned against unseemly "guessing games," published biographies of no fewer than twenty-five cardinals said to be *papabili*.

And what did Angelo Roncalli think as the days of the *novendialia* went by? To one visitor he quoted, somewhat ambiguously, the old maxim that he who goes into the conclave a pope comes out a cardinal. Following the requiem for Pius XII, he caught a glimpse of his old secretary, Msgr. Thomas Ryan, then posted at the Vatican, and called out spontaneously, "Don Tomaso, come to see me in Venice after the conclave!"

But from the first, there were some signs of what was to come. A certain group of cardinals, among them the six from France, went out of their way to hearten the patriarch of Venice. By their particular deference they conveyed something that required no further explanation. And there are meaningful lines in Roncalli's letters.

To Enrica, on October 20, he wrote that the family must not believe any newspaper gossip. "These will be days of mystery to me and for many, in fact for all the cardinals. . . . We must look to the Lord and to no one else and not think of any honors or undertakings for the years that still remain to us. . . . So, courage. I am more than ever confident, almost certain, of returning to Venice and Camaitino."

To Montini in Milan he wrote, "I have great need of the help of the saints. Therefore I apply to you, who are very near to the saints of my special devotion (who are buried in Milan). . . . Commend my soul to Saint Ambrose and Saint Charles Borromeo."

On October 24, a day before he entered the conclave, Roncalli sent a letter to Msgr. Giuseppe Pazzi, bishop of Bergamo, which perhaps comes nearest to revealing his feelings in those final hours before the cardinals shut themselves away from the sight of men: "One point about my entrance into the Conclave: it is like an invocation made to all that is dearest to my heart as a good Bergamesque. . . . But it matters little whether the new pope be of the Bergamo region or not. Our combined prayers should be to ensure that the new pope be a wise and gentle leader, that he be a holy man and one who spreads holiness. You will understand what I mean, Excellency. Greetings and an embrace. . . ."

What did Angelo Roncalli think? Certain superficial writings have painted for us a straightforward and simple soul who thought of nothing but the will of God as he disappeared into the Vatican for the vote. But it is a sterile and curiously unsatisfying portrait that takes no account of Roncalli as a human being with private feelings and sensibilities, as a shrewd observer of men and events. And what about his clear references, negative though they were, to his chances of becoming the choice of his brother cardinals? The new pope *need* not be from the Bergamo region. He was *almost* certain of returning to Venice.

But in conceding the alternate possibility, does he not also illuminate some secret corner of his heart for us? Beyond question, he *wanted*, most of all, to return to Venice. But he seems to have been well aware that a certain special series of circumstances, already in the making, might deny him this wish. God's will would be done, yes, of that he was convinced. But as the *noven-dialia* ended and the cardinals, now wearing scarlet robes, gathered in the Pauline Chapel, Angelo Roncalli surely recognized the clear chance that he might well be the instrument of God's will.

In the year 1404, when the sacred college chose Innocent VII to be pope, a contemporary account of the election included this description of the rules of the conclave: "It is a close-built place, without anything to divide it, and it is set apart to the cardinals for the election of the pope; and it must be shut and walled in on all sides, so that, excepting a small wicket for entrance, which is afterwards closed, it shall remain strongly guarded. And therein is a small window for food to be passed in to the cardinals, at their own cost, and this window is so fitted as to open or shut as required. And the cardinals have each a small cell on different floors for sleep and rest."

More than five hundred years later, the essentials of procedure remained unchanged. Each of the fifty-one cardinals who entered the conclave area on the afternoon of Saturday, October 25, was permitted to bring with him two aides, "conclavists." There was also a small work force—two doctors, a clerical staff, firemen, barbers, plumbers, carpenters, and cooks. In all, perhaps 250 people were confined in the sealed-off section of the apostolic palace.

Roncalli had been first among the cardinals to arrive. A little before 3:00 P.M. he passed through the low Archway of the Bells with his conclavists, Capovilla and Gusso. The office of the commandant of the Noble Guard, Cell No. 15, had been designated as his quarters, a small, bare room into which an iron cot had been moved. Capovilla had been assigned to the anteroom. Gusso took one look around, ducked out and returned with a pitcher and wash basin. "At least you will be able to wash here, Eminence," he said.

Roncalli took no notice. Some of the cardinals, the most aged and infirm, had fared better, but most, like Roncalli, were in improvised bedrooms with communal bathing facilities. The bearded, regal Tisserant, dean of the sacred college, was in a corner of the Borgia armory. But no one complained. It was another principle of the conclave that creature comforts should not give the cardinals cause to dally at their task.

Having arranged Roncalli's things as best he could, Gusso went to find his own room, according to the identifying number given him. It turned out to be a tiny kitchen used by the Noble Guards to make coffee. Beyond it was an equally small room, but the second at least had the virtue of privacy. "Well, after all, I can tell about it now," Gusso later revealed with a broad smile. "I didn't know anything about the Vatican, but the aide of Cardinal Ruffini knew it well and he had chosen the little room beyond the kitchen. I saw at once that every time he went in or out he would have to cross through my room and, as he hadn't arrived yet, I asked no questions and just changed the numbers on the doors. I put my suitcase in the other room and left him the kitchen. When he got there he was very shocked, poor fellow, but I just said, 'Well, the numbers—look at the numbers, my friend.' And that was it."

With the conclave area locked from within and without, the cardinals sat down to a simple meal in a refectory set up in the Borgia apartments. Then they went to their separate quarters. The following morning, at exactly 10:00 A.M., they assembled in the Sistine Chapel to begin the voting. Thrones of purple damask were arranged around the walls for them, a canopy above each one. Roncalli sat near the door, next to Cardinal Valeri, his predecessor as nuncio in France.

The Sistine Chapel, built during the papacy of Sixtus IV in the late fifteenth century, is one of the glories of our civilization. Its design is a simple rectangle, 133 feet long and forty-five feet wide. But its lofty vaulted ceiling and the golden light that falls on its magnificent frescoes, on Michelangelo's awesome and incomparable *Last Judgment* at the end wall, make it eminently appropriate as the place where the supreme pontiff of the world's 500 million Roman Catholics is chosen.

On that Sunday, October 26, the patterned stone floor was covered with wood and the wood with green carpet. Before the altar stood an ancient silver chalice into which the cardinals would drop their paper ballots. Behind them, beyond the marble transenna that divides the chapel, was an old black stove in which the ballots would be burned. An improvised chimney, vented through one of the tall windows, was the link between the conclave and the waiting world. White smoke would signal the election of a pope; black smoke meant that no one had yet gained the necessary two-thirds plus one of the votes cast.

Four ballots were taken on Sunday, two in the morning and two in the afternoon, and the smoke was black. Monday it was the same. To the thousands in Saint Peter's square and the millions around the world who hovered around radios and television sets, the days passed without change or hard news. The game of *papabili* went on. New favorites were said to be forging forward, but it was no more than guesswork.

And yet something highly significant *was* happening behind the silent stone and the blank windows. By Monday night the main contending forces, and it is important to remember that the contention was never anything but sedate, had reached an impasse. A mood of compromise prevailed. Perhaps there was one among their number not readily identified with this faction or that. And the name that was often heard in the little informal conferences after the balloting was that of the patriarch of Venice.

According to Capovilla, Roncalli was now shown "the most delicate attention" by the cardinals, as if to "sustain him with the warmth of their filial piety and the promise of devoted attachment." There was a flurry of coming and going around Cell No. 15, the office of the Noble Guard. When someone wondered aloud whether the sign on the door, "*Comandante*," could be an omen, Roncalli said bluntly that he did not believe in omens.

But the archbishop of Turin, Cardinal Maurizio Fossati, assigned to Cell No. 16, watched the activity next door and came to his own conclusion. Later, writing of those pivotal hours, he said, "I do not think I am violating the obligation of secrecy, from which, moreover, I should feel certain of being absolved by the great and kind goodness of the Holy Father [Pope John], if I say that at a particular point a friend felt it necessary to enter a friend's cell *confortans eum*, by way of comforting him."

But the fact is that Roncalli slept well that night. He had listened in silence to the cardinals and now faced the prospect of the next day's vote with a certain detachment. He had put behind him the terrible sense of dread that he was not worthy of the fearsome responsibility, not strong enough for the crushing burden. For as he sat alone, at last, in the little office of the Noble Guard's commander, he felt himself in God's hands. In a personal diary which he had begun to keep in a big desk agenda, and which remains unpublished, he wrote on the night of October 27, "But who is it that rules the church? Is it you or the Holy Ghost? Well, then, Angelo, go to sleep!" And apparently content, added, "I feel as if I were an empty bag that the Holy Spirit unexpectedly fills with strength."

The secrets of a papal election are supposed to be held inviolate by the participants, all of whom are sworn to silence on pain of excommunication. But an assiduous questioner has been known to glean a few facts—though obviously his sources must be protected—and by using this information to supplement what is apparent about the personalities and forces at work, can sometimes reconstruct the essential story.

The first thing that must be understood is that the serviceable labels being bandied about Saint Peter's Square and in much of the world press were arbitrary and generally inapplicable. There were no clear-cut groupings of "reactionaries" or "progressives" among the cardinals, nor were there candidates who could be counted on to become "pastoral" or "political" popes. The distinctions between them were infinitely more subtle, inextricably bound up with theology and doctrine and social leanings, and where there were differences in one area there could easily be overlapping consensus in another.

But there were differences. For the largest part they were between those who wanted to loosen the iron grip of the curia and those who, having gained unusual power in Pius XII's last years, were unwilling to let it go. It was all akin to the not unfamiliar friction between the field forces of an army, here represented by the cardinals with Sees, and its headquarters, or the curia. Confined to the Vatican, the curial cardinals were somewhat removed from the realities of life and tended to oppose change, whereas the cardinal-archbishops of the great cities were every day hard-pressed by life and its modern complications and saw an urgent need for the church to keep up.

The early polling did not reveal the favorite of either side. It was confined to the traditional courtesy ballot, the French voting for Tisserant, many of the Italians for Ruffini, some of the Americans for Spellman, and some for Cardinal Wyszinski of Poland, a victim of both the Nazis and Communists. None could be considered a serious candidate. Roncalli voted for Valeri to emphasize again his belief that the one-time nuncio had been unfairly expelled from France. It was the only vote Valeri received.

But by the time the first day's balloting ended on Sunday afternoon, some illusions had been shattered and a myth dispelled. The advocates of Cardinal Gregory Peter Agagianian, pro-prefect of the Congregation for the Propagation of the Faith, had done nothing to discourage the rumor that he had come into the conclave "more than halfway to Saint Peter's throne." Indeed, he seemed brilliantly suited for the papacy—cultured, learned, pious, an Armenian who had become thoroughly Romanized, a member of the curia with a modern outlook. But though Agagianian was high on everyone's list of *papabili*, he was opposed by Tisserant and others as having become more Roman even than the Italians, or as someone remarked, "more doctrinaire at sixty-three than Pius had been at eighty." In any event his candidacy collapsed on Sunday afternoon when he received only a handful of votes.

Then there were those who clung to the notion that the next pope waited in Milan. There were several versions as to why Pius XII had not conferred the red hat on Giovanni Battista Montini when he sent the faithful *sostituto* off to be archbishop of Milan, the most prevalent theory being that Tardini, the other *sostituto*, somehow prevented it, but to those who favored Montini's more open, innovative social views, this made no difference. There was nothing in canon law that said a pope had to be chosen from the college of cardinals, they repeated to whoever would listen. Any male Catholic was eligible. And apparently there were many who did listen—Montini's name, too, was prominent on the list of *papabili*—but they were all on the outside. Within the conclave, the sacred college was not ready to violate a six hundred-year-old tradition by electing a noncardinal. Montini, who would finally be given the red biretta by John XXIII and become the overwhelming choice of the 1963 conclave, received no votes at all in 1958.

Other frequently mentioned contenders saw their chances blocked on Sunday, too: Ruffini and Ottaviani because they were considered too rigidly conservative; Lercaro, archbishop of Bologna, because of his flamboyant nature. In this connection, Vittorio Gorresio, among the most knowledgeable of the Vatican commentators, quotes a colorful estimate of Lercaro by one of his intimates, Luigi Santucci: "Cardinal Lercaro is—how shall I put it?—an after-school cardinal, a holiday-excursion cardinal, standing outside the gate next to the ice-cream man's cart at the streetcar stop with a packet of sandwiches and a slingshot." Gorresio succinctly concludes, "Lercaro could not be made pope."

Finally, there was some earnest talk about the possibility of a non-Italian pope. But again, such talk was confined to those with a limited grasp of papal politics. For although the non-Italian cardinals were indeed a two-to-one majority of the sacred college, they were scattered among twenty-two nations, hence agreed that, for the time, at least, it was better to continue an old tradition rather than risk stirring new nationalistic passions.

On Monday morning, the real candidate of the curial cardinals was revealed. He was Benedetto Aloisi Masella, aristocratic member of Rome's exclusive ecclesiastic society, one-time nuncio of Portugal, Chile, and Brazil, choice of the sacred college after Pius's death to be *camerlengo*, interim ruler of the Holy Roman church. When the ballots of Monday's second poll were counted, Aloisi Masella seemed certain of election: He had nearly half of all the votes and his supporters were confident of gaining the necessary two-thirds plus one in the afternoon.

But in the afternoon, as one source put it, "we were all at sea again." Aloisi Masella's strength had peaked and begun to recede. For stubbornly, skillfully, a small group led by Tisserant and the French cardinals, determined to loosen the curia's hold on church affairs, clustered their vote on a single candidate, someone they had reason to believe amenable to change, Angelo Roncalli. And holding fast, they began to gain votes. In a fresh effort to win the day, the more conservative cardinals now threw their forces behind Giuseppe Siri, archbishop of Genoa. But Siri was only fifty years old and the possibility that he might still be pope in the year 2000 did not greatly appeal to a body of men whose average age was seventy-three. It was this moment, the final vote on Monday, to which Roncalli referred when four years later, in a "summary of great graces bestowed on a man who thinks poorly of himself," he wrote of his first grace, "To have accepted with simplicity the honor and the burden of the pontificate, with the joy of being able to say that I did nothing to obtain it, absolutely nothing; indeed I was most careful and conscientious to avoid anything that might direct attention to myself. As the voting in Conclave wavered to and fro, I rejoiced when I saw the chances of my being elected diminishing and the likelihood of others, in my opinion truly most worthy and venerable persons, being chosen."

But if on Monday afternoon he still thought Siri or Aloisi

Masella might prevail, the unavoidable truth must have come clear to him by evening. Later he would say, "I knew by certain signs that I would be chosen." These signs were the visits to Cell No. 15 by so many of his colleagues. Although his final vote total of the day was modest, no more than twelve or fifteen, the cardinals came to urge courage on him, to express confidence, to pledge their loyalty.

In the two ballots on Tuesday morning, gaining the votes of nearly all the moderates as well as a few from the curial contingent, he passed ahead of the other candidates. In the Sala Ducale of the Borgia apartments, where Capovilla waited nervously with the other conclavists, a rumor that a "Roncalli tide" had begun was whispered along. And during luncheon, while Roncalli concentrated on his food, Tisserant, at the far side of the table, said with some satisfaction that this might well be the cardinals' final meal together.

Why, to the great surprise of the waiting millions, did the sacred college turn to Angelo Roncalli? He was, after all, little known to the outside world, rarely seen at the Vatican and less understood there. Was it only that the cardinals sought a *papa di passagio* (a transitional pope) as has been so widely reported, an elderly, essentially harmless caretaker to bridge the gap between Vatican moderates and conservatives, someone to hold the creaky machinery of the Holy See together for a few years while the church fathers weighed what to do next and prepared for the succession of an activist pope? For Montini?

There are elements of truth in all this speculation. But there was no shortage of suitably aged worthies among the princes of the church and the reason Roncalli was elected and the others were not is disarmingly simple—which may explain why it has been generally overlooked. In the end, he not only had the least opposition, but his positive virtues began to look more and more attractive to the deadlocked electors. No one any longer disputed his natural gifts as a statesman. His goodness and simplicity had always been apparent. The French had not forgotten his courage in the matter of the accused bishops and the worker-priests. The cardinal-archbishops believed he would close the gap between the church and a swiftly changing world. And even the curial conservatives valued his loyalty and unwavering obedience to Pius XII.

So, as the cardinals gathered again on the afternoon of Tuesday, October 28, a different excitement, not doubt but anticipation, held sway in the majestic Sistine Chapel. And as the eleventh ballot began, as the reverend fathers once more marked their voting papers and one by one carried them forward to the altar, it was clear that the elaborate ritual of election was moving into its last culminating moments. Each cardinal in turn knelt in silent prayer, then said aloud, "I call to witness Christ the Lord, my judge, that I am electing him who I believe should be elected by God's will." His ballot was then placed in the chalice. When all had voted, three cardinal-scrutineers read out the name on each ballot, the others keeping count in their canopied thrones. And time after time the name called out was, "The very reverend Cardinal Roncalli." When they had finished, the patriarch of Venice had many more than the requisite thirty-five votes.

In a sudden stillness, in the moment that became a prelude to history, Cardinal Tisserant, with that proud bearded head that might have been one of Michelangelo's frescoed prophets come to life, walked slowly to where Roncalli sat pale and silent and, in the midst of all the others, already alone. Tisserant, dean of the sacred college, stood before him and spoke in traditional Latin. "Do you accept your election, which has been performed canonically?" he asked.

Again the silence hung quivering among them. It seemed to last a long time but was only a moment frozen in the minds of those who listened so intently. Then Angelo Roncalli replied, "Listening to your voice, 'I tremble and am afraid' and what I know of my own poorness and insignificance is enough to explain my confusion. But seeing in the votes of my brother cardinals of our Holy Roman church the sign of God's will, I accept the choice they have made. I bow my head and my shoulders to the chalice of bitterness and the yoke of the cross. On the solemnity of Christ the King we have all sung: 'The Lord is our judge, the Lord is our lawgiver; the Lord is our King. He will save us.' "

In the instant that he spoke the words, "I accept," he became the pope. The other cardinals pulled the cords that lowered the canopies over their thrones in signal that they were no longer his equals. Now Tisserant asked, "By what name do you wish to be called?"

"*Vocabor Johannes*" ("I will be called John").

It was the first surprise of his papacy. In breaking with the succession of Piuses that, with few exceptions, had ruled the church for nearly two hundred years, he turned not to Benedict or Leo, the great popes of his youth, but all the way back to the John XXII of the fourteenth century. A hundred years later, when there had been three rival claimants to the crown of Saint Peter, there had even been an antipope John XXIII. Now Angelo Roncalli produced some notes and told why he had chosen this name: "The name John is dear to me because it is the name of my father. It is dear because it is the title of the humble parish church where we received baptism. It is the solemn name of innumerable cathedrals throughout the world, and first of all the blessed and holy Lateran basilica, our cathedral. It is the name which, in the long series of Roman pontiffs, has been most used. Indeed there have been twenty-two unquestionably legitimate supreme pontiffs named John. Nearly all had a brief pontificate."

This was his little joke, irresistible even on so solemn an occasion. He went on:

> We have preferred to shield the smallness of our own name
> behind this magnificent succession of Roman pontiffs. . . .
> But we love the name of John, so dear to us and to all the
> church, particularly because it was borne by two men who
> were closest to Christ the Lord, the divine Redeemer of all
> the world and Founder of the Church: John the Baptist . .

and John the disciple and Evangelist. . . . May God dispose
that both these Johns shall plead in all the church for our
most humble pastoral ministry. . . .

My children, love one another. Love one another, because
this is the greatest commandment of the Lord. Venerable
brethren, may God in his mercy grant that, bearing the name
of the first of this series of supreme pontiffs, we can, with the
help of divine grace, have his sanctity of life and his strength
of soul, unto the shedding of our blood, if God so wills.

So, in this first little address, widely reprinted the following
day, Pope John revealed the essential faith, the simple spirit of
love, to which the millions around the world of every religion and
of no religion soon responded.

When John had finished speaking, Msgr. Alberto di Jorio,
secretary of the conclave, approached bearing the white zuchetto,
or skullcap, worn by the popes. John immediately took off his
own red biretta and put it on di Jorio's head. It was another
surprise, revival of a custom fifty years in disuse. It meant that in
reward for his services to the sacred college, di Jorio would be
elevated to cardinal at the next consistory.

Now John went alone to the main altar to pray, returning then
to sign the Act of Acceptance before retiring to the little sacristy
of the Sistine Chapel to change into papal vestments. It was then
that Capovilla and Gusso learned that *their* cardinal was now the
pope. While the other conclavists were ushered into another
room, they were led through the Sistine Chapel to the sacristy. It
was an emotional moment. "Well, you see what has happened to
me," said Pope John.

Capovilla was too overcome to speak, but automatically began
helping the pontiff into the white robes. Unhappily, though the
official tailors had provided pontifical habits in a variety of sizes to
fit the other *papabili*, Roncalli's more than two hundred pounds
defied the largest of them. "I feel trussed up and ready for delivery," John quipped as Capovilla drew the cassock as tight as he
could and concealed the gap with the surplice.

Gusso, meanwhile, had been sent back to the Domus Mariae to

fetch some things needed by the pope, particularly his own shoes, as he could barely squeeze into the ones provided. But Gusso returned disconsolately in just a few minutes. As the conclave was still closed, he reported, Cardinal Tisserant refused to let him leave. John cleared his throat and gave his first pontifical order, "You may say to His Eminence Cardinal Tisserant that, as the pope requires his shoes, he has given you permission to leave the conclave."

As it happens, the conclave was not to be broken until the following day. Returning to the Sistine Chapel to bless the kneeling cardinals, Pope John asked them to remain with him inside the conclave area for one more night. It was the last time he would have them all together, he said, and before they went off in their separate directions, while they were still undistracted by the world around, he wanted to seek their counsel in a series of "family gatherings."

This unprecedented departure from tradition provoked a moment of comic drama. A sizable group of prelates, Tardini among them, having seen the white smoke and eager to offer obeisances to the new pope, burst in upon the conclave through the door Gusso opened to leave. Appalled at this breach of canon law, the stately Tisserant stopped them in their tracks and solemnly proclaimed that they had incurred the punishment of excommunication. Later, when someone, in awestruck tones, told John what had happened, he smiled amiably and said, "Well, we shall have to use our new influence to absolve the unfortunates."

It was now nearly 6:00 P.M. Standing on the central balcony of the basilica, Cardinal Canali was looking out over that expectant sea of faces in Saint Peter's, the voices suddenly stilled, the tension almost audible as the hundreds of thousands strained to hear the name of the new pope. "*Habemus Papam!*" Canali said, and they cheered. "He is my most eminent and revered lord, Cardinal Angelo Giuseppe Roncalli." And behind the whispered surprise came the thunder of approval. "*Habemus Papam!*"

Pope John was making his way to the balcony. Any number of officials swooped around him, darting in to adjust his robes or to remind him of this or that nicety of protocol. Suddenly he scattered them with a vigorous, "That's enough! No more fussing over me! Do you want me to trip in front of all these people?" Then he stepped into the glare of the lights, into the gaze of the whole world.

Meanwhile the news had reached Sotto il Monte. Zaverio and Alfredo, having come in from a hard day's work in the field, heard it on the radio just as they sat down to supper. They were stunned into silence. They sat listening a while longer as the soup grew cold, then went to put on their good dark suits, bought for the trip to Paris. By the time they had dressed, the first of the excited neighbors was already pounding on the door of the Colombera.

Assunta was out buying bread when the news came over the baker's radio. "My God," she gasped aloud, "little Angelo!"

Another shopper, alarmed at the way her face had paled, asked, "What's the matter?"

"My brother has just been elected pope," she said.

And Battista, driving back that night from Faenza to Fusignano, a small working-class town where he had been posted as chaplain, saw a crowd gathered in front of the rectory. He thought at first that they might be local Communists come to agitate over some issue or other. And indeed he recognized the faces of a good many Communists among the people who rushed to swarm around his little Fiat 500, but it was not agitation that they had in mind.

"Your uncle has been made the pope!" someone shouted. And there were other voices calling, "It's true! It's true!" as he got out of the car. Hands groped for his and other hands pounded his back in congratulation.

"I couldn't believe it," he recalled. "I didn't want to believe it. At his age I wanted for him a little rest and comfort, not all those new burdens."

He heard the church bells ringing and still didn't believe it.

Inside the rectory, some priests were bent over a radio and he recognized the voice of his sister Enrica. She was being interviewed at the Camaitino, explaining that this was the dining room, and this the study of her uncle, Cardinal Roncalli.

"Pope John," the announcer corrected.

"Pope John," she said, hesitantly, as if she did not believe it either.

Don Battista felt confused and light-headed. *What is she doing?* he wondered. *What is it all about?* Then someone handed him a telegram from Rome and finally he understood:

"First blessing/Come at once/Capovilla."

The new pope had completed the traditional *Urbi et Orbi*, his apostolic blessing on the city and the world. He stood a little longer in the blaze of lights on the balcony, looking out on the thousands who rose from their knees and gazed back at him. Then he went back inside. And the people began to leave, to return to their homes and their own lives. But they spoke only of the new pope, John XXIII, as they moved slowly out of the piazza, and they asked, "Will he be good?"

XII

THE VATICAN CITY

"Today they made me pope," he wrote in the diary on October 28. But even in those first hours of dash and drama following his election, there welled up in him again the black doubt, the human inability to grasp and hold to so stunning a truth: that he, Angelo Giuseppe Roncalli—"the poor son of [Giovanni] Battista and Marianna, certainly both good Christians, but so modest and humble!"—was now the pope.

In the evening he sat down to a last meal in the company of the cardinals, but took only a cup of tea. Then he retired with Monsignor Dell'Acqua, who had been his aide for a time in Turkey and was now in the Secretariat of State, and together they composed a first message to the world. It was to be a plea for peace. Later, in the stillness of the middle of the night, he sat alone in the unfamiliar surroundings of the first-floor Vatican apartment normally occupied by the cardinal secretary of state, a post Pius had long left vacant. During the conclave it served as the quarters of Aloisi Masella, the cardinal *camerlengo*, and now had been hastily made ready for the new pope until he took over the papal apartments on the fourth floor.

Here Capovilla found him, long past midnight, quietly reading his breviary. When the secretary asked whether there was anything more to be done and urged him to retire, John replied that the events of the day had caused him to fall behind in his devotions. "I will say vespers, then go to bed," he said.

Still he did not sleep. "I spent the entire night in prayer," he later confided to the French author Henri Daniel-Rops. "It was such a burden that I now had, such a weight. But the Lord wished it."

In the morning, following a mass for the cardinals in the Sistine Chapel, John delivered his appeal for peace. It was broadcast in thirty-six languages by Vatican Radio and addressed directly to the rulers of nations:

> Why is it that our divisions and disagreements are still not able to be settled on the basis of fairness? Why should the resources of human ingenuity and the riches of nations turn so often to the production of arms—pernicious instruments of death and destruction—instead of improving the welfare of all classes of citizens, and particularly of those who live in poverty? . . . Take action, boldly and with confidence, and may heaven's inspiration be given to each of you, and may divine aid be yours. Look at the people entrusted to you and listen to their voices. What do they seek? What do they implore of you? Not these new monstrous instruments of war which our times have produced and which can annihilate us all—not these, but peace.

Soon after, the conclave was officially ended. Vatican Radio announced, "The pontificate of John XXIII has begun."

Among his first visitors was a delegation of clerics and lay friends from Bergamo, one of whom was the journalist Gabriele Carrara. John was still wearing the improvised white robes in which he had greeted the faithful in Saint Peter's Square the evening before, safety pins tucking folds of fabric up under his armpits, and on his face, according to Carrara, "the look of a man who walks with a heavy load." He greeted them all warmly, struggled with the strange new intricacies of proper papal address, which requires the pontiff to refer to himself by the imperial "we," then, typically, gave in to his irrepressible and sometimes antic wit: "I ask you to forgive me if I have not yet mastered the ceremony and protocol of this new office. As you know, the gifts of the Holy Ghost do not, unhappily, include the gift of papal style. But my good collaborators will educate me and we are confident that slowly, slowly, we shall grow accustomed to the standards of dignity and tact one expects of a pope."

But his diary notes for October 29, a plaintive cry for the spiritual support of departed loved ones, reflect his continuing anxiety. "Today the whole world is talking and writing only about me, my name and myself. O Mama, O Father, Grandfather Angelo, Uncle Zaverio, where are you? Who brought us to such honor? Pray for me!"

And then, sometime during those crowded hours, he found the strength he needed. Capovilla has told how John finally confronted his apprehension by resolving to speak to the pope about it. And as the realization that *he* was the pope finally sank in, he squared himself and said aloud, "Very well, I will speak to our Lord God about it!" and turning a serene and confident face to the world, he took up the awesome burdens of his office.

The press, captivated by his unassuming openness and peasant vitality, soon went about demolishing the myth of John as a transitional or interim pope, which the journalists themselves, in astonishment at the election of this comparative unknown, had earlier conjured up. Now, as the new pope broke with one time-encrusted precedent after another, more than one Vatican observer was reminded of Felice Peretti, the remarkable Franciscan who became Pope Sixtus V in 1585. Peretti had entered the conclave bearing down on a cane, feeble, seemingly ill beyond hope of recovery. But as soon as the ballots were counted, he straightened up, threw away the cane and began a five-year reign of robust reform, animating the church with his great spirit and restoring the splendor of the pontifical state.

The very choice of his papal name characterized John as his own man. Most often, the name by which a new pope chooses to be known is that of the recent predecessor whose program or personal style he most valued, so that this first decision may well suggest something about the nature of policies to come. In going back to a name that had been in disrepute for more than five centuries, Roncalli was not only braving the ghost of the antipope who had usurped the papal throne as John XXIII, but he was also declaring that he meant to be free to shape his own pontificate. His devotion to the name, borne by his father and saints close to his heart, is unquestioned. But there were seasoned students of the church who guessed at once that the choice also marked John as a pope about to set out on a course unimagined by the Piuses and Leos of the past two hundred years.

There were other signs. As popes are traditionally crowned on Sunday, all Rome and most of the Vatican court assumed that John's coronation would take place on November 9. Instead, he fixed the date for the fourth, a Tuesday—the Feast Day of Saint Charles Borromeo. In his first major appointment, he named his one-time superior, Tardini, to be pro-secretary of state. As a *sostituto*, Tardini's responsibility had been limited to the Office of Extraordinary (foreign) Affairs, while for nearly fifteen years Pius XII himself tried to direct even trifling details of the church's inner workings. Now Tardini, the tough and forthright old Roman, would head both sections of the Secretariat of State and, as the new pope's closest policy adviser, be assured the red hat at the next consistory. John further opened the papal doors by reestablishing *di tabella* audiences, those at which congregational heads and curial officials could count on meeting with the pope at fixed times during the week. These had been suspended during Pius's illness in 1954 and never restored.

On October 30, John sent for Count Giuseppe della Torre,

editorial director of *L'Osservatore Romano*, the semi-official
voice of the Holy See. If the venerable count was surprised by
the summons—he had not been honored by a private audience
with the pope in twelve years—he was stunned speechless when
its purpose came clear to him.

With tradition-bound obduracy, *L'Osservatore Romano*
flowered its every reference to the pope with such phrases as
"The Illuminated Holy Father" and "The Highest Pontiff," and
prefaced accounts of his public statements with the likes of, "The
chosen one, in his inspired and sublime discourse . . ." or, "As
we gathered from the august lips. . . ." Now, having congratulated della Torre for long and distinguished service, John came
briskly to the point: He wished an end to this inflated and
convoluted terminology.

"This is the twentieth century," he said pointedly. "Let us have
a style that suits the times. Wouldn't it be better simply to write,
'The pope said this,' or 'The pope did that.'?"

The stricken look on della Torre's aristocratic face impelled
John to soften his words. "I myself would prefer it," he said
gently. And, at the other's final wince of pain, hastily corrected
himself: "*We* would prefer it."

His nephew Battista arrived amid the chaos of that second day,
around seven o'clock in the evening. But having forgotten to
bring Capovilla's telegram and being somewhat intimidated by the
impersonal grandeur of the Vatican Palace, which he was seeing
for the first time, poor Battista failed to excite any interest with
his wan assertions about who he was and that he had come to see
his uncle the pope. The fact that the mother tongue of most Swiss
Guards is German did not help. Finally he found someone who
could be persuaded to let him use a telephone and he called
Capovilla.

"Where are you?" the secretary cried out at once. "The Holy
Father keeps asking for you!"

"I am down here—somewhere. They won't let me pass."

Soon enough his whereabouts were pinpointed and a moment
later Guido Gusso came hurrying down to usher him up through

the maze of marble loggias. Then came the emotional first meeting. This is how Battista remembers it:

> There were so many important people in the antechamber, monsignori and other men who must have been ambassadors, and they did not look at me kindly when I passed in front of them. The door of his study was open and I could see him there, all dressed in white, and I stopped, for I wanted to cry for him, knowing what a burden he must now carry to the end of his days, and that he would never see Sotto il Monte again. He looked so tired. Then Gusso told me to go ahead, he was waiting, and someone called out, "Don't forget to kneel three times!" and all of a sudden—I don't even remember if I kneeled or not—he was embracing me.

There was a moment of awkward silence. The pope stood beaming at his nephew while Battista, by now turbulently unsettled, groped for something to say. "I couldn't think of anything. I didn't know whether to sit or stand. I didn't even know what to call him—uncle, Your Holiness, what."

Finally John spoke, "Are you hungry? You have had a long trip."

"No, no."

"Thirsty, then?—it is so hot."

And despite Battista's protests he bustled about trying to order something to drink, glaring first at a bewildering array of bells and buttons on the desk, then striding back to the door to summon one of the dignitaries from the antechamber. The poor man, a monsignor who was clearly not of the household staff, listened dumfounded as the Holy Father, feigning vast indignation, exclaimed, "What kind of place do they run here? Here is my nephew, who has come all the way from Faenza for a visit, and there is no one to offer him a bit of refreshment."

"I will see to it at once, Holiness," the disconcerted cleric said. "Whatever Your Holiness desires."

"What would you like, Battista? An orangeade?"

"Yes, an orangeade."

Still, nearly an hour passed before an attendant finally brought the drink. By this time uncle and nephew were engrossed in a member-by-member survey of the Roncalli clan. John, who had isolated himself from the world at the moment of his arrival in Rome two and a half weeks before, now wanted all the news of Sotto il Monte, and of the relatives who had scattered from the native village. He asked particularly about Battista's sister Giuseppina, to whom he had given the sacred veil and who now, as Sister Maria Angela, served as a nurse with the Daughters of Our Lady of the Sacred Heart of Issoudun at nearby Monte Sacro. Why hadn't she come to see him? he asked. She was so close. When Battista replied that it must be because she was too shy to dare the complexities of the Vatican alone, John said at once, "Very well, you must spend the night here and go and fetch her tomorrow!"

This Battista did, but again there was difficulty in gaining admission to the inner sanctums. Waiting forlornly in a corridor, the brother and sister were lectured by an overprotective monsignor who, taking no note of their explanations, kept droning, "It is simply not possible to open these doors to every priest and nun who want to see the pope."

This time, though, it was John himself who rescued them. Marching by in the midst of a solemn cortege, he spied despairing Battista and Sister Angela and immediately broke out of the procession, throwing chamberlains and assorted ecclesiastics into confusion. "Here are my niece and nephew!" he beamed, introducing them amid a nervous swirl of cassocks. Someone tugged at his sleeve and whispered urgently, "Your Holiness, we are awaited—the benediction. . . ."

But he would not stir until assured that Battista and Sister Angela would be properly looked after. They were brought to him later on and, after another happily distracted hour of family talk, Battista was cheered: Today his uncle seemed truly at peace. When he asked, "How did you sleep this night, Holiness?" John replied with the ancient Italian expression of well-being: "Just like a pope."

But there were complications, sudden and inevitable pressures in the once easy relationships with his family. John was approached by officials who, in the traditional manner, asked whether he would elevate his brothers to the nobility and invest them with some princely title. It was even within his power to move them to quarters inside the Vatican where they could hold court. John brushed all this aside. His brothers would be known as the brothers of the pope, which is what they were, no more, and that was enough. Their greatest nobility, he said, would be that they would remain in their meager homes in Sotto il Monte, as they wished to do. Zaverio, Alfredo, and Giuseppe themselves declined when the mayor of Bergamo proposed to honor them with the title of *Cavalieri della Repubblica Italiana.*

Then there was the matter of John's housekeeper. There was a spate of early rumors that Sister Angela would succeed to the post. But it was a sensitive matter, particularly in view of the storms stirred up by the late Pope Pius's housekeeper, the imperious Sister Pasqualina. A Bavarian nun who had zealously guarded Pius's health and private life for forty years, Sister Pasqualina had no qualms about intruding into church affairs when what she conceived to be the pope's welfare was at issue. This was no secret. John Foster Dulles, then American secretary of state, told how she once marched into the pope's study and interrupted their conference to announce that Pius's lunch was ready. Whereupon His Holiness rose and, apologizing to Dulles, said, "There is no power on earth that would stay our good mother Pasqualina when soup is on the table."

As it turned out, Sister Angela was not appointed John's housekeeper. As her training was in surgical nursing, it is doubtful that she was ever seriously considered, nor was any member of the Roncalli family employed in the Vatican. Eventually three Bergamo nuns were chosen to see to the new pope's meals and housekeeping needs, and served in contented anonymity.

John took over the papal apartment on October 30. The seals, affixed at almost the moment of Pius's death, were broken and the new pope, with his books, some family photographs, and little else, moved in. Actually, although the entire papal suite consisted of some twenty-two rooms, John was to confine his nonpublic life to a sparsely furnished bedroom, study, and dining room, the same ones used by his two predecessors. In the bedroom, which overlooks Saint Anne's Gate and the vast piazza, he hung pictures of his mother and father. Then, in the afternoon, he set out to inspect the Vatican City-State, of which he was now absolute ruler.

The pope is supreme pontiff for the world's 500 million Catholics; he is primate of the Italian nation and bishop of the city of Rome. And the Vatican, a tiny temporal kingdom of not quite 110 acres, is the core of this wider sway, the nerve center and beating heart of the church. John, the first twentieth-century pope never to have lived or worked there before his election, knew little about its geography and inner mechanisms and, curious about all of it, turned up in the most unexpected places. In the carpentry shop, he ordered wine for the startled workmen, and they toasted his health. At the Vatican Radio, whose broadcasting station is built on the high ground at the extreme western end of Vatican City, the sole occupant when he arrived was an announcer, so undone by the sudden appearance of the pope that he stammered, "N—no one is here, Holiness."

"Nonsense, you are here," John replied affably. "Come, show me how things work."

A story told by the journalists Charlotte and Denis Plimmer about these days of orientation has it that a visitor, lost in the complex of corridors and courtyards, wandered into a huge and splendid chamber of mirrored walls. It was a room in which an outsider clearly had no business, but once he had closed the ornate door behind him the hapless soul could not find his way out. Wherever he turned, his own agonized image gaped back at him until, defeated, he watched his reflection helplessly. There he stood in terrified expectancy, as one of the great mirrors slowly swung toward him, and into the room stepped the pope. Evaluating the situation at a glance, John roguishly put a finger to his lips and whispered, "Shh, I'm lost too."

There were aspects of the rigorous protocol to which he could not accustom himself. One was the tradition that the pope must eat alone, a long-ago and long-redundant reform that had been intended, centuries before, to guard against orgies of unseemly feasting in the seat of Catholic Christianity. This was absolutely contrary to John's gregarious nature. After suffering through a week of solitary meals during which he felt, he said, like a seminarian under punishment, he simply gave it up. "I searched all through the sacred scripture for whatever it is that requires the pope to eat alone and I found nothing. So now I have an occasional guest and am much more comfortable."

It troubled him, too, that even intimate aides dropped to their knees every time they came into his presence. It was a custom so firmly fixed in the Vatican routine that in the time of Pius XII, it is said, officials knelt even when the pope called them on the telephone. John could not abide that sort of exaggerated ceremony. It ran counter to his Bergamesque sense of brotherhood and he was continually ordering people to their feet. When an aged reporter from L'Osservatore Romano assured him that he was perfectly comfortable conducting an interview from his knees, John threatened to leave the room unless the man sat in a chair. Guido Gusso, who genuflected three times on each of the dozen or more occasions that he saw the pope in the course of the day, protested that he could not help himself. "It is a force stronger than I am, Holiness."

"Very well, but once is enough," John said wearily. "Don't you think I believe you the first time?"

The ambassador of an Arab country arrived to present his credentials. He began by reading a long and predictably florid speech, which John interrupted at the first pause: "Come, Your Excellency, let us hand these formal addresses to our aides. Then you and I can go into my library and have a good talk."

But he could not change everything. He was too sensitive to the feelings of others. One was the maestro di camera, or chief chamberlain, Msgr. Mario Nasalli Rocca di Corneliano, who had to contend with this new pope's stubborn egalitarian streak. Once Nasalli Rocca followed in numb amazement as the Holy Father escorted a visitor from the library through a series of ante-chambers and all the way out to the stairway leading down to the Saint Damasus courtyard. Returning, the chamberlain gently explained that this sort of thing simply was not done: people, no matter what their rank, came to the supreme pontiff, who received them and bade them farewell in his own quarters.

"But this is my house," said John. "I was merely showing a guest to the door."

Nonetheless, soon after, John shook a visitor's hand in the doorway of his private library and said ruefully, "I'd like to show you out but Monsignor Nasalli Rocca doesn't like me to do that."

The first time he was carried aloft in the *sedia gestatoria*, the golden throne chair, he looked down on the heads of the people below and sadly remarked, "It's windy up here."

.

On the evening of November 3, the family of Pope John—the three remaining brothers and his sister Assunta, and perhaps thirty nieces and nephews—arrived from Sotto il Monte at the Termini Station in Rome for the coronation of their beloved Don Angelo. They were dressed in somber Sunday black and held their straw suitcases and paper packages close. It is not surprising that the stir and bustle of a metropolitan railroad station bewildered them. But when a covey of Vatican ministers and prelates swooped down to escort them into the dignitaries' lounge and peppered them with deference—including the honorary title, Your Excellency, accorded to close relatives of a reigning pontiff —they were too stupefied to speak, even to each other. And so the ill-matched assemblage sat nervously perched on chair edges, the simple country people unsure of what to do with their hands, and the church officials straining to make polite conversation. Eventually two buses arrived to transport them to the Vatican. At the moment they were led into the pope's presence the tension was broken.

"He was the same as always," Enrica said, "full of tenderness for each one and little jokes for all. He could see that some of us had tears in our eyes and he said, 'Come, come, no crying. After all, it is not so bad what they have done to me.'"

Zaverio recalled his remark that so many young men from Bergamo had taken holy orders that "one of us was bound to grow up and become pope."

Later they were taken for the night to the Domus Mariae, the same pilgrim center where John had been quartered on his arrival from Venice in what now seemed to them all like another lifetime. Early next morning they were driven to Saint Peter's and, in the basilica, seated in a special tribune near the papal throne, in the midst of the thousands—royalty, ministers, diplomats, representing the sovereigns and heads of state of fifty-one nations—all come to see Pope John XXIII crowned as the 262nd supreme pontiff of the Roman Catholic church.

For John, the day had begun before dawn when he wakened to study again the long and complex coronation ritual. Throughout the service, he was to have at his side Msgr. Enrico Dante, prefect of pontifical ceremonies, the ranking authority on liturgical procedures, but was still bent on mastering the details himself. Soon after 8:00 A.M., the papal procession of nearly three hundred, having assembled in the Sistine Chapel, marched to Saint Peter's in majestic and rigidly prescribed array, breastplated Swiss Guards, members of the papal court and household, the sacred college of cardinals in capes of ermine-trimmed red silk, various patriarchs and bishops, more Swiss Guards. Eight strong men bore the *sedia gestatoria* which swayed perceptibly as Pope John, wearing the sacred vestments, blessed the crowd.

When the cortege reached the atrium of the basilica, a choir burst into triumphant song, *"Tu es Petrus"* ("Thou art Peter"), and the multitudes that spilled from the piazza out into the Via della Conciliazione roared in insistent cadence, *"Viva il Papa! Viva il Papa! Viva il Papa!"*

Twelve silver trumpets rang out, then sounded again in Saint Peter's echoing heights. Three times before the procession reached the main altar it was halted by the pontifical master of ceremonies, who then touched flame to a handful of flax. As the ball flared and swiftly burned itself out before the pope's eyes, Monsignor Dante intoned the ancient reminder that men are short-lived and their works ephemeral: "*Pater sancte, sic transit gloria mundi*" ("Holy Father, so passes the glory of the world").

The basilica blazed with the light of ten thousand electric candles. The pillars were hung with crimson and gold, and the bronze statue of Saint Peter draped with full pontifical robes and crowned with a triple miter. Television cameras beamed the spectacle across Europe and an American motion picture crew, in that time before satellite relay, was prepared to rush its film across the Atlantic for broadcast in the United States that very night.

The coronation mass lasted nearly five hours. It was noted that, throughout, the seventy-seven-year-old pontiff drank only one glass of water and that his voice remained sonorous and strong. From time to time his eyes sought out the weathered faces of his brothers and sister and, after the singing of the gospels—"Thou art Peter, and upon this rock I will build my church; and the gates of hell shall not prevail against it"—he surprised the entire assemblage and the ten million distant watchers by speaking directly to them, revealing something of the kind of pope he hoped to be: "There are those who expect the pontiff to be a man of state, a diplomat, an organizer, or one whose mind is attuned to every form of modern knowledge. Oh, venerable brothers and beloved sons . . . the fact is that the new pope, through the happenings of life, is like the son of Jacob who, meeting with his brothers, showed them the tenderness of his heart and, bursting into tears, said, 'I am Joseph, your brother.' The new pope, let us repeat, holds in his mind's eye the splendid image drawn by Saint John, the image of the Good Shepherd."

After the mass was ended, the pontiff was presented with a white silk purse filled with twenty-five historic coins, traditional payment at Saint Peter's "for a mass well sung." Then the procession reformed and Pope John, in the *sedia gestatoria*, was carried up the broad Scala Regia to the Hall of Benedictions and out to the central balcony where a platform had been built so the papal throne could be seen by the surging mass in the piazza. The most auspicious moment, the actual coronation, had been saved for the people, and as John took his place on the throne they waved and cheered and some wept.

The choir sang but one hymn, "Crown of Gold upon His Head," and Cardinal Tisserant uttered the only prayer, the Lord's Prayer. Then Cardinal Canali placed the jeweled triple crown, symbolizing the sanctifying, ruling, and teaching powers of the church, upon the pontiff's head. At the same time, he recited the ancient Latin formula: "Receive the tiara adorned with three crowns and know that thou art the father of princes and kings, pontiff of the whole world, and vicar on this earth of our Savior Jesus Christ, to whom is honor and glory, world without end."

It was nearly 1:00 P.M. Wearing the tiara, John stepped to the balustrade and gave his blessing to the hundreds of thousands whose faces were turned expectantly to his. Many had arrived before daylight and waited through a wet gray morning for this moment. Then, as they cried again and again, "*Viva il Papa!*" he passed through the open doors into the Hall of Benedictions.

He found time to express his gratitude to everyone who had had a part in the ceremonies. For the eight men who had carried the *sedia gestatoria* he had special thanks, and a broad smile, "You should really be paid extra for carrying us since we weigh so much more than our predecessor." Turning to a group of friends from Bergamo and Venice, he again referred to being borne about by uniformed men, which he really did not like. He noted that seventy years had passed since he had been carried on his father's shoulders. They had been seventy years of service to God, he said, then added, "The secret of all this is to let oneself be carried by God, and to carry him."

A visitor asked how he found Rome compared with other cities in which he had lived. His agile mind called up the names of two Vatican aides, Cardinal Canali and Monsignor Dell' Acqua, which, in Italian, mean canals and water, and he punned, "Rome is most like Venice. Here, too, we are surrounded by Canali and Dell' Acqua."

But of course it was not like Venice at all, nor like any of the other far-flung places where he had served the church. Here, in Rome, in a very real sense, he *was* the church, and all its world-wide problems were his. He didn't flinch, mainly because he had no conscious plan to revolutionize the church, nor even any expectation that he would greatly change it. Wherever he had gone he had exercised his authority according to a favorite maxim: to see everything, to turn a blind eye to much of it, to correct a little. Now, in Rome, in the beginning at least, it seemed that this same gentle patience would mark his papacy.

His style, however, was something else, and stood out at once in stark contrast to that of the austere and long-ailing Pius XII. John liked having people around him and soon filled the apartments on the second and third floors with new appointees to long-empty offices. Now the windows of the apostolic palace, shrouded in darkness during all the last years of Pius's reign, beamed cheerily down on Saint Peter's square, conveying to the populace something of the lively new spirit of this new regime. Although John took to calling himself the prisoner of the Vatican, he left it often enough to cause those responsible for his security anxious moments. If there was one symbol that marked his unwillingness to submit to the customarily passive papal life-style, it was his shoes. Every pope in living memory had worn slippers of red velvet. But these would hardly have served for John's frequent forays beyond the Vatican walls, and early on he commissioned a shoemaker to make him some good stout walking shoes, which were then dyed the required red hue.

Monsignor Heim, the Swiss who had been John's secretary when he was nuncio in Paris and had since become an expert at heraldry, was chosen to design a coat of arms for the new pope. It turned out to be much like the one he had used as patriarch of Venice, a tower symbolizing his family origins, lilies for service in

France, and the winged lion of Saint Mark of the Republic of Venice. John asked for only a single change: the lion, he said, looked too fierce; he wanted "a gentle Venetian lion that doesn't frighten anybody."

He was aware of his surging popularity among the people and concerned from the first lest his person, as opposed to his spiritual authority, become a cult object. Through God's divine intervention he had succeeded to the throne of Saint Peter, but he could not forget that beneath the fine red stole he was still Angelo Roncalli whose people for generations had worked the Lombard soil. Once, visiting a hospital, he was surrounded by a group of nursing sisters who presented him with a white skullcap. By long-standing custom, he ought to have given them his in exchange, but did not.

"I will not give you my cap for two reasons," he told the nuns gently. "The first is that I have no wish to create need for a capmaker with nothing more to do than make caps for the pope. And the second is that this sort of thing can lead you into idolatry and superstition."

He liked to walk in the Vatican gardens and did so at odd hours, whenever he felt the need to turn from the unending problems that were brought to his study, to refresh his mind and his spirit. This troubled the functionaries in charge of Saint Peter's. Pius had walked in the gardens, too, but always at the same hour every day, during which time they would close the cupola of the basilica to the public. John's habits, though, were unpredictable and they did not know what to do.

"Why must you do anything?" the pope asked when they came to him about this. "Why must you close the cupola at all?"

"Because otherwise they would see you, Holiness!" replied one aghast. "The people, all the tourists . . ." His voice trailed off in horror.

John thought this over for a moment, then said, "Don't worry about it. I promise not to do anything that would scandalize them."

And clearly perceived beneath the wit was the great human being. It was Angelo Roncalli, unwilling to veil himself in mystery, saying again, "I am Joseph, your brother."

Tardini, long accustomed to the glacial rhythms of the Vatican under Pius XII, was sometimes unsettled by the sudden acceleration and unexpected turns of John's papacy. Officials in the ground-floor Secretariat of State soon grew accustomed to the old Roman's crusty remarks and the way his eyes rolled upward when he referred to the new pope as, "The one up there." Inevitably, John heard about it.

"*Caro* Tardini," he said when they were alone one day, "let me set you right about something. 'The one up there' is the Lord God of us all. I am only 'The one on the fourth floor.'" And as Tardini's mouth dropped open, amiably added, "I beg you, please don't throw confusion into the ranks."

In the beginning, Vatican gardeners, having been carefully trained to respect Pius XII's penchant for solitude, scurried away when the new pope appeared on his walks. But John sought them out. He wanted to know about their work and their families and whether they managed well on their salaries. And so he came to find out that the wages paid by the Holy See were appallingly low, even considering the tax-free shops and low-rent apartments available to many Vatican employees.

To someone like Pope John, steeped in the Bergamesque tradition of Catholic Action and social justice, the thought of a man struggling to support a wife and children on as little as $85 a month was intolerable. He ordered an immediate study which, soon enough, led to pay increases. When some curial officials protested that this additional financial strain on an annual $7,250,-000 payroll would cut into Vatican charities, John accepted this unhappy consequence. "The wage increase is a matter of simple justice," he said, "and justice comes before charity."

Although the pay raise benefited everyone, ecclesiastics as well as lay employees—the base pay of a cardinal, for example, went from $560 to $650 per month—the largest percentage increases went to those who earned the least. With the addition of special family allotments for dependent children, the Vatican wage scale rose from the lowest in Rome to respectable middle ground.

In theory, the Lateran Treaty of 1929 between the church and the Italian government freed the pope from self-imposed confinement inside the Vatican. In practice, however, neither Pius XI or Pius XII often ventured beyond the Leonine walls. Then, suddenly, to the enchantment of the Roman crowds, here was this new one, this "Papa Giovanni," walking among them in his white soutane and wide-brimmed white hat, standing in his car to wave and turning up unexpectedly in unlikely places. John had decided that to truly exercise his episcopate as bishop of Rome, he would visit every one of its 192 parishes. He might have done it, too, despite the brevity of his pontificate, were it not for his weakness for going back to some of the same parishes again and again.

Guido Gusso, who now became the Holy Father's chauffeur, tells how they would slip out of the Vatican alone in the shiny black Mercedes Benz with the SCV-1 license plate, leaving pandemonium in their wake.

According to the rules, he was supposed to announce his intention of going out at least two hours in advance so that the *carabinieri* could be informed. But that meant that a big train of autos and motorcycle police would go with him and he didn't like that because then he would cause traffic jams and the police wouldn't let the people come near him and the monsignori were always rushing him to go back. What he liked was to stop at the red lights, like everyone else, and if it happened that the people recognized him he would wave and bless them. So sometimes, when he wanted to visit somebody, he quietly sent me for the car and we just went out by ourselves.

Among those they went to visit was the English ambassador to the Holy See, Sir Marcus Cheke, lately fallen ill. This was doubly disconcerting to ruffled Vatican officials, who learned first that the Holy Father had driven off without notice or proper escort, and then that he had gone to visit an Anglican! Later, John went alone with Gusso to a home for aging priests at Monte Mario, simply ringing the doorbell and waiting patiently until an astonished caretaker responded. In a single brief period during those hectic first months, he paid a visit to the Pontifical Roman Seminary, where he had studied for the priesthood well over half a century before, turned up to watch a troupe of circus performers, and attended the concert version of T. S. Eliot's haunting drama about the death of Thomas à Becket, *Murder in the Cathedral.* During Lent he revived a thirteen hundred-year-old papal custom by taking his place among the processions of parishioners walking to the stations of the cross. These good Romans, though properly astonished at the sight of the supreme pontiff leaving his sleek limousine to join them on foot in narrow, twisting little streets, were not beyond a bit of affectionate irreverence. Among themselves they nicknamed him "Johnnie Walker."

But there was no question that he had touched their hearts. Even when he visited the working sections of Rome that were strongholds of the Italian Communist party, the people surged close to cheer him—to the great and growing nervousness of his security force—and hung bedspreads and colored tablecloths from the windows of their bleak tenements in a gesture of greeting. In the small church of one such district, the hundreds crowded inside applauded wildly when he rose to speak and he tactfully reminded them, "In church there can be only two things: prayer and silence."

In the summer he journeyed to Roccantica in the Sabine Hills, further than any pope had traveled in a hundred years. He prayed in the seminary chapel and gave a little talk to the townfolk who gathered in great excitement. But it is not unlikely that his thoughts were lost in that long ago evening in August 1904, when he had come to this same place, having only the day before celebrated his first mass as a priest, and where the other students, awaiting him, stood together by the little bridge and sang, "Thou art a priest forever."

Of all his visits to churches, seminaries, shrines, and hospitals, none is so well-remembered, or so characteristic, as the two he made during the first Christmas of his papacy. Immediately following the Christmas mass at Saint Peter's, he went to the Gésu Bambino, a hospital for sick children. It had not been planned. He simply decided to go and did so, and the nurses and attendants, when confronted by their distinguished visitor, did not know what to do. The children, though, responded with natural and uninhibited enthusiasm: "*Papa! Papa!* Come over here, to us!"

And John replied, "Quiet now, I'm coming. I'm coming to see all of you."

He made his way from bed to bed, chatting with them, beaming. To one little boy who reported that his name was Angelo, the pope plaintively said, "We used to be called Angelo once, too." He sat for a long time by the side of a child who had lost his sight, stroking the boy's hand and talking earnestly with him. When he rose, subdued and obviously affected, those nearby heard him say, "We are all blind sometimes, my dear child. Perhaps it will be given to you to see more than others."

Next day, December 26, he left Vatican City again, this time to visit the prison of Regina Coeli. "You could not come to see me so I have come to see you," he told the hastily assembled prisoners with a broad smile. When they cheered lustily, he called out, "Are you glad that I came? Are you glad?"

"*Viva il Papa!*" they yelled back.

He stood in the rotunda, four tiers of cells rising above him and all around him, and the men pressing close to the gallery rails to see. "My dear sons, my dear brothers, here, in this place, we are in Our Father's house, too." There was more cheering and, again, John asked, "Are you glad that I came? I knew that you wanted me to come, and I wanted to see you." He told them that he had a kinsman who had once been jailed for hunting without a license, a confession that was chastely omitted from *L'Osservatore Roma-*

no's account of the visit, and added, "Things like that can happen sometimes, even if one's intentions are not wicked. But if one makes a mistake, one pays for it, and we have to make our sacrifices to the Lord."

Then he raised his arms and his face to them, saying, "To tell you what is in my heart as I speak to you would be impossible. . . . My eyes look into yours—no, no, do not weep! Be glad that I am here! Are you not glad? I have pressed my heart against yours. The pope has come—here I am among you—and, with you, I am thinking of your children, who are your poetry and your sorrow, and of your wives and sisters and mothers."

He insisted on walking among them, and had his photograph taken with them. When he came to a section reserved for incorrigibles, sealed off from the rest of the prison, he asked that the gate be opened. "Do not bar me from them—they are all children of the Lord." Inside, a convicted murderer fell to his knees and begged, "Can there be forgiveness for such as me?" For answer, John raised the convict and embraced him.

Soon his travels led to rumors of wider travel, stories that the pope meant to journey beyond Rome, perhaps even to go abroad. His old friend, Monsignor Spada, editor of *L'Eco di Bergamo*, has said that this was truly John's great hope. Only his preoccupation with the historic Second Vatican Council, and then his final illness, kept him from visiting the United States, a land that intrigued him, as part of a world tour. But the effect in history is the same. By visiting the parishes of his Roman diocese, John freed future popes from their confinement to the Vatican. By going to the Regina Coeli prison, he made it possible for Paul VI to go to America and the Holy Land.

In the numbers and diversity of those he received in audience, Pope John sometimes made it seem as though he had taken the whole world for his flock. Indeed, in response to his homely, sometimes rambling little talks to foreign visitors, there surfaced the first signs that this pope, this Papa Giovanni, was reaching out to touch people who lived half a world away and who had no commitment to Catholicism, or to any formal religion at all.

It began on November 6, just two days after he had been crowned, when the hundreds of journalists, come to Rome to cover the conclave and coronation, were invited to an audience in the Clementine Hall. Pope John acknowledged the great power of the press—"Even in numbers you resemble an army!"—and the high distinction of their calling. Then, smiling and speaking extemporaneously in French that was occasionally larded with an Italian pun, he said that in recent days he had read many accounts of his election. "Well, this was the constantly recurring theme: every one of you was busy trying to guess the secrets of the conclave." The smile widened. "Even though the ability of journalists to see in the dark is well known, perhaps in this case a learned silence would have been wiser." The reporters laughed self-consciously. The pope went on, "One newspaper even purported to give an hour-by-hour account of what went on in the conclave, and do you know"—at this point he bounced forward on his throne with delight—"there were not two lines of truth in the whole thing!"

And having won them with humor, he proceeded to implant some thoroughly serious thoughts in now-fertile ground: "You write about a political pope, a scholarly pope, a diplomatic pope. But the fact is that the pope is simply the pope, the 'good shepherd' who looks for ways to bring souls to truth. 'Truth and goodness' are his two wings. No one should construct a pope according to any other ideas, and especially not to a private one."

He reminded them that the tremendous power of the written word entailed a responsibility, quoting the words of Alexander Manzoni, "Truth is holy and I have never betrayed it." Finally he said, "Now I will give you a small blessing, if you wish to receive it. And this blessing will carry to all those who are dear to you."

There was a burst of spontaneous applause, and when John rose and left the room, he carried off the hearts of a press corps representing half a hundred nations.

By the end of the first year of his papacy, he had received in audience more than 240,000 people, a greater number by far than any earlier pope had seen in a single year. They ranged from Europe's royalty to the simple faithful of countless Italian country towns. No visiting bishop ever left Rome without seeing the Holy Father, and time was found for such astonishingly diverse groups as American astronautical researchers, African poets, Japanese pilgrims, Italian farmers, and the student firemen of Rome.

He spoke to all without special preparation or notes, and often wandered along in warm, friendly fashion until he was far from his conversational starting point. This posed a particular problem when he had foreign visitors, for then his interpreters had to sum up in a minute or two the essence of a discourse that might have rambled around the subject for half an hour. Msgr. William Carew, the young Canadian who served as John's English interpreter, recalled the day after one such audience, when the Holy Father said to him, "You know, you did a wonderful interpretation yesterday. It was only after I read your summary that I realized what I was trying to say in the first place."

And yet he almost always managed to find the inimitable word or gesture that linked him, human to human, with his visitors. Before the wife of President Kennedy came, he wondered whether she should be addressed as Madame President. Advised that simply Madame, or Mrs. Kennedy, was proper, he worried the choice around in his mind until she appeared in his doorway. Then he rushed toward her with extended arms and exclaimed, "Jacqueline!"

American Congressman Brooks Hays arrived and nervously blurted, "I'm a Baptist." The pope, smiling in welcome, replied, "Well, I'm John." To the president of Turkey he spoke a greeting in the Turkish language, remembered from his years in Istanbul: "May God guard you and roses bloom along your way." And to a horny-handed group from the working-class districts of Rome, he said, "You have not come to see the son of a king, or an emperor, or one of the greats of this earth, but only a priest, the son of poor people, who was called by the Lord and carries the burden of being the supreme pontiff."

But in the end, of course, what he said on such occasions, formalized as they were, mattered less than the glow of his presence. He radiated a charismatic warmth. He was interested in everyone, not in the detached, protocol-ridden manner of statecraft, but in the human way. And as word of his friendly accessibility spread across the world, the most diverse figures in the mainstreams of religion and politics and the arts found reason to come to Rome. Surely no previous pontiff had received so many notables; there were more in John's four and a half years than in Pius's twenty, and some of these papal visits made history. Never before had the presiding bishop of the Protestant Episcopal church of the United States met with a reigning pope. Not since the fourteenth century had an archbishop of Canterbury set foot inside the Vatican, nor any Greek Orthodox sovereign since the time of the Byzantine Empire. Now all these came to see Pope John.

Well before the announcement of the Vatican Council, those who watched for such things saw in the mood and manner of this new episcopate the prospect of a new era between the churches. And soon the Patriarch Athenagoras of Istanbul would say, "The pope of Rome is the first leader of Roman Catholicism who has grasped the mystery of Christ's seamless robe, fingered intuitively its warp and woof and its seamless wondrousness."

Early in 1963, a certain Soviet citizen, Aleksei Adzhubei, together with his wife, asked to be received by Pope John. Since the wife was the daughter of Nikita Khrushchev, and since Adzhubei himself was no ordinary Russian—as a member of the Supreme Soviet and editor of *Izvestia*, the government newspaper, he was a power in his own right—the request sent shock waves through innermost Vatican circles: Surely the Holy Father would not grant an audience to so prominent a Communist official.

But the Holy Father did. He did not hold with closed doors. He could oppose the doctrine of communism but could not muster any personal animosity against individual Communists. And so, while the hand-wringers worried and fussed up to the moment that the Adzhubeis were shown into his study, John remained his open, affable self. Typically, he asked first about their children. Rada Adzhubei replied that they had three sons: Nikita, Aleksei, and Ivan.

"They are fine names," said the Pope, noting that Ivan was the Russian equivalent of his own name, John. "You must embrace them for me when you return," he went on, "particularly little Ivan." Then smiling, "But in such a way that the other two are not offended."

With only Father Kulik, the interpreter, present, they talked comfortably for a quarter of an hour. When Adzhubei asked whether he thought East and West could reconcile their differences, John replied, "You are a journalist and surely know the Holy Bible. The Bible tells us God created the world in six days. The days actually were epochs, an infinite space of time. On the first day the Lord said, 'Let there be light.' Today we are at the first hour. It is God who is giving us light. Do not doubt it, my son—he will give us the rest."

At another point, John said, "You say you are atheists. But surely you will receive the blessing of an old man for your children?" At the end, he blessed the couple, too. Disarmed, they stood with bowed heads as he said with infinite kindness, "That was only a little blessing. Such a little one can't hurt. Receive it as it was intended—and all your relatives at home were included—in a spirit of reconciliation. May peace and justice be with you always."

Afterward, Rada Adzhubei remembered his hands, "fine big peasant hands" that reminded her of her father's. Elsewhere in the world, the meeting gave rise to some sweeping speculations: Khrushchev himself would come to the Vatican; under John's aegis, Khrushchev and Kennedy would meet and resolve the great differences between East and West. If there was little of substance in these expectations, they nonetheless reflected John's genius for inspiring the best of men's hopes: Millions had come to believe that if anyone could achieve the miracle of a lasting peace between the nations, Pope John could.

There were other, less happy reactions to the Adzhubei meeting. When the Italian Communist party registered distinct gains in the election that followed, John was openly and often bitterly attacked from the Right. The conservative press charged that by granting the Adzhubeis an audience he had somehow clothed all Communists in a mantle of respectability. Those within his own court who opposed him for turning the church outward now sneered about "the red Pope." And John, when all this came to him, wept. They misunderstood. They did not see what he was trying to do, he said.

Some time earlier, John began a friendship that was to become the subject of a perceptive and moving book by the Rome-based journalist and author, Curtis Bill Pepper, *An Artist and the Pope*. The artist was Giacomo Manzù, one of the world's great sculptors, creator of innumerable clay Christs and cardinals commissioned by the Vatican. But in the spring of 1960, when the two first met, Manzù was still laboring to realize a set of bronze doors for Saint Peter's begun twelve long and frustrating years before. For at some point after beginning the work that was to have been his magnum opus, the artist had become alienated from his faith, had turned to communism, and the louder the wardens of Orthodoxy in the curia railed, the farther fled his inspiration.

None of this troubled John. As he had to have an official portrait done, a bust, he chose Manzù, a gifted sculptor, to do it. That Manzù came from Bergamo, that John had known his father—this was clearly more important to the pope than the artist's political views. So they became friends, and the story of their remarkable relationship—closer, as Pepper points out, than any reigning pope has had with an artist since the time of Michelangelo—ended only when Manzù sped to the Vatican on another spring night, three years later, to make John's death mask. But the power of their friendship lived on. It provided Manzù with the elusive spark he needed to finish the doors for Saint Peter's—the Doors of Death—and their towering beauty is both an eternal memorial to his sense of loss, and the world's, and a tribute to man's unconquerable spirit.

Monsignor Carew recalls the time Yousuf Karsh, the great Canadian photo-portraitist, came to photograph Pope Pius XII. At the sitting, Karsh said that he had observed the pontiff at mass the previous day, and that there had been a particularly evocative moment when, hands joined and eyes turned upward, the Holy Father seemed to personify the ineffable mystery of religious faith. Could His Holiness assume that pose now? Pius immediately fell into such an attitude of prayer, and the result was another Karsh triumph, perhaps the most beautifully spiritual photograph ever made of Pius XII.

Years later Karsh returned to Rome to photograph the new pope. Again he quietly observed the pontiff on the day before the formal sitting, this time at a general audience, and finally noted that single instant when the warm and paternal look on John's face revealed the pastor and shepherd of souls. But next day, when he recalled the moment— "It was when you were blessing the people, Holiness, and turned to them, so—" —John could not respond. His reactions had to be natural and spontaneous. He could not wave to a nonexistent crowd with enough conviction to fool the camera, or bless an empty room. This contretemps was resolved, finally, when he rang for Capovilla and said to the secretary, "Would you be good enough to kneel here, monsignor, as I have to give you my blessing." And in the real circumstances, the special look returned to his face, and Karsh photographed that beatific smile the world remembers.

Under the tutelage of Monsignor Ryan, who then headed the English-language section of the Secretariat of State, John took up the study of English, tentatively begun in Istanbul fifteen years. before. It was not a marked success. Monsignor Carew, then also in the English section, had the impression that the two old friends might spend ten minutes studying English grammar and half an hour reminiscing in lively Italian about days in the Near East.

Ryan, now a bishop in his native Ireland—this appointment was one of Pope John's last acts—recently conceded that this was so. A huge and still hearty man, Monsignor Ryan said, "I believe Pope John felt a bit less of a father to the English-speaking people he met because he could not say anything to them in their own tongue. So he tried to learn, not to make speeches, but just to say a few words of greeting. But of course he was past seventy-seven and when we got together he was much happier telling stories about the olden days."

Ryan remembered the meeting with Eisenhower, immortalized by the famous photograph of pope and president, heads thrown back laughing, when John fumbled the laboriously rehearsed English greeting. "*Era di belli!*" ("That was a beauty!") he then exclaimed, and his tone clearly conveyed his chagrin to Eisenhower as the camera clicked.

Even more characteristic, says Ryan, were the heavily accented words he did manage for a group of Americans during an audience in 1960. "I do not speak English well," he said, "but my heart speaks to you."

His warmth and wit were such that, inevitably, the stories about him proliferated. Of course some are apocryphal and some sheer inventions. But the best ones are well-attested, and everyone who ever came into contact with John XXIII seems to have a favorite.

Cardinal Vagnozzi: "I arrived back in Rome in 1959, when he appointed me apostolic delegate to the United States, and freely expressed my nervousness to him. America was such a huge country, and the problems were many, and I said to him, 'Your Holiness, this new job is so big that it frightens me.' Whereupon he nodded sympathetically and said, 'I know just how you feel, *caro amico*, for I am in the same boat.'"

Monsignor Carew: "He had received a diplomat who was not very diplomatic. He kept asking the pope questions about how many buildings there were in Vatican City, and how much it cost to run, and whether the Vatican museum earned a profit. Then he said, 'Tell me, Your Holiness, how many people work in the

Vatican?' and John ended that line of questioning altogether by replying, 'I assume about half.' "

Monsignor Spada: "When he had been stationed abroad, he used to stop in the office of *L'Eco di Bergamo* on his way home to Sotto il Monte to chat with the journalists. He was much drawn to them, and was quite knowledgable about their craft. He once told me that he loved the very smell of printer's ink, and over the years he contributed many articles to *L'Eco*. Of course all that ended when he became pope. Afterward, when I was visiting him in the Vatican once, he had just finished writing a letter and had gotten some ink on his fingers. Almost instinctively, he started to wipe them on his cassock, as priests wearing black habits so often do. Suddenly realizing that he now wore white, he looked at the inky hand and thoughtfully said, 'Well, now I can't do *that* any more either.' "

Journalist Alice Leone-Moats: "Pius XII looked like a casting director's dream of a pope, lean, remote, scrupulously ascetic in gesture and expression. John looked like a country priest who had wandered into the Vatican accidentally. He was not intimidated by it, but it certainly never seemed like his natural habitat. And of course he was well aware that, in appearance, he was *nobody's* dream pope. There is a story that in prayers once he asked God—in the friendliest way—why, if He knew that Angelo Roncalli was going to be pope He had to make him so ugly. And following his election there was the time he looked at his image in a mirror—the squat form and face, the overly generous ears, the huge hooked nose—and, amiably resigned, said aloud, 'Oh Lord, this man is going to be a disaster on television!' "

There were those, particularly in certain circles of the Roman aristocracy, who took the stories and the pope's homely appearance as evidence of his limitations. This was a mistake. John XXIII was no simple rustic, as even the sophisticates would come to realize. In an incredibly short time he had become the most universally beloved pontiff in history, not because he told funny stories, but because his essential faith reached across countries and creeds to win the world's heart. "I am Joseph, your brother," he called out to all men, and gave them a sense of belonging to the human family.

And no simple rustic could have led the Catholic church along those new paths, from which there is no turning back, toward honest confrontation with the desperately relevant questions of the atomic age. No one yet knows whether the answers bode good or ill for the church, but most agree that the questions had to be faced. Pope John heard the voices of dissent from within the Vatican Council but they did not frighten him. "We are not friars singing in a choir," he said, and so the bishops spoke out, and led by a brave man, a brave beginning was made.

Less than a year after he ascended the throne of Saint Peter, John wrote Enrica, his niece, "I forgive from my heart those who never, or hardly ever, came to see me in past years. But now I seem to belong to no one. In his great kindness, the Lord has wished to make use of my humble person to do great things. I must do all I can in his service."

A few months later, during a retreat at the Vatican, this theme was still much in his thoughts: "Since the Lord chose me . . . I feel I have no longer any special ties in this life, no family, no earthly country or nation. . . Now, more than ever, I see myself only as the humble and unworthy 'servant of God and servant of the servants of God.' The whole world is my family."

And in August 1961, he made his understanding of his earthly mission indelibly clear: "When on 28 October, 1958, the cardinals of the Holy Roman church chose me to assume the supreme responsibility of ruling the universal flock of Jesus Christ, at seventy-seven years of age, everyone was convinced that I would be a provisional and transitional pope. Yet here I am, already on the eve of the forth year of my pontificate, with an immense program of work in front of me to be carried out before the eyes of the whole world, which is watching and waiting. As for myself, I feel like Saint Martin, who 'neither feared to die, nor refused to live.' "

XIII

OPEN WINDOWS

On the first anniversary of his elevation to the papacy, John responded to the congratulations of some visitors from Bergamo by wryly noting that one who is pope at seventy-eight does not have a great future. But the truth is that his pontificate was already marked for history. Even if the triple tiara had passed to another on that very day, the winds of change loosed when John XXIII summoned the twenty-six hundred bishops of the Roman Catholic church to meet in ecumenical council—only the twenty-first such gathering in the two thousand-year life of the church, and the first since 1870—these winds were flying free. He had called for a spirit of *aggiornamento*, a renewal to affect the life and worship of every Catholic, a regeneration that would direct the church toward a distant, triumphant end: the unity of Christian people. Such a spirit is not easily stifled.

At the outset, John had pledged his papacy to "new development in the eternal youth of our holy church." Ancient, anachronistic traditions were shattered. Two weeks after his coronation, on the very day he conferred on Tardini the full title of secre-

tary of state—"because there are too many *sostituti* around
here"—he announced that he would create twenty-three new
cardinals at a consistory to be held December 15. This was stunning news. It was generally agreed that the sacred college was
overdue for an infusion of fresh forces; it had shrunken to fifty-
two, of whom twelve were past eighty, but what John proposed
was to exceed the limit of seventy cardinals set by Pope Sixtus V
in 1586.

Nor was he finished. Over the next three years, he held four
more consistories, creating fifty-five new cardinals in all. Among
them were Bishop Valerian Gracias, the first Indian to be given
the red hat, and Bishop Laurean Rugambwa of Tanganyika, the
first African; Father Augustin Bea, the brilliant Biblical scholar
who had been Pius XII's confessor; Bishop Julius Doepfner of
Berlin, who was only forty-five and became the youngest among
the princes of the church; and of course Tardini.

"I refused the red hat from Pope Pius XII because I wanted to
be let alone," the old man growled privately. "But there is no way
of refusing *this* one." And, as always, his eyes rolled upward
toward the fourth floor in silent identification of "this one."

At the top of Pope John's first list of cardinals-elect was the
name of the archbishop of Milan, Giovanni Battista Montini. Had
Montini been a cardinal at the time of the last conclave, John once
revealed to Capovilla, he would have voted for him to be pope.
Now, by making him his *prima creatura*, John was signifying
something not lost on seasoned observers: the archbishop of
Milan was his choice as a successor.

Small acts to set right what he once referred to as "our own
bad habits" illuminated his sensitivity to the feelings of others. At
the pope's direction the baptismal ceremony for converts to
Catholicism was revised to eliminate the condemnation of former
faiths. Parts of a liturgical prayer to the Sacred Heart of Jesus
which were offensive to Jews and Moslems were likewise
changed. On his first Good Friday as supreme pontiff, John
expunged from the traditional Good Friday prayer the reference
to "perfidious Jews and infidels." That his own true feelings on

this matter ran deep was demonstrated some years later when a cardinal, celebrating the Good Friday liturgy in the pope's presence, referred to "perfidious Jews" from force of habit. John stopped him on the spot, commanding the celebrant, "Say it over—the new way!"

No modern pope so endeared himself to non-Catholics. But sometimes it seemed as though even as John captivated the imagination of the outside world, elements in the Roman Curia, the central administrative body of the Holy See, moved to obstruct him within the church. They were satisfied with things as they had always been, attentive to their personal fiefs and resistant to the forces of change unleashed by "il buon Roncalli." And John, who knew all this, did nothing. It was not in his nature to lend himself to a power struggle. To an American prelate who once complained of curial machinations, he said, "My dear young man, when you face Jesus Christ in eternity as one of his bishops, he is not going to ask how you got along with the Roman Curia but how many souls you saved."

On the other hand, there was no confusion in his mind about who was in charge. Speaking of the curial fathers, he said, "They are zealous men, but it is not they who rule the church. That post is mine." And armed with his inherent goodness and a gift for conciliation and persuasion, rule he did.

Cardinal Alfredo Ottaviani, secretary of the Holy Office and perhaps the most doctrinaire of the traditionalists, once came to see him about a political matter. The Christian Democratic party led by Premier Amintore Fanfani had formed a coalition with the socialists and there were those, Ottaviani among them, who believed this to be a challenge which the church must take up. In the same sort of situation a few years before, during the reign of Pius XII, the Holy Office had issued decrees of excommunication against Italians who voted for the Communists.

John listened sympathetically as Ottaviani detailed his position. He said nothing. Then, unexpectedly, he rose, took the cardinal's arm and led him to the library window. They looked out over the city, and John spoke of how beautiful it was, how golden and peaceful in the light of the afternoon sun. Soon Ottaviani left, somehow satisfied that Pope John had understood him. But there was no Holy Office statement about the coalition, no Vatican involvement in the politics of the republic.

Certainly Tardini's views were conservative, but he too, for all his grumbling, served John loyally and well. When he did try to give up his position over some disagreement in 1960, John accepted the resignation, and immediately reappointed him. "Here is the old secretary of state and the new one," he announced to the assembled cardinals, and Tardini stayed on.

He died the following summer, and John was deeply grieved. He himself made the announcement from a balcony overlooking Saint Peter's Square: "The angel of death this morning carried away with him the cardinal secretary of state, Domenico Tardini, who was the closest and strongest helper of the pope in the government of the church. Our heart is afflicted. . . ."

That evening he called on Cardinal Amleto Cicognani, who had long served as apostolic delegate to the United States, to accept the vacant post. Cicognani was dismayed. He pointed out that he was past seventy-eight, that his energy was not what it had once been, and asked, at the very least, for time to consider the offer. Undiscouraged, John said that age had nothing to do with the matter at hand: he himself was older than Cicognani and still in harness. He talked on—it was a trait he had perfected to bridge such tentative moments—noting, among other things, that Cicognani's American experience would be invaluable in the Secretariat of State. Then he said, "Well, now you have had time to think the whole matter over, and I know you will say yes." And Cicognani did.

Pope John has been called a revolutionary. A remark attributed to Cardinal Siri, that it would take the church fifty years to recover from the aberrations of John XXIII, calls up the image of a stormy, swath-cutting pontiff with wrecked institutions and discredited dogma strewn in his wake.

This was not John. He believed that the church needed to be brought into the twentieth century, but stood firm against any impulse to discard two thousand years of teaching in the effort. He sought to make the church more Catholic and less Roman, and to embrace a social doctrine that had consequence in the real world. But he turned a deaf ear to certain clerics who would have junked everything—dogma, doctrine, discipline—in a frenzied experiment at popular Catholicism.

The Diocesan Synod summoned together by John in January 1960, the first in the long history of Rome, was to demonstrate his undiminished faith in the old verities. Called to consider major diocesan reform, and widely considered to be a sort of preliminary to the upcoming worldwide Vatican Council II, the Synod restricted itself to producing a series of trivial rules pertaining to lay and clerical behavior, with an inflexible emphasis on self-denial: Priests were forbidden to attend movies, theater or opera, or to watch too much television, or to be seen in a bar or restaurant "except for very good reason," or to travel in an auto with a lady. John admitted to disappointment in the narrowness of the synod's scope, but he did not challenge its decrees.

It was a time when some clerics had begun raising the first tentative objections to the law of ecclesiastical chastity. During the synod, one well-known priest even published an article arguing that obligatory celibacy was not dogma but simply judicial training, hence open to questioning. John responded in a much-anticipated address, during which he made no overt reference to the issue of celibacy, but concluded by asking God's blessing on the church, "one, holy, apostolic, Catholic"—adding, after a pregnant pause, and with emphasis—"and chaste."

For one of Pope John's generation and training, it could hardly have been otherwise. And yet, even at eighty, his inherent sensibility helped him to understand the special dilemma of a priest in the unconstrained and compliant 1960s. It distressed and grieved him, he said, to hear "the lament of priestly souls for their burden of loneliness and celibacy." In an eloquent and compassionate letter to an American order devoted to helping fallen priests, he wrote, "These men are our brothers, pilgrims in life. In the dedication of their young lives they did not count the cost. If now they have been wounded in the fray, it is our duty to help them, for they are our brothers, our sick brothers."

So he believed that priestly discipline must be tempered by human love and an understanding of modern-day pressures. Similarly, he believed that the church must recognize that larger contemporary problems would not be resolved in the old ways, not by papal thunderings or curial condemnations or by again sealing off the Vatican from a confused populace and a turbulent world.

Almost a century had passed since the popes' loss of secular power had led to an uncompromising reliance on ecclesiastical power. From the time of Vatican Council I in 1870 (so named because it was the first ecumenical council held at the Vatican), the doctrine of papal infallibility had produced a single answer to every question: "*Roma locuta; causa finita*" ("Rome has spoken; the case is closed"). Now, as the pontificate of John XXIII commenced, the church had never been more powerful in terms of nominal adherents and potential influence. And yet it was still tilting at the windmills of Modernism and dissent.

Meanwhile the world had changed. More than a third of mankind was under Communist rule. In France and Italy barely one Catholic in three attended mass with any regularity. Everywhere commitments to the priesthood were on the decline, while in the disadvantaged nations the gap between priests and people widened. And inside the Vatican, curial fathers listened nervously as contentious talk from beyond the wall, arguments for decentralized authority and a reformed liturgy, grew more insistent.

What to do?

On the morning of January 20, 1959, just three months after his election to the papacy, John was discussing these matters with Cardinal Tardini. What to do? "Suddenly," as John himself was later to describe the moment, "an inspiration sprang up within us as a flower that blooms in an unexpected springtime. Our soul was illuminated by a great idea. . . . A word, solemn and binding, rose to our lips. Our voice expressed it for the first time—a council!"

How the conservative Tardini reacted to this thunderbolt is open to question. John, though, with his usual generosity, put it this way, "To tell the truth, we feared that we had aroused perplexity, if not dismay. . . . But a clear expression appeared on the cardinal's face. His assent was immediate and exultant, the first sure sign of the Lord's will."

On the following Sunday, January 25, a darkly cloudy day heavy with the threat of a winter storm, John attended mass at the patriarchal basilica of Saint Paul's-Outside-the-Walls. It was one of his favorite churches in Rome, but those who watched the pontiff closely noticed that he seemed distracted. Kneeling before the papal throne during a prayer for persecuted Christians, he lowered his face into his hands. After the mass, together with a group of cardinals who had accompanied him, John withdrew to the adjoining Benedictine monastery. And it was there, speaking to the cardinals, and through them to the world, that he made the historic announcement.

"We are aware," he began, "that the new pope is being watched, in many quarters with friendship and devotion, in others with hostility or some hesitation." He spoke of his dual and inseparable responsibilities as bishop of Rome and supreme pontiff of the universal church, and referred to the immensity of difficulties in "a city transformed completely in the course of the forty years from the time we knew it in our youth . . . a veritable human hive, from which issues an endless and confused murmur of voices, seeking for agreement." And when the pope views the whole of his spiritual domain, he sees, on one hand, the noble efforts of those, graced by Christ, to multiply the fruits of salvation and sanctity; and on the other, human freedom abused and men in the thrall of the prince of darkness, struggling only for earthly goods. "All this," John said, "evoked a response in the heart of the humble priest whom the manifest will of Divine Providence has lifted, unworthy though he may be, to the heights of supreme pontificate."

It was at this point that John looked directly at the seventeen members of the sacred college of cardinals before him, and then exclaimed, "Beloved sons and venerable brethren! Trembling a little with emotion, yet at the same time with a humble resoluteness of purpose, we pronounce before you the name and plan of a double endeavor: A Diocesan Synod for Rome, and an Ecumenical Council for the Universal Church."

The immediate response was a stunned and stony silence. One senses John's disappointment in later musings: "Humanly, we could have expected that the cardinals, after hearing our pronouncement, might have crowded around to express approval and good wishes." But again he put the best face on it. "Instead, there was a devout and impressive silence. Explanations came on the following days."

The cardinals' shock was understandable. A synod in Rome, where it had always been assumed that the pope could resolve all diocesan problems without need to consult his bishops, was extraordinary enough. But a council—a summoning together of all the archbishops, bishops and heads of the religious orders in the whole world—what was the use of a council? Councils of the past had dealt with the dangers of heresy or doctrinal conflict, or with the menace of some temporal power. Since there was now no external threat to the church, and since in 1870 Vatican I had decreed the dogma of papal infallibility in matters of faith and morals, what earthly—or heavenly—purpose could a council now serve?

Later, when someone put this question to John, when they asked him what he expected the council to do, he strode to a window of his study and threw it open. "We expect the council to let some fresh air in here," he said.

For him, typically, that was enough. He imposed no program, content to have opened a way to let the spirit of inspiration enter. But as soon came clear, Vatican Council II was to be a forum free to reexamine almost every aspect of Catholic life. Modification of everything from the liturgy to the eating of fish on Friday became possible. And in a larger sense, the church prepared to study itself in the context of a bewilderingly new universe, seeking to relate in meaningful ways to an industrial surge and urban growth and decay, to an explosion of scientific knowledge, to a new morality and the politics of a world that had come to a balance of terror, and in which the tactics of the cold war, if not yet discredited, were already irrelevant.

Was the unity of all Christian churches a possibility too? In the great spiritual renewal envisioned by Pope John, nothing was beyond hope. The council, as Peter Nichols of *The Times* of London put it, was to be John's means of breaking through the sealed walls of the curia. It was to be the way in which he would involve the whole church in his aspirations, not only for his lifetime but for generations to come.

The voices of opposition were soon snapping along Vatican corridors, and gathering volume. "We are paying for fifteen minutes of insanity in our pope," curia wits muttered behind their hands. Speaking quite openly in New York, Cardinal Spellman said, "I do not believe that the pope wanted to convoke a council, but he was pushed into it by people who had misconstrued what he said." And Archbishop Lercaro of Bologna declared: "How could he have dared to convoke a new council after one hundred years and within less than three months after his election? . . . Either Pope John has been rash and impulsive, with a lack of breeding and experience . . . or else in actuality Pope John has done this with calculated audacity, though obviously not capable of foreseeing all the details . . . or future developments."

This sort of resistance could not fail to draw blood. John was both too astute not to sense the backlash of scorn precipitated by his ecumenical call, and too sensitive not to be wounded by it. But he went serenely on his way. When a curial elder protested that it would be impossible to organize a council by 1963, John replied, "Good, then we will have it in 1962."

In June he established an Ante-Preparatory Commission to circulate the necessary information to the thirty-five hundred bishops, prelates, heads of the religious orders and the thirty-seven Catholic universities of the world, and to solicit from them suggestions for an agenda. Their replies filled two thousand file folders, eventually to be bound into twelve great volumes. It took a year to prepare the needed reports from this mass, whereupon Pope John created ten commissions, whose chairmen were cardinals of the curia, charged with preparing the schemata, or draft proposals, for the council's consideration.

At the same time, John announced the formation of a Secretariat for Promoting Christian Unity and named as its head Cardinal Bea, who was adept and long active in maintaining contacts with non-Catholic Christians. It was this new body that arranged the historic meeting between Geoffrey Francis Fisher, archbishop of Canterbury, and Pope John in November 1960. More to the point, it served as the link between the council and invited observers from other Christian communions.

This, too, was John's own idea. Once again he was moving to free the church from the stigma of doctrinal absolutism, from that translucent sheath of mystery it held up to outsiders. As nearly as he could manage it, John was asking the whole world to participate in this council. And though the logistical problems would be awesome—accommodations would need to be found for ten thousand people; somehow thirty-five hundred of them, including bishops and their assistants, would have to be seated in the nave of Saint Peter's—he himself intervened to assure that the observers would be given the best places.

The council was to be forty-five months in preparation. Meanwhile the conduct of church affairs commanded the attention of the pope. John's daily schedule differed little from what it had been in Venice, having been shaped by nearly eighty years of living. It suited his bodily rhythms.

He was awake at 4:00 A.M. to pray, then to celebrate mass. After a breakfast of warm milk and coffee, rolls, some fruit, Capovilla brought him the newspapers and his agenda for the day. By nine o'clock he was in the papal library on the second floor, ready to receive Tardini in the first audience of the morning. The library is a vast room, eighty feet long and forty feet wide, with walls of red silk damask and ornate, outsized furniture. The pope's desk is covered with red leather, on which John kept a small gold crucifix, some pencils, and two telephones.

The audiences were supposed to last until two, but not infrequently, engrossed in conversation, John would lose track of time and, despite Capovilla's best efforts, luncheon had to be delayed. Afterward, John rested or walked in the gardens, returning to work alone in his small study, a room he much preferred. In the evening, before dinner, there were more prayers, usually with servants and the household nuns. Most often he was in bed by ten, but sometimes he would waken around midnight and go to his desk for another two hours of work.

Walking in the gardens one day, near the base of the Tower of San Giovanni, he remarked to Capovilla that the gaunt, cylindrically shaped old pile of bricks, built to withstand the Saracen invasions and unused in all the centuries since, seemed to him the most peacefully secluded place inside the Vatican walls. From the top, one might look out over the city and see the children playing in the streets, and lose for a little while that heavy sense of being shut away from the people. Soon Capovilla proposed that an apartment be built in the tower for the pope's use. John agreed, and although the construction took a long time and cost far more than anyone anticipated (the foundations had to be strengthened, and electricity and an elevator installed), it became, in the last years of his life, a retreat and a solace. Standing on the terrace, often with a pair of binoculars, he could gaze out on the people of Rome, his neighbors, and feel as though he were walking among them without guards and monsignori to nay say him. Here in the tower, too, during a private retreat just before the opening of the council, he made the final entry in his journal:

"Without any forethought, I put forward, in one of my first talks with my secretary of state, on 20 January 1959, the idea of an Ecumenical Council. . . . Now, after three years of preparation we are on the slopes of the sacred mountain. May the Lord give us strength to bring everything to a successful conclusion!"

In the face of protocol and the relentless press of duty, he clung doggedly to the ties of family. He encouraged Battista to come often, and these visits, filled with gossip about relatives and small talk from the parishes of Faenza and Sotto il Monte, were a particular joy. At first Battista worried that his uncle invited him out of politeness, and that perhaps he was really imposing on precious time. "But then I realized that every time I arrived there was something special to eat, a cake or ice cream, and the sisters would tell me that the Holy Father himself had asked that it be prepared. So I knew he was really glad to see me."

As Battista was a priest, and a favorite of the pope, a room was set aside for his use at the Vatican, and often he stayed two or three days. But relatives beyond the immediate family circle had to be gently informed that propriety kept John from extending the same hospitality to all, and this task was entrusted to the ever-faithful Enrica.

"Nothing is more welcome to me than these visits from our own kith and kin," John wrote to her from Castel Gandolfo during the summer of 1959. "I am willing to pay everything for them, their fares and lodging, but I cannot put them up here, or keep them here for long with me. A visit lasting a few minutes, during which they can tell me of any particular needs—in this way I shall always receive them very willingly. I want you, dear Enrica, to explain this to all our dear relatives. . . . I should like to be kind and generous to all, but when people turn up here suddenly and without any warning they are disappointed and I am distressed. . . ."

He was concerned, too, lest certain promoters play on the innocence of the family and persuade them to lend the Roncalli name to dubious projects. Nor did he want his brothers or sister beguiled into posing as public figures. In September he wrote firmly to Assunta:

> For some time past you have been seen here and there, even at Lourdes, and recently at Fiera di Primero. No harm in this, and indeed a great deal of good in the pilgrimage to

Lourdes. But you should not show yourself in public here, there and everywhere, even if they pay all your expenses and shower compliments and gifts upon you. Your place as the pope's sister is in *retirement, almost seclusion, in your own home*. Every time you show yourself, even with due decorum, it causes some petty gossip and a mocking spirit with regard to you and the pope himself. Do not trust anyone, my dear Assunta. Whoever *invites or favors you in any way is doing it merely for his own interests*. And when these reports come to my ears from here or there I am grieved and distressed. . . .

On May 15, 1961, Pope John issued the first of the two towering encyclical letters which, if he left no other heritage, assured his brief papacy long life in the memory of men. Its subject was Christianity and social progress, but its title, *Mater et Magistra*, is taken from the opening sentence, "Mother and teacher of nations —such is the Catholic church established by Jesus Christ."

Mater et Magistra voices the church's concern for the exploited poor in the factories of industrialized nations, and for the forgotten poor in the colonial and emerging nations. It speaks not only for their need of basic necessities, but for human dignity as well, and redefines social justice in the mid-twentieth century to mean that all men must share in the wealth produced by modern technology. "Socialization," a word that might once have struck terror into the hearts of church elders, was now specifically endorsed, so long as it was achieved in freedom and full consideration for the rights of all. Socialization, wrote John, is an "expression of the tendency in human beings to join together to attain objectives which are beyond the capacity and means of single individuals."

Even more striking was the section of *Mater et Magistra* dealing with the great disparities between the economically advanced nations of Europe and North America, and the underdeveloped lands in the rest of the world: "The solidarity which binds all men and makes them members of the same family imposes upon political communities enjoying abundance of material goods the obligation not to remain indifferent to those communities whose citizens suffer from poverty, misery and hunger, and who lack even the elementary rights of the human person. This is the more so since, given the growing interdependence among the people of the earth, it is not possible to preserve lasting peace if glaring economic and social inequality among them persists."

As a young priest in Bergamo, Angelo Roncalli had been imbued with the spirit of *Rerum Novarum*, Pope Leo XIII's great encyclical which first formulated an enlightened church attitude toward labor and social progress. Nor had he ever forgotten that long-ago strike at Ranica, and the moral pointed by his beloved bishop, Radini-Tedeschi: "Prudence does not consist in doing nothing. It means to act, and act well."

Now, as pope, John had acted, and with *Mater et Magistra*, he brought up to date the tradition of Catholic social concern enunciated by Leo seventy years before. Robert Neville called it the most impressive statement of John XXIII's reign. And *The New York Times* wrote, "No document of our times is more apposite to contemporary problems, or more socially advanced."

There seemed no end to his stock of surprises. Only a week before the opening of the council, it was announced that the pope, traveling by train, would make a pilgrimage to the tomb of Saint Francis at Assisi, and to Loreto, the shrine of the Holy Virgin. Today, such a journey, perhaps 250 miles in all and measured against the world-wide travels of Pope Paul, seems insignificant. But when John went to the Vatican railroad station on the morning of October 4, 1962, it marked the first time a reigning pope had traveled by train in ninety-nine years, and centuries had passed since one ventured so far from Rome by any mode of transport.

All along the route the crowds lined the tracks to wave and cheer, and at every station they surged toward the open window where he stood smiling at them and blessing them. At Loreto,

where fifty thousand waited, he stood before the shrine of Our
Lady and prayed for the success of the council, "May it be said in
future years and centuries that through your motherly interces-
sion the grace of God crowned the work of the twenty-first
Ecumenical Council, imparting to all the children of the Holy
Church new fervor, generosity and firmness of intention. . . ."

On the return trip he stood again, waving to the people, who
had waited through the afternoon into umber evening. "This date
in my life should be written in gold," he said.

Only a few knew that he was already fatally ill.

Back inside the Leonine walls, he retreated to the Tower of
San Giovanni, canceling all audiences for a week of prayer and
meditation. Elsewhere in Rome, clerics and laymen also asked
God's blessing on the deliberations of the council fathers, and
countless millions of non-Catholics, heartened by the new mood of
the mother church and touched by the warm humanity of its
leader, joined in prayers for the triumph of the ecumenical spirit.

Meanwhile the immense work of preparation went forward.
Inside Saint Peter's, carpenters installed the last seats of the
benched tiers, each 300 feet long, that faced each other across the
nave. Outside, the organizing committee bustled to find rooms
for latecomers, and to assign them to one of the one hundred
rented buses that would carry the fathers back and forth from
their quarters to the Vatican. Joked one longtime resident of the
Eternal City: "If the police can get the bishops through Rome's
traffic jams it will be a real demonstration of divine intercession."

Already foregathered were the cardinals, archbishops, bishops,
abbots, and superiors of religious orders and congregations who
would attend the opening session. Nearly three thousand had
been invited, but restrictions in some countries under Communist
rule cut the final attendance. Thirty delegate-observers representing seventeen different Christian denominations—all but the Greek
Orthodox and World Baptist Alliance—were also on hand. (There
would be ninety-three official observers by the time the fourth
session convened.) Though they would not have the right to vote
or speak in the public sessions, they could make their views

known through Cardinal Bea's Secretariat for Promoting Christian Unity.

Thursday, October 11, dawned dark with rain, but in a remarkably short time the sun shone. At eight o'clock, Pope John, wearing the heavy white ritual robes of the Pontifex Maximus, joined the cardinals and bishops in the Hall of Benedictions and summoned the spirit of the Holy Ghost with the ninth-century hymn, "*Veni Creator Spiritus.*" Then the solemn procession to the basilica began, ranks of white-robed bishops marching down the Scala Regia (the Royal Stairway) and through the crowds in the piazza to the great bronze doors, standing open to reveal the ceremonial splendor of the largest church in Christendom.

Pope John insisted on walking among the bishops, one among brothers, though his slow, painful descent of the long marble sweep of the Scala Regia was now clearly a test of his strength and courage. Beyond the curving line of the Bernini columns, he stepped into the *sedia gestatoria* and was raised to shoulder height, content to be carried thus across the piazza so the people could see him. Once inside Saint Peter's, he descended and walked the length of the nave.

Cardinal Tisserant, dean of the sacred college, celebrated the solemn pontifical mass. Except for the television cameras and the sober-suited Protestant observers, it seemed a moment lost in time, a scene of baroque pageantry and brilliance, preserved through the centuries and unchanged by the years. Then Pope John began to speak and "a gust of fresh air" quickened the mood in Saint Peter's: The venerable fathers were summoned up from the glorious past of the universal church and into the troubled but hopeful present, and then gently made to look, not backward, but ahead.

"Illuminated by the light of this council, the church, we confidently trust, will become greater in spiritual riches, gaining the strength of new energies from it. She will look forward to the future without fear."

A moment before, in the unforgiving television lights, his face had been chalky white and worn by fatigue. His eighty-one years bore down heavily. But now as he read his sermon, peering through old-fashioned gold-rimmed spectacles, and flicking the pages away as he finished them, his voice rang out bravely, strongly, along the colossal nave, and his shoulders seemed to straighten, and his look was enlivened by the bold vision of his address:

> In the daily exercise of our pastoral office, we sometimes have to listen, much to our regret, to voices of persons, who though burning with zeal, are not endowed with much sense of discretion or measure. In these modern times, they can see nothing but prevarication and ruin. They say that our era, in comparison with past eras, is getting worse. And they behave as though they had learned nothing from history, which is nonetheless the teacher of life, and as if at the times of other councils, everything was a full triumph for the Christian idea and for proper religious liberty.
>
> We feel that we must disagree with those prophets of doom, who are always forecasting disaster as though the end of the world were at hand.

As many of the good fathers glanced irresistibly in the direction of Ottaviani, Siri, and others among the acknowledged "prophets of doom," John imperturbably explained why he had summoned the council, and what he expected of it: "In the present order of things, Divine Providence is leading us to a new order of human relations." Differences were not to be feared, for even differences could lead to the greater good of the church. And in order to spread her message to all men throughout the world, the church would have to bring herself up to date wherever it was required. "The Church should never depart from the sacred patrimony of truth received from the Fathers, but at the same time she must ever look to the present, to new conditions and new forms of life introduced into the modern world, which have opened avenues to the Catholic Apostolate."

He had not called the council for "a discussion of one article or another of the fundamental doctrine of the church which has repeatedly been taught . . . and is presumed to be well-known and familiar to all. For this a council was not necessary. . . . The world expects a step forward toward doctrinal penetration and a formation of consciences . . . which should be studied and expounded through modern research and scholarship." In other words, doctrine must now be evaluated in terms of contemporary learning, and so made more readily understandable to present-day worshipers.

Next he turned his attention to the inquisitorial spirit that often animated the Holy Office and certain curialists, who were so quick with their denunciations. "Often errors vanish as quickly as they arise, like fog before the sun," he said. And though, in the past, the church condemned these errors with the greatest severity, nowadays it "prefers to make use of the medicine of mercy rather than that of severity."

Finally he came to his last and greatest hope, that the council would enlist the Catholic church in a movement for worldwide reunion. He envisioned "a triple ray of beneficent, supernal light: in the unity of Catholics among themselves; in the unity of prayers and ardent desires with which those Christians, separated from this Apostolic See, aspire to be united with us; and the unity in esteem and respect for the Catholic church which animates those who follow non-Christian religions. . . . God grant that your labors, toward which the eyes of all peoples and the hope of the whole world are turned, may abundantly fulfill the aspirations of them all. . . ."

There had been those among his advisers who warned that all the talk about renewal and reform might shake the fundamental faith of the people. As if in answer, the people gathered that night in the square of Saint Peter's and along the Via della Conciliazione, five hundred thousand strong according to the police, to celebrate the opening of the council, and to express their love for the man called John, sent by God to be their pope. He appeared on the central balcony and called out, "Dear children, dear children, I hear your voices!"

They fell silent. He could see them in the light that flooded the great basilica, and in the light of torches that hundreds of exuberant young men held up high. And he could feel their love pouring out to him, strengthening him for this last and greatest endeavor. He spoke to them of his hopes for the council, using the plain, everyday language of the people. Then he said, "Now go back to your homes and give your little children a caress and say it is from the pope."

On Saturday, October 13, Pope John spoke to the delegate-observers in the Consistorial Hall. He did not sit on his throne, but took one of the chairs arranged in a square, as he was accustomed to do when he met with the cardinals in consistory. This brotherly gesture was underscored when he said, "As for my own humble person, I don't like to claim special inspiration. I am content with the sound doctrine that everything comes from God." He could tell them that he drew extraordinary comfort from their presence, "but if you would but read my heart you will understand more than words can say."

They could read his heart well enough, these men whose creeds had heretofore shared with Rome only a mutual antagonism. "If we should pray for anyone in the world today," said the Protestant theologian Paul Tillich later, "we should pray for Pope John. He is a good man."

And if any among them had believed that John convened the council simply to ratify some high-flown but harmless theological precepts, they learned differently that very afternoon, almost immediately after the first general congregation of the bishops was called to order. Handed a list of 160 curia-approved candidates for the ten permanent commissions, the bishops refused to vote their approval. Demanding a voice in the all-important organization of the council's administrative structure, they adjourned the meeting after only twenty minutes—and returned a few days later to elect men of their own choosing to the key committees.

It was a heady moment. "We found we were a council," said

American bishop Robert J. Dwyer, "called here not as school-boys, but rather to give considered opinion."

They had come together strangers, these far-flung and disparate fathers of the church, accustomed to dealing with superiors and with the curia but not with each other. Now they were learning that, African or American, missionary or metropolitan, theologian or pastor, they shared a broad and vital community of interests. The myth of the monolithic church was shattered. The council was a reality.

Not that its deliberations went smoothly. John, watching on closed-circuit television (after his inaugural sermon, he did not return to the conciliar hall until the end of the first session in December), noted the contention between the Italian traditionalists and the more progressive-minded churchmen from beyond the Alps, but he did not intervene. Quoting Pope Pius XI, he remarked placidly, "There are three periods in a council: that of the devil, who tries to mix up the papers; that of man, who contributes to the confusion; and that of the Holy Ghost, who clears up everything."

In the beginning, Vatican Council II seemed to be putting the Holy Ghost to a severe test. Following the excitement of the opening—what the newspaper headlines had called the "Revolt of the Bishops!"—the fathers moved on to high drama: the debate over the first schema, a proposal for liturgical reform.

There were few outside the clergy, and not all in it, who really understood the core significance of this issue. On the surface, it sounded like little more than an idea for dropping the traditional Latin in certain parts of the mass and permitting those parts to be said in the language of the people. But most of the council fathers, and certainly all of the traditionalists among them, understood clearly that to deprive the curia of its historically held right to decide all liturgical matters was to open the door to decentralization. If, as proposed, national conferences of bishops could choose when to use Latin and when to use the vernacular, wouldn't they soon also want a voice in missionary activities and the control of seminaries?

As the language of the council was Latin, it was a particular irony that many of the Italians who rose to uphold its exclusive use in the mass spoke it badly. And at one point, an American traditionalist, Cardinal Spellman, required someone to speak in his place, as the council was unable to understand his Latin at all. On the other hand, the northern European prelates, whose Latin was generally good and sometimes impeccable, pointed out that neither Christ nor his followers for the first two hundred years spoke Latin, and that the Catholic churches of the Eastern rite had always had their own languages.

Then Cardinal Ottaviani, who had been waiting a turn to speak, went to the microphone and curtly demanded to know whether the fathers were planning a revolution. The liturgy was sacred ground, he said. Changes in the mass would scandalize and alienate the faithful.

Unfortunately, as Ottaviani grew more impassioned, he spoke on beyond the ten minutes each advocate was allowed by the rules. Though Cardinal Bernard Alfrink of the Netherlands, who was presiding that day, politely reminded him that he had exceeded the time limit, Ottaviani continued in mounting anger. At last, after seventeen minutes, Cardinal Alfrink turned off the microphone. For another pathetic moment, the seventy-two-year-old head of the Holy Office went on speaking, although now no one could hear a word he said. Then, finally aware of what had happened, he returned to his seat, flushed and deeply hurt. When the fathers began to applaud Alfrink's action, thereby signifying disagreement with Ottaviani's extreme position, the old man rose and left the council hall, not to return for two weeks.

After nearly a month of intense debate, the council approved certain limited liturgical reforms, among them the right of the bishops to decide whether parts of the mass could be said in the language of their own countries. But the important thing was that the vote was 1,922 to 11; it was an emphatic sign that change *was* possible.

The next schema, On the Sources of Revelation, plunged the council into crisis. It had been prepared by the Theological

Commission, whose chairman was Cardinal Ottaviani and whose dominant members were like-minded, and it unequivocally reaffirmed one of the sharpest points of difference between Catholic and Protestant theology: How has God spoken to man?

Protestants recognize only one source of revelation, the Bible. But the Catholic church holds that a certain body of religious truth, passed down by the Apostles and called Tradition—the Assumption of the Virgin Mary, for instance—is equally valid. Many of the council fathers believed that the church's ancient definition of the nature of revelation needlessly stressed religious differences and also obstructed modern Biblical study. In the quest for Christian unity, they wanted a schema that would present Scripture and Tradition as parallel paths between the same places.

But Ottaviani was inflexible. His schema came down hard on the distinction between the beliefs of the separate faiths, and was even written in a terminology largely unfamiliar to non-Catholics. Its supporters—Siri, Ruffini, and Cardinal James McIntyre of Los Angeles—defended the schema on grounds that it represented centuries of Catholic thought; and its challengers cautioned that its adoption would strike down any hope for Christian unity in this century. Pleaded Cardinal Bea: "Do not close the door to intellectual Europe and the outstretched hands of friendship in the Old and New World."

Pope John watched the unhappy proceedings on the television set in his apartment, and knew that the Protestant observers were watching with particular interest, too. On November 20, he saw the fathers vote, 1,368 to 822, in favor of a proposal to reject Ottaviani's schema—but the motion failed to pass because it fell narrowly short of the required two-thirds majority. And at this point, John intervened to save his council.

He had not wanted to influence the fathers, which is why he kept to his apartment during the conciliar sessions, and it was surely not in his nature to impose his will on them. But the alternative was continued wrangling as the schema was debated section by section, dulling, scarring, and, in the end, perhaps destroying the fine spirit of ecumenism in which the council had begun. After a night of anguish and prayer, he sent word to Saint Peter's that because so clear a majority of the bishops was opposed to the schema, he was withdrawing it despite the vote: A new commission would be appointed to redraft it.

What he did cannot be overestimated. No victory was won, but certain defeat was staved off. Vatican II would proclaim no ringing decrees of irresistible universality, not in Pope John's lifetime, but it had spoken out in the name of "holy liberty," as he had urged it to do.

And it would convene again after he was gone. The bishops had come to know each other and their strength. They had dealt a death blow to the creaky dictum, "Rome has spoken; the case is closed." In its place, a certain optimism, an aspiration, a divine audacity was in the air, and would haunt the Vatican and inspirit the world.

Some windows, once open, can never be closed again.

The last general congregation of the council was held on December 7. Unexpectedly, Pope John entered Saint Peter's through a side door and took his place on the papal throne. The fathers, all of whom had heard the rumors and now saw the pope's white and wasted face, burst into emotional applause, then stood, and those not choked by love and sorrow, cheered aloud. John prayed with them and blessed them, then left the platform without help.

On the following day, the Feast of the Immaculate Conception, the first session of Vatican Council II was solemnly closed. A coordinating committee under Cardinal Cicognani had been established to prepare for the second session, scheduled for September 8, 1963. Again John appeared, and seeming more his old self, addressed the fathers in Latin: "Now that the bishops of the five continents are returning to their beloved dioceses . . . we should like to dwell a little on what has been done so far, and to map out the future. . . .

"The first session was like a slow and solemn introduction to the great work of the council . . . it was necessary for brothers, gathered together from afar around a common hearth, to make each other's close acquaintance; it was necessary for them to look at each other squarely in order to understand each other's hearts."

The second session, he said, "will be a new Pentecost indeed, which will cause the church to renew her interior riches and to extend her maternal care in every sphere of human activity. . . . In this light we look forward to your return, we salute all of you 'with a holy kiss,' while at the same time we call down upon you the most abundant blessings of our Lord, of which the apostolic blessing is the pledge and the promise."

Rising, he stood looking at them for a moment, then with some effort walked from the basilica. It was understood that the fathers, his beloved brethren, would not see him there when the council reconvened.

XIV

I AM YOUR BROTHER

In November 1961, on the occasion of Pope John's eightieth birthday, Chairman Khrushchev tendered personal greetings and good wishes through the Soviet embassy in Rome. Ignoring the advice of timorous aides to reply with caution—or even, as some counseled, not to reply at all—John promptly sent forthright thanks for the thought and added, "I will pray for the people of Russia."

Nearly a year later, just as Vatican Council II was about to convene, two Russian Orthodox priests arrived in Rome, having at the last minute secured government permission to attend as observers. John had given his assurance that an attack on the Communist system was not on the council agenda, and Khrushchev, having perhaps puzzled over what to make of a Roman churchman who did not parade his anti-communism like a battle flag, decided to trust him.

This was soon to have consequences reaching far beyond

Moscow and the Vatican, for the council had barely gotten under way when President Kennedy made a stunning announcement to the world: The United States had learned that the Russians were engaged in constructing missile sites in Cuba, a grave threat to American security, and he had ordered the navy to intercept approaching Soviet vessels. Civilization was face to face with nuclear catastrophe.

At this point in the crisis, Pope John assumed the obligation of speaking for mankind. Thus he became the third member of what Norman Cousins, then editor of the *Saturday Review*, called "one of history's most implausible triumvirates: an American President, a Pope, a Communist [brought together by] the vulnerability of civilization to modern destructive power."

Cousins himself played an unanticipated catalytic role in the brief alliance of this trio, for it was he who set off the interaction among them. That he was on hand to record the ensuing events with sensitivity and journalistic skill is posterity's good fortune.

Through a friend, Father Felix P. Morlion, president of the Pro Deo University in Rome, Cousins learned of Pope John's willingness to make a public appeal for peace if it would help the antagonists to back away from the brink. He immediately conveyed this word to the White House and the Kremlin, and both Kennedy and Khrushchev agreed that such an initiative might indeed strengthen their hands in the search for a peaceful solution.

Late on the night of October 25, 1962, only the light in the pope's study broke the dark facade of the apostolic palace as John worked on the momentous address. The next day, seated before the radio microphones and speaking in French, he appealed to the conscience of the great leaders. Not only American and Russian lives were at stake, he said, but the lives of all the people in the world, and their fate must not be ignored. History would laud those who understood this, and who put the fate of men before national interests.

"Hear the anguished cry which rises to heaven from every

corner of the earth," he beseeched them, "from innocent children to old men, from the people in the cities and villages: Peace! Peace!"

Newspapers over the world, even those in the Soviet Union, headlined John's plea. On that same day, October 26, there was a marked easing of the tension that had been building between East and West. On the 28th, Chairman Khrushchev announced that the Russian missiles would be withdrawn from Cuba and President Kennedy praised him for an act of statesmanship. The crisis was over.

The will to peace, having brought these three into improbable communion, provided the impetus for further explorations along their frontiers of disagreement. And again Cousins was their agent. Before the year 1962 was out, he was in Moscow to press Kennedy's proposals for a nuclear test ban, as well as Pope John's interest in establishing a tentative contact with the Russians. In a meeting with Khrushchev, Cousins conveyed the pope's concern for the religious well-being of the Russian people, not only Catholics, but all who sought to worship God in their own way. A particular expression of the chairman's commitment to religious liberty, said Cousins, would be the release of Archbishop Josef Slipyi, a Ukrainian imprisoned since 1944 when he was charged by the Stalin regime with Nazi collaboration.

Khrushchev made no promises. But as Cousins later wrote, he did express genuine admiration for Pope John, saying, "He made a big contribution to world peace during that terrible time of the Cuban crisis," and that he would welcome good relations with the Catholic church. Smiling, he added, "This doesn't mean that I'm going to become a Catholic any more than the pope is going to become a Communist." Then he wrote out an unusual personal message for Cousins to give to John, making unmistakable religious allusions in wishing the pope good health for the Christmas season.

A few days later, Cousins sat in Pope John's study reporting on his encounter with the Russian leader. He recalls how the supreme pontiff, whom he had never met, went to pains to put him at ease. "We have much to talk about," John said. "Just remember, I'm an ordinary man; I have two eyes, a nose—a very large nose—and so on. . . . You must feel completely relaxed. We will talk as man to man."

John was especially grateful for Khrushchev's Christmas greetings. "I get many messages these days from people who pray that my illness is without great pain. Pain is no foe of mine. . . . I have lived a long life, and I have much to look back upon. These memories give me great joy now and fill my life. There is really no room for the pain."

When their long discussion was over, John gave Cousins two papal medallions. One was for him, for his efforts on behalf of Archbishop Slipyi. Then, noting that it was "not appropriate for the Holy Father to bestow awards on heads of state," John said that the second was for *anyone*—and he emphasized the word— who Cousins felt had deserved it.

Not long afterward, having returned to the United States, Cousins heard from Soviet ambassador Anatoly F. Dobrynin that as a direct result of Chairman Khrushchev's interest, Archbishop Slipyi was to be freed. Elated, Cousins immediately telephoned the news to the Vatican, where arrangements had to be made to bring the aged and ailing prelate to Rome.

Then he sent the second medallion to Khrushchev.

The end of the story is best told in Cousins's own words:

> Several months later, I returned to Moscow carrying a message from President Kennedy that sought to unblock an impasse at that time in the test ban negotiations. . . .
> Mr. Khrushchev was in good spirits. He began by thanking me for the Pope's medallion.
> "I keep it on my desk at all times," he said. "When Party functionaries come to see me, I play with it rather ostentatiously. If they don't ask me what it is right away, I continue to let it get in the way of the conversation. . . .

Inevitably I am asked to explain this large engraved disc. 'Oh,' I say, 'it's only a medal from the Pope.' "

"Peace! Peace!" he had implored the nuclear superpowers, and now, as winter softened into the final spring of his life, the quest for a just and lasting peace in a world sown with the seeds of its own destruction was his most tormenting concern. On April 11, 1963, Holy Thursday, he put his name to his eighth and last encyclical letter, *Pacem in Terris* (Peace on Earth). It was the magnum opus of his pontificate. And because the yearning for peace was common to people of every faith, John spoke to them all: *Pacem in Terris* was the first papal encyclical addressed not only to the bishops and Catholic faithful, but to "all men of good will."

It was as brilliantly reasoned as it was boldly conceived, a blueprint for a world community in which men of different religious and political persuasions could live in harmony, justice, security, and freedom. With an unerring sense of history, John perceived the shifting nature of the Communist monolith. "False philosophical teachings" may remain constant, he wrote, but the historical movements they inspire are affected by a world in constant evolution, and hence they are subject to profound change. "Moreover, one must never confuse error and the person who errs . . . not even in the moral or religious field. The person who errs is always and above all a human being who must be regarded with dignity . . . and who, at a future date, can learn and believe the truth." He advocated continued meetings and agreements with nonbelievers, not for the sake of mere coexistence, but in active collaboration "in pursuit of the common universal goal."

He saw how racial discrimination and the old despotic, exploitive colonialism fed on each other, and he condemned both. "It is not true that some human beings are by nature superior and others inferior. All men are equal in their natural dignity. Consequently there are no political communities that are superior by nature and none that are inferior by nature." Already fading was a world in which some countries ruled others. Now, discrimination on account of race or social standing had to go, too: "Not until a man becomes fully conscious of his rights can he be equally aware of his duties."

Finally, he turned to the clash of nations when, striving for advantages and sometimes only for conveniences, they fell into contention, one with another. "The warning of Pius XII still rings in our ears," he wrote: *"Nothing is lost by peace; everything is lost by war."* Reason and restraint were needed for the reconciliation of national differences, and a "public authority of the world community, not imposed by force," to resolve broader economic, social, political or cultural problems. "It is our earnest wish that the United Nations organization—in its structures and its means—may become ever more equal to the magnitude and nobility of its tasks."

If he credited the mounting, monstrous power of modern weaponry with a deterrent influence, he came down far more emphatically on its wastefulness and ultimate danger. "While the people of these countries [those stockpiling nuclear armaments] are loaded with heavy burdens, other countries as a result are deprived of the collaboration they need in order to make economic and social progress. . . . Justice, then, right reason and humanity urgently demand that the arms race should cease; that nuclear weapons should be banned; and that a general agreement should eventually be reached about progressive disarmament and an effective method of control."

Wherever men and women longed to live free of the threat of war, Catholics or not, believers or not, *Pacem in Terris* struck a responsive chord. According to an editorial in *The New York Times*, it was one of the "most profound and all-embracing formulations of the road toward peace that has ever been written."

But not everyone applauded, not even all Catholics. A dissenting minority, small but shrill, lamented John's open acknowledgment that civilization might fare better if the Communist states were let out of political purgatory. This was craven surrender, they held. But as most of the rest of the world had recovered from the trauma of the Russian Revolution and cherished the hope of peace above the luxury of implacable hatred, the overwhelming reaction to *Pacem in Terris* was praise, enthusiasm, and gratitude.

On May 10, Pope John was awarded the Balzan Peace Prize. By this time he was severely ill and almost always in pain. But when the doctors tried to persuade him not to attend the award ceremony, which had been arranged as part of the regular weekly general audience, he said, "But why not? What could be finer than for a father to die in the bosom of his assembled children?"

His illness had begun around the time of his eightieth birthday, November 1961. Late that month he wrote in the journal, "I notice in my body the beginning of some trouble that must be natural for an old man. I bear it with resignation, even if it is sometimes rather tiresome and also makes me afraid it will get worse. It is not pleasant to think too much about this; but once more I feel prepared for anything."

By summer he felt the first clear symptoms of an intestinal growth. Later, it would be said that months passed before he realized the gravity of his illness. But it is hard to believe that a man who had lost a mother, a brother, and four sisters to cancer would be taken completely unaware by the onset of the disease in his own body. A certain elegiac note crept into his public statements, not yet a good-bye, but rueful acknowledgment that the end of his glorious adventure on earth must be nearing an end.

"We are entering our eighty-second year," he told a group in Saint Peter's that winter. "Shall we finish it? All days are good for being born, all days are good for dying."

To several hundred children gathered in the courtyard of Saint Damasus not long after, he spoke of Pope Leo XIII, who lived to the age of ninety-three: "Still, at last he had to undergo that which happens to all of us, and probably soon to the pope who stands before you today."

But his homely good humor never deserted him. Told by the doctors that he had a "gastropathic condition," he laughed aloud and said, "That is because I am pope. Otherwise you would call it a stomach ache." After the early reports of his illness called forth the predictable Roman rumors that he was already at death's door, he said wryly, "Tell them the pope still lives. And there is no reason to bury him before he dies."

Throughout the summer of 1962, while the council weighed the future course of the church, John followed their deliberations from his quarters, and though pale and perceptibly weaker, maintained a regular schedule of audiences and conferences. In November he chose his old friend from Bologna, Professor Antonio Gasbarrini, to be his personal physician, replacing Dr. Filippo Rocchi, who had died. An extensive series of x-rays and tests was undertaken. Some of Italy's leading specialists were called into consultation. And the ultimate diagnosis was unsparing and unmistakable: inoperable cancer. Only palliative treatment was possible and, at best, Pope John had perhaps half a year to live.

In the evening of that shattering day, Gasbarrini told John that he was suffering from a tumor. "A tumor," the old man repeated, understanding everything, and at the same time full of concern for his friend. "*Ebbene*, very well, let God's will be done. But don't worry about me because my bags are packed. I'm ready to go."

A gifted young anesthesiologist, Dr. Piero Mazzoni, moved into the apostolic palace to provide the close, constant attention Pope John would require over the next months. Only a few days later, during the night of Tuesday, November 27, Mazzoni was awakened by a distraught Capovilla: the Holy Father was in desperate pain. He went running, and saw at once that John was in the grip of a massive intestinal hemorrhage. He administered coagulants, blood plasma, and morphine, and by daylight the bleeding was under control. His face drawn and haggard by the struggle, John slept for a few hours, his strong peasant sinews gathering fresh strength for the struggles yet to come.

As the public audience scheduled for that Wednesday had to

be canceled, the Vatican press office began issuing a series of vague and contradictory reports that served only to feed the rumor mills of the city. The pope had a bad cold, said the first announcement; was "indisposed," said the second; and, on November 29, that there were "symptoms of a gastropathy . . . which has provoked a fairly intense anemia." This last was just ambiguous enough to touch off the wildest public speculation: The pope had undergone radical surgery; the pope would not survive the week; the pope was already dead.

But on Sunday, miraculously, the pope appeared at his study window, as usual, to recite the Angelus with the crowd gathered in the square below. Smiling wanly, he said to them, "Good health, which was threatening to leave us, is returning—has returned!"

They cheered, as had the council fathers when they were informed that the Holy Father was resuming his usual activity. Moved by their affection, John wept.

Under Dr. Mazzoni's care and with regular periods of rest, he rallied remarkably. Although he was still not strong enough to attend the regular Wednesday audience at Saint Peter's, it was announced that he would offer the papal blessing from his window. The council adjourned their session so the bishops could join the crowd, and by noon that day the piazza was filled. As soon as the study window on the fourth floor was opened, a great joyous burst of horns and bells and cheering swept up toward it. Finally it was quiet, and John said, "My children, as you see, Providence is with us. From day to day there is progress . . . *piano, piano*, sickness, then convalescence. And your presence gives us joy and strength and vigor."

And, indeed, that was true. Incredibly he worked on. His bags were packed, he had said, but it was as though, on the eve of his departure, he remembered some urgent matters that required his attention. He would go, and willingly, of course, but in those last months, when he was never really free of pain, and sometimes tortured by it, he would see to the resolution of the council's gravest conflicts, to the writing of *Pacem in Terris*, and to the personal good-byes of a man who had never forgotten, amid the press of highest duty, that he was also a son and a brother and an uncle and a friend.

He had written a long letter to his family at Sotto il Monte, a valedictory. He considered it his spiritual testament, and though he addressed it to Zaverio, his eldest brother, it was clearly intended for all the Roncallis:

> I think it is three years since I last used a typewriter. I used to enjoy typing so much and if today I have decided to begin again, using a machine that is new and all my own, it is only in order to tell you that I know I am growing old—how can I help knowing it with all the fuss that has been made about my eightieth birthday?—but I am still fit, and I continue on my way, still in good health, even if some slight disturbance makes me aware that to be eighty is not the same as being sixty. . . .
>
> This letter which I was determined to write to you, my dear Savero, contains a message for all the members of our large family, and I want it to be to all of them a message from my loving heart, still warm and youthful. Busied as I am, as you all know, in such an important office, with the eyes of the world upon me, I cannot forget the members of my dear family, to whom my thoughts turn day by day.
>
> It is pleasant for me to know that, as you cannot keep in personal correspondence with me as you did before, you may confide everything to Msgr. Capovilla, who is very fond of you all, and speak to him just as you would to me. . . .
>
> My eighty years of life completed tell me, as they tell you, dear Savero, and all the members of our family, that what is most important is always to keep ourselves well prepared for a sudden departure, because this is what matters most: to make sure of eternal life, trusting in the goodness of the Lord who sees all and makes provision for all. . . .

Go on loving one another, all you Roncallis, with the new families growing up among you, and try to understand that I cannot write to all separately. Our Giuseppino was right when he said to his brother the Pope: "Here you are a prisoner *de luxe:* you cannot do what you would like to do."

I am well aware that you have to bear certain mortifications from people who like to talk nonsense. To have a Pope in the family, a Pope regarded with respect by the whole world, who yet permits his relations to go on living so modestly, in the same social condition as before! But many know that the Pope, the son of humble but respected parents, never forgets anyone; he has, and shows, a great affection for his nearest kin; moreover his own condition is the same as that of most of his recent predecessors; and a Pope does not honor himself by enriching his relations but only by affectionately coming to their aid, according to their needs and the conditions of each one.

This is and will be one of the finest and most admired merits of Pope John and his Roncallis.

At my death I shall not lack the praise which did so much honor to the saintly Pius X: "He was born poor and died poor."

As I have now completed my eighty years, naturally all the others will be coming along after me. Be of good heart! We are in good company. I always keep by my bedside the photograph that gathers all our dead together with their names inscribed on the marble: grandfather Angelo, "*barba*" Zaverio, our revered parents, our brother Giovanni, our sisters Teresa, Ancilla, Maria, and Enrica. Oh what a fine chorus of souls to await us and pray for us! I think of them constantly. To remember them in prayer gives me courage and joy, in the confident hope of joining them all again in the everlasting glory of heaven.

I bless you all, remembering with you all the brides who have come to rejoice the Roncalli family and those who have left us to increase the happiness of new families, of different names but similar ways of thinking. Oh the children, the children, what a wealth of children and what a blessing!

Now, with the prognosis of his illness apparent to all those around him, he did his best to lift their spirits. He kept urging Capovilla to get more rest, "or you will go off before your boss." Guido Gusso recalls that, out of John's sight, both he and Capovilla wept a good deal. "I lost all interest in food and drink," he said. "All I could do was smoke cigarettes, four packages a day, so that now I cannot even bear the smell of them. In those seven months that the Holy Father was dying, I lost thirty-five pounds."

Then one day John asked Gusso to bring his small son to see him. The child was not yet three and spoke in the Veneto dialect, so that communication between the two was difficult. But when the boy, who was named Giovanni, said that he wanted to become a priest, John, laughing, replied, "You are too handsome. When the time comes you will want to marry."

The little visit seemed to cheer John, and it helped Gusso accept what had to come. "He did it for that reason, so that I could see he was really at peace, and that his only concern was for the rest of us."

Not long after, he told Dr. Mazzoni that he would like to meet his family. They came on a Sunday, the doctor and his wife and two young daughters. "He was so kind, so *interested* in them," Mazzoni recalled. "He talked to them for half an hour and afterward, when I took them home, I asked my younger daughter, who was then eight, what she thought of the pope. She said that he looked like an ordinary priest, and I could tell she was disappointed. But when she is older and can understand such a thing, I will explain to her that that was Pope John's glory, that he was just an ordinary priest—who took Christianity seriously."

John had no interest in the clinical aspects of his illness. At the very beginning, he had told Mazzoni, "You will do what you must do, and I know you will do it well. But for myself, I ask only one thing: that you tell me honestly when the end is at hand."

Early that spring John received Father Pietro Bosio, he parish priest of Sotto il Monte, who had brought for his blessing the first stone of a seminary for foreign missions, to be built adjacent to the pope's birthplace. There were many in Sotto il Monte who wanted to come and see him, Father Bosio said, to which John replied, "Well, tell them to come quickly. Are they waiting until I am dead?"

Inspecting a model of the proposed seminary, he made this little address: "Let the people of Sotto il Monte rejoice, not so much because one among them was born one of the successors to Saint Peter, but because the Lord has deigned to arrange that among those fields and vineyards, future missionaries will be prepared. Let them rejoice to house in the ample circle of their lovely hills a lighthouse of missionary light, young hearts vibrating with love for God and souls who, in their eagerness, beat in unison with the heart of the pope."

Then he added plaintively, "If you hurry up and build it, maybe I will come personally and dedicate it."

On April 30 he suffered another hemorrhage. This time he required several blood transfusions, as well as the coagulants and morphine for the pain, and for twenty-four hours Dr. Mazzoni did not leave his side. There was some talk among the doctors of attempting radiation therapy. But they quickly agreed, as each, secretly, had known in his heart from the first, that it would be futile, and might even provoke more severe bleeding.

But again John found the strength to weather the storm. On May 5 he received a group in audience at Saint Peter's, and a week later, over Mazzoni's objections, went to the Quirinal to be present for the conferral of the Balzan prizes for music, mathematics, and chemistry. He was the first pope to visit the seat of the civil government since it was taken from the papacy in 1870.

It troubled him to hear of the predictions, some from inside the Vatican, that once he was gone everything he had brought to the church would go, too: the spirit of *aggiornamento*, the council, everything. He did not believe it, but of course he could not be sure. "May it be God's will that the council fathers be able still to crown the great work that they have begun," he prayed. "I offer all my suffering *ut unum sint* [that they may be one], that all may be a sole entity in Christ."

On May 20, Cardinal Stefan Wyszynski, primate of Poland, came to see him. Capovilla had suggested that he be received in the bedroom, but John flatly refused. "We haven't come to that yet," he said, and walked purposefully down the stairs to his library. When their talk was over, Cardinal Wyszynski, referring to the next session of the council, said, "Until September, Holy Father!"

And John, with a small smile, replied, "In September you will either find me here, or another. You know, in one month they can do it all—the funeral of one pope, the election of another."

That night he had another hemorrhage and more transfusions. Now, as his stomach would tolerate no food at all, he had to be fed intravenously. On the morning of Wednesday, May 22, preparing for the audience at Saint Peter's, he fainted. But he recovered quickly and went to the window to tell the people that the audience would have to be canceled: "I was expecting to see you at noon, but instead we are advancing our appointment a bit. So here I am. I know that our meeting was to have taken place inside Saint Peter's, but what's the difference, inside or out. As long as it is at Saint Peter's it's all right."

The next day, the celebration of the Ascension, he appeared at the window again to pronounce a blessing. His voice trembled and the crowd, seeing how weak he was and that he spoke only with enormous effort, was solemn and still. And that was the last time anyone ever saw him from the square.

There was yet another massive hemorrhage on the twenty-sixth, and Gasbarrini was hurriedly summoned from Bologna. But it was not the end. By Thursday, May 29, John's astonishing stamina—what Gasbarrini called "a constitution of iron"—had fought the ravaging disease to a momentary standstill, and he got out of bed and conferred with Vatican aides. Gasbarrini returned to Bologna and, for the first time in a week, Mazzoni, red-eyed with exhaustion, left the apostolic palace for a few hours respite.

But what Pope John had reverently spoken of as Sister Death was now close at hand. That night, Mazzoni was dozing in the study when John's feeble cry for help wakened him shortly before midnight. The bleeding had begun again, and this time the cancerous mass burst the intestines and flooded the abdominal lining with poison: peritonitis. For four more days John would drift between coma and agonizing consciousness, but this time Sister Death would not be denied.

In the morning, he lay spent and gaunt, the white linen night-shirt hanging slackly on his shrunken frame. A flight of swallows swept by as he gazed through the window, free and untroubled in the spring sky. Then he turned again to the ivory crucifix on the wall opposite the bed, placed "so I can see it with the first glimpse in the morning and the last one at night."

Mazzoni came in with Capovilla. The secretary, torn with anguish, tried to speak and could not. Mazzoni went to the edge of the bed. "Holy Father," he said, "you have asked me, many times, to tell you when the end was near, so you could prepare."

The wasted face on the pillow fixed itself into a gentle smile. "Yes," John said. "Don't feel badly, doctor. I understand. I am ready."

Capovilla fell to his knees by the side of the bed, burying his face in the covers, sobbing. John caressed the dark head. "Courage, courage, my son," he said softly. "I am a bishop and I must die as a bishop, with simplicity but with majesty, and you must help me. Go, get the people together."

"*Santo padre,* they are waiting."

The smile widened, the smile of a father suddenly and greatly moved by the love of a beloved son. "Send in the confessor," he said.

After his confession and last Communion, he received the holy oil of extreme unction. Again and again he whispered the words of Jesus after the Last Supper, "*Ut unum sint*" ("That they may be one"). Slowly the small room filled up as cardinals and monsignori gathered to witness the death of the pope.

In the afternoon, Battista, now a canon in Bergamo, arrived, stricken and distraught. John asked him for news of Monsignor Spada and others at *L'Eco di Bergamo*, and Battista could not believe that his uncle was dying. But by evening, when Assunta, Zaverio, Alfredo, and Giuseppe were brought to the bedside by Cardinal Montini, John had slipped back into coma. Later, Battista described the scene in the bedroom as the pope's family tried to find a place among the worthies of the church. "The first thing they were told is that they must not weep. If it turned out that they could not hold back their tears, they were to leave. Those four poor old souls were trembling and still upset from their airplane trip, which was the first for any of them. There was only a dim light in the room. We were all standing back because we were given the impression that the pope was having great difficulty breathing, that he needed air, and that if we stood too close we would deprive him of it."

He recovered consciousness again and embraced his brothers and sister. "Do you remember how I never thought of anything else in life but being a priest?" he whispered. "I embrace you and bless you. I am happy because in a little while I shall see our mother and father in heaven. Pray. . . ."

On Sunday, June 2, with his temperature at 104 degrees, he told Dr. Mazzoni, "I am suffering with love, but with pain, too, so much pain." He wanted the faithful doctor to have something of the pope's as a keepsake and, fumbling, he found his fountain pen on the night stand. "Take it," he said to Mazzoni, who was now crying, too. "It is nearly new."

To Capovilla he said, "I am sorry to have kept you from your mother such a long time. Promise me when this is over that you will go to see her."

On Monday he lost consciousness for the last time. He lay back on the pillow gulping for air and sometimes they put an oxygen mask over his face. His false teeth had been removed and a stubble of white bristles lined his jaw.

In the evening, Cardinal Luigi Traglia, John's vicar for Rome, celebrated an outdoor mass for the thousands drawn to Saint Peter's Square. The spring breeze was so soft that the altar candles barely flickered, and the murmur of prayer seemed to hang in the air even after the mass ended. A little before eight, Cardinal Traglia spoke the traditional words of dismissal, "*Ite, missa est*" ("Go, the mass is ended").

And at that same moment, upstairs in the dimly lit bedroom where Sister Death waited, the man born Angelo Roncalli and destined for sainthood as John XXIII, took a last gasping breath and died.

The Vatican press office issued the final bulletin: "He suffers no more." Beyond the bedroom window, television lights swept across the piazza, packed with people, grieving, many on their knees. And beyond the piazza, the world grieved, too.

Other popes had decried war and defended peace, praised virtue and condemned evil. But in the experience of living men, none before John XXIII had ever moved the church toward the mainstream of human endeavor, or welcomed all men and all creeds to the good fight, or made it seem even remotely possible that they could win.

And even more deeply, the world's millions were caught up with the man who had lived beneath the robes of the supreme pontiff of the universal Church, bishop of Rome, vicar of Jesus Christ and sovereign of Vatican City. To the multitudes, some devout, some disaffected, the peasant face with its undisguised warmth meant more than all the weighty titles. "I am your brother," he had told them. And they had come to believe him.

BIBLIOGRAPHY

Aimé-Azam, Denise. *L'Extraordinaire Ambassadeur*. La Table Ronde, Paris, 1967.

Algisi, Leone. *John the Twenty-Third*. Darton, Longman & Todd Ltd., London, 1963.

Aradi, Zsolt. *The Popes: The History of How They Are Chosen, Elected and Crowned*. Macmillan, London, 1955.

Aradi, Zsolt; Tucek, Msgr. James I.; O'Neill, James C. *Pope John XXIII: An Authoritative Biography*. Burns & Oates, London, 1961.

Arendt, Hannah. *Men in Dark Times*. Jonathan Cape, London, 1970.

Attwater, Donald, ed. *Catholic Encyclopaedic Dictionary*. Cassell, London, 1958.

Bacchion, Eugenio. *Papa Giovanni: Patriarca a Venezia*. Editrice Triveneta, Venice, 1964.

Balducci, Ernesto. *John "The Transitional Pope."* Burns & Oates, London, 1965.

Blanshard, Paul. *Paul Blanshard on Vatican II*. George Allen & Unwin, London, 1967.

Capovilla, Msgr. Loris. *Giovanni XXIII: Sette Letture*. Libreria Editrice Vaticana, Vatican City, 1963.

    The Heart and Mind of John XXIII. Corgi Books, London, 1964.

Cousins, Norman. *Present Tense: An American Editor's Odyssey*. McGraw-Hill, New York, 1967.

    The Improbable Triumvirate. W. W. Norton, New York, 1972.

De Luca, Don Giuseppe. *Giovanni XXIII: In Alcuni Scritti di Don Giuseppe De Luca.* Casa Editrice Morcelliana, Brescia, 1963.

Fesquet, Henri. *Wit and Wisdom of Good Pope John.* Harvill Press, London, 1964.

Franck, Frederick. *Outsider in the Vatican.* Collier-Macmillan, London, 1966.

Giovannetti, Msgr. Albert. *We Have a Pope: A Portrait of His Holiness John XXIII.* The Newman Press, Westminster, Md., 1959.

Gorresio, Vittorio. *The New Mission of Pope John XXIII.* Funk & Wagnalls, New York, 1970.

Gritti, Jules. *Jean XXIII Dans L'Opinion Publique.* Editions du Centurion, Paris, 1967.

Hales, E. E. Y. *The Catholic Church in the Modern World.* Eyre & Spottiswoode, and Burns & Oates, London, 1958.

Pope John and His Revolution. Eyre & Spottiswoode, London, 1966.

Hatch, Alden. *His Name Was John: Life of Pope John XXIII.* George G. Harrap & Co., London, 1963.

Hirschmann, Ira. *Caution to the Winds.* David McKay Co., New York, 1962.

Hughes, Philip. *A Short History of the Catholic Church.* Burns & Oates, London, 1967.

John XXIII, Pope. (*Seven Great Encyclicals*) *Mater et Magistra, Pacem in Terris.* Paulist Press, Glen Rock, N.J., 1963.

Mons. Giacomo Maria Radini-Tedeschi. Ed. di Storia e Letteratura, Rome, 1963.

Journal of a Soul. Geoffrey Chapman, London, 1965.

Mission to France. Geoffrey Chapman, London, 1966.

Prayers and Devotions from Pope John XXIII. Burns & Oates, London, 1967.

An Invitation to Hope: A Spiritual Biography. Simon & Schuster, New York, 1967.

Letters to His Family. Geoffrey Chapman, London, 1970.

Kaiser, Robert B. *Inside the Council.* Burns & Oates, London, 1963.

Klinger, Kurt, ed. *A Pope Laughs.* Collins, London, 1965.

Lapide, Pinchas E. *The Last Three Popes and the Jews.* Souvenir Press, London, 1967.

L'Arco, Adolfo. *Il Segreto di Papa Giovanni.* Piero Gribaudi Editore, Turin, 1967.

Lees-Milne, James. *Saint Peter's.* Hamish Hamilton, London, 1967.

Levine, Irving R. *Main Street, Italy.* Doubleday, Garden City, N.Y., 1963.

Morlion, Felix A. *Freedom's Challenge and Pope John.* Harper & Row, New York, 1963.

Murphy, Francis X. *John XXIII: The Pope from the Fields.* Herbert Jenkins, London, 1959.

Neuvecelle, Jean. *Jean XXIII.* Gallimard, Paris, 1962.

Neville, Robert. *The World of the Vatican*. Harper & Row, New York, 1962.

Nevins, Albert J. *The Story of Pope John XXIII*. Wonder Books (Grosset & Dunlap), New York, 1966.

Nichols, Peter. *The Politics of the Vatican*. Pall Mall Press, London, 1968.

Pallenberg, Corrado. *The Vatican from Within*. George G. Harrap & Co., London, 1961.

The Making of a Pope. Macfadden-Bartell, New York, 1964.

Pepper, Curtis G. *The Pope's Backyard*. Farrar, Straus & Giroux, New York, 1966.

An Artist and the Pope. Peter Davies, London, 1969.

Pichon, Charles. *The Vatican and Its Role in World Affairs*. E. P. Dutton, New York, 1950.

Picker, Henry. *Johannes XXIII: der Papst der Christlichen Einheit und des 2. Vatikanischen Konzils*. Ketwig, Blick und Bild Verlag fuer Politische Bildung, 1963.

Pucci, Eugenio. *The Vatican City*. Bonechi, Florence, 1967.

Rynne, Xavier (Pseud.). *Letters from Vatican City*. Faber & Faber, London, 1963.

Serafian, Michael. *The Pilgrim: Pope Paul VI, the Council and the Church in a Time of Decision*. Farrar, Straus & Co., New York, 1964.

Sheehan, Elizabeth Odell. *Good Pope John*. Vision Books (Burns & Oates), London, 1967.

Sugrue, Francis. *Popes in the Modern World*. Thomas Y. Crowell Co., New York, 1961.

Sullivan, Kay. *Journey of Love: A Pilgrimage to Pope John's Birthplace*. Appleton-Century, New York, 1966.

Trevor, Meriol. *Pope John*. Macmillan, London, 1967.

Van Lierde, Peter Canisius. *The Holy See at Work*. Hawthorne Books, New York, 1962.

INDEX

327

Luther
GERHARD EBELING

'On reading this book one recovers a sense that theology is
about what really matters ... Although it is a deeply serious
book it is very readable and deserves a wide public.'
A. D. Galloway, Glasgow Herald

Erasmus of Christendom
ROLAND H. BAINTON

'In this book, which carries lightly and easily the massive
Erasmian scholarship of the last half-century, Erasmus comes
to life. He speaks for himself and, speaking, reveals himself.'
Hugh Trevor-Roper, Sunday Times

Calvin
FRANCOIS WENDEL

'This is the best introduction to Calvin and his theology that
has been written, and it is a work of scholarship which one
salutes and admires.' *Professor Gordon Rupp*

The Religious Experience of Mankind
NINIAN SMART

In this study of great world religions the author shows that
religions grow and change and affect each other just as living
organisms do. He points out that one cannot understand
human history without knowing something about man's
religion.